MISBEHAVING
AT THE
CROSSROADS

MISBEHAVING AT THE CROSSROADS

Essays & Writings

HONORÉE FANONNE JEFFERS

HARPER

An Imprint of HarperCollins*Publishers*

HarperCollins books may be purchased for educational, business, or sales promotional use. For information, please email the Special Markets Department at SPsales@harpercollins.com.

Some material has been previously published in another format.

FIRST EDITION

Library of Congress Cataloging-in-Publication Data has been applied for.

ISBN 978-0-06-324663-8

$PrintCode

Mama, with the sun
Mama, with the moon
Mama, my beginning
Mama, never-ending

Contents

PART III: RED DIRT: INTERLUDE

PART IV: OF POWER AND OTHER INNOVATIONS

PART V: BLUES FOR BOYS, BLUES FOR MEN

PART VI: MISBEHAVING WOMEN

PART VII: IN SEARCH OF OUR MOTHERS' FORGIVENESS

Honorée's Family Tree

Paternal Side

Hugh Flippin (1814–1882) unmarried liaison with Veta Denipplf (birth and death dates unknown)
- Charles Albert Flippin

Charles Albert Flippin (1844–1930) married Mahala K. Anderson (1839–1871)*
- George Albert
- Florida Ellen

George Albert Flippin (1868–1929) married Georgia Lela Smith (1879–1951) *
- Dorothy Mae
- Robert Browning

Dorothy Mae Flippin (1899–1991) married Henry Nelson (1894–?)*
- Lance Henry Nelson

Dorothy Mae (Flippin) Nelson married Forest Jeffers (1900–1993)**
- Lance Flippin, adopted by Forest Jeffers (last name legally changed)

Lance Flippin Jeffers (1919–1985) married Trellie Lee James (1933–2023) ***
- Valjeanne Michelle (1959–2022)
- Sidonie Colette (1963–2014)
- Honorée Fanonne (1967–)

Maternal Side

Luvenia Thomas Napier Paschal's branch

John Thomas (1842–?) married Mary Thomas (1842–?)
- Richard
- David
- Wyatt
- Elizabeth
- Henry
- Catherine
- Caroline
- Mary
- Washington
- Jessee

Henry Thomas (1868–1944) married Unknown Woman (?–?)
- Luvenia
- [No records located for other children]

Jenkins Napier Paschal's branch

Richard Napier (1837–?) married Clarissa Napier (1841–?)
- Ann
- Davis
- Nace
- Caroline
- Amanda/Mandy
- William
- Lula
- Dock
- Lou

Amanda/Mandy Napier (1868–?) unmarried liaison with
Ambrose Hutchinson Paschal, Sr. (1859–1924)

- Jenkins Napier, later Jenkins Paschal

Luvenia Thomas (1891–1981) married Jenkins Paschal (1884–1952)

- Crawford
- Florence
- Henry
- Iola
- Elconia
- Ambrose
- Jinks, Jr.
- Dave
- Lillie
- Lewis
- Delores
- Oris
- Morris
- Helen
- Flossie

Florence Napier Paschal (1909–2000) married Charlie James (1909–1961)

- Trellie Lee
- Alvester
- Thedwron
- Edna
- Charles
- Florence
- Larry Paschal (adopted)

* First marriage
** Second marriage
** Third marriage

I

IN SEARCH OF OUR MOTHERS' CROSSROADS

My dearest Honorée, your mother meant Life to me. I wish you could have seen the two of us—from your heavenly, pre-birth perch—as we sallied forth to Butler Baker High School. Me a shattered but recovering little bird, your mother stalwart, a warrior, a fiercely focused driver over the red dirt rutted road on our way to school.

—ALICE WALKER

For certainly every Afro-American is descended from a *black* black woman.

—TRELLIE JAMES JEFFERS, "THE BLACK BLACK WOMAN AND THE MIDDLE CLASS"

1

That Day in January

On January 6, 2021, I was in the master bedroom of my home in Norman, Oklahoma, listening to *MSNBC Live with Katy Tur* on my laptop. I had settled in for what I knew would be a very boring certification of the electoral vote for the forty-sixth president of the United States, Joe Biden. I'd never watched the certification, though, and I wanted to be a responsible citizen. I felt very proud of myself.

I lay across my bed, scribbling something I don't even remember in a notebook. Then something happened: a discordant word from Tur. A wrong string plucked in the tenor of her voice. I looked up from my notebook as Tur began to narrate that protesters of the presidential certification were marching toward the US Capitol building—they were protesting what they believed was the theft of the election from President Trump, our forty-fifth president.

On my laptop the screen split, between Tur and the events at the Capitol. The crowd increased in size. The people in the crowd insisted that, all legal, material, and documentary evidence to the contrary, President Trump hadn't lost the presidential election to Joe Biden on November 3, 2020. Actually—this was shouted by people in the crowd—the election had been stolen, and they were at the Capitol to "stop the steal."

I put aside my notebook and began paying attention to the images moving across my laptop screen, noticing that the burgeoning crowd appeared to be nearly all White men. Here and there, I saw a White woman. The few Black men were even easier to count, only three or four that I could spot. As violence erupted, I screamed as White men pushed past the flimsy barrier in front of the Capitol. They began beating Capitol police officers. They crushed those same officers between doors.

A group broke the glass in the Speaker's Lobby of the Capitol. Pointing a gun at the group, a Capitol police officer ordered them not to enter, but shockingly, a young White woman kept crawling into the space where glass had shattered.

A crack: The policeman shot the woman. Then another rioter proclaimed her dead.

⋙⋘

We have a country named the United States because of a war that officially started in 1776—a revolution of angry men—that was fought on this soil and over the sea. If you want to name the White men who met in the Continental Congresses—or the White man who wrote the Declaration of Independence—as founders of this country, I can agree with you.

And if you call the names of those creators of the United States, those who wrote us into existence as Americans, the way a Christian God breathed life into Adam, "our fathers," as a series of White men did—George William Curtis, Abraham Lincoln, and Warren G. Harding—I won't dispute you, either. They are the authors of cherished, mythical narratives. The ones who collected us as kin, as family, in this country. Not in the stuffy, distant way of history, but when you are joined by the gristle of blood and experience and shared outcomes.

But what is *family*, here in this place we now call America?

We are supposed to be a national marshaling of 350 million kindred, "from sea to shining sea." Our nation is supposed to be our home—and to speak about home is to speak about the interior of where you live. A bedroom with a place to hold your weariness, to wrap you in clean sheets and a blanket. A kitchen where sustenance bubbles in a pot, fragrant and eventually delicious. A cup, a plate, a glass, a fork, blunt knife, and spoon on a table. An inviting meal.

An image of home is coziness. Domestic bliss. A protective roof and rooms conjured in the mind of the receiver: "Home is where the heart is." The folding of laundry—the shirts, the pants, the dresses that keep bodies warm. Inside the home is a family, and in our American minds—no matter how altered by political and social discourse—many still think of a family as nuclear and old-fashioned.

Many still consider a family as patriarchal. Father is the head and the ruler. Mother is the helpmeet. Children take their guidance from Father; they take his last name, the name that his own father gave him, and so on and so forth. And isn't that true? Whatever our original ancestors—African, Italian, Asian, Indigenous, Latinx—our last name is *American*. In this country's dining room, a long table, reaching across thousands of miles, is set for millions of people, made kin by the title of "American." At the head of this table is our president, who with one exception has always been a White man. All this is brought forth when we speak of a nation.

But what happens when, instead of that meal on that three-thousand-mile-long table—that sustenance, that food for the citizens—many plates remain empty? Or even when those plates are picked up and smashed on the floor? Even for those who carry "American" in their identity? When some of citizens who sit down at the table—say, we *Black* citizens—are dragged away from that table by others, usually by White men, because Father is the head of our national family? We must bow to his will.

After a few hours of suffering—or days or months or years or decades or centuries—the door to the nation again opens wide. We Black citizens are welcomed back inside with smiles and promises, but no apologies or any acknowledgment of what happened.

"That was in the past. Stop bringing up what is done."

We're invited to sit down at the table. The entire scene plays out once more: We Black citizens are dragged away. We are pushed outside. We are beaten or shot to death. There is no logic or reason to what happens. There is only the power of those White men who hold it by force, a recitation of their self-interested logic: Their past is the only past that matters.

The document that heralded our national revolution, the Declaration of Independence, was penned by Thomas Jefferson. Within that text, he did not cover any Indigenous peoples, or White women, or Black folks with the grace of liberty.

Jefferson wrote, "We hold these truths to be self-evident, that all men are created equal." Yet the presence of that "we" that held "these truths to be self-evident" in those words that are considered sacred spoke an *absence*: Non-White, non-male people didn't establish this nation. They merely lived here.

I won't descend into tortured explanations for Jefferson's wording. (I will leave that to his apologists.) He was who he was—a rich man who would own approximately six hundred enslaved African Americans during his lifetime—and he wrote what he wrote: All *men* are created equal. Jefferson meant *White* men, not Indigenous men and not Black men—despite the fact that Crispus Attucks, an Afro-Indigenous man, was the first to fall in the Boston Massacre in 1770, an essential lead-up to the Revolution. "Men" did not include women, either, of any cultural background. Jefferson's purpose in the *Declaration* was to establish White men as ultimate fathers, second only to God. White men as the authors of the limbs and blood and lineage of this nation. Jefferson didn't need to *state* his purpose—his purpose is implied.

This was the brand of patriarchy created in this nation. Though patriarchy surely existed around the globe, our United States' brand of that system was never meant to include—or benefit—anyone else but White, straight, cisgender men. The laws and practices of this country placed those men on the top of nation's hierarchy.

 ❧

On January 6, 2021, when recently elected Colorado congresswoman Lauren Boebert declared on the site formerly known as Twitter that "Today is 1776," she wasn't including Black people in that statement of a second founding.[1] I don't believe she was including White women, either.

It wasn't a coincidence that the majority of those storming the Capitol were White cisgender men, for what happened wasn't only a political decision about who would become president and who would not. It was about maintaining the rule of White men, a rule that many believed had been broken when Barack Obama was elected president eight years before Donald Trump: *Father is the head.*

To Boebert and others who think like her, this was a White-owned country. Might made (and continues to make) right, "right" in terms both of political views and of the entitlement to ultimate power. That means that nobody BIPOC can be right, unless they agree that Whiteness is the logical conduit to moral and political authority in the United States.

Ever since the campaign of businessman Donald Trump began in 2015, I had tried to ignore what was happening. Mentally, as things got worse, I clung faithfully to the previous picture of Barack Obama and his family. I tried to accept the illogical logic of America, the logic telling me that despite all that I'd read in the historical archives, things had changed for the better; that the presidential administration of Donald Trump was a hiccup.

After all, I'd believed that the election of Barack Obama in 2008 would change three centuries of American history. And so had my mother. And so had so many other African Americans. I'd believed in that change in his first term.

My letting go of the fantasy was gradual. Bits and pieces of trust died off, and after January 6, 2021, my fantasy was completely dead. I'd been tricked too many times—my ancestors had been tricked— and though I was anguished by what I saw on my laptop, in the days afterward, I felt as if I was awakening from a short illness; several years might seem long to some, but for me, it appeared to pass quickly. I felt calm, superior even, because I wasn't lying to myself anymore. I scoffed at the shock of White anchors on the left-leaning news shows that I watched on CNN, on MSNBC. I snorted with laughter as I read the *New York Times* and the *Washington Post.*

These folks didn't have the same experience as me, of being dragged from the American table, repeatedly. They truly believed that all would be well. Or they blamed Donald Trump, as if he were Lucifer in the garden, convincing millions of Americans to taste a particularly juicy, White supremacist fruit. Or they blamed progressive Democrats for pushing for too much change too soon.

~≈~

I wish that I could unknow the lessons of that January day in 2021.

For two hours, there was chaos at the Capitol. In those hours before Vice President Pence stood again on the dais in the House Chamber and finally certified Joe Biden as the president and Kamala Harris as the vice president of the United States, I kept asking, where was the National Guard? Where were the DC city police? Where was anybody to stop this violence?

I was fifty-three years old. I had entered the last third of my life, for most folks in this country don't live past eighty. I didn't know how to raise a garden (then). I didn't own a gun (then). I didn't live with another grown person who could join with me in defending a home, should anyone break in to kill. I had no family members and only one close friend in the university town in which I lived.

I was panicked, imagining what would happen to me if a war broke out—because war appeared to be fulminating on my laptop screen. How would I survive? Writing poems or stories or novels is not a practical skill set in a postapocalyptic society.

It was when I saw the gallows that had been erected that I apprehended the reality: This was a lynch mob, as of old. Many might die. I closed my eyes but could not escape an image of a photograph from the early 1900s: a dead Black man, hanging, and in the foreground smiling White onlookers.

At the Capitol, the mob growled in fury. Cameras cut to a light-skinned congresswoman praying fervently in a gallery, her eyes closed, her hand raised, like the women I remembered from my early childhood, the church sisters at Flat Rock Primitive Baptist, my grandmother Florence's sanctuary in Georgia. I believe I heard the congresswoman call the name of Jesus, as those old ladies had. I prayed along with her, hoping for someone to save her. Begging for grace. I curled into a ball, rocking myself for comfort.

I felt the closest I ever had to my ancestors, but instead of a connecting joy stinging my veins, I felt only my vulnerability: I was Black. I was a woman. What did it mean to inhabit this nation's static image? The joining of those two identities meant that I'd always been an abomination in my country.

I shook and I moaned, chanting the name of God. I clutched at scant blessings: Though History stalked me, at least I recognized its face.

2

Our Fathers Who Rewrote Our Mothers

You already know that before there was an "America," there were inhabitants here already, the Indigenous peoples of many, many tribes. Then came the invaders: White colonizers who smiled at and tricked and murdered some of those Indigenous people. They were English, French, Spanish, Portuguese, and Dutch, but—after too many years and wars and land theft to mention—the English mostly would prevail. That first colony to survive had named themselves Virginia, after Queen Elizabeth, who called herself untouched by men.

But they don't teach about the displaced Indigenous people who lived in that territory, the Algonquian, Iroquoian, and Siouan, other than the fact that *they were conquered.* You don't learn much about the African people who ended up on this side of the water, other than that we were "slaves", to be seen with farming implements or platters of food. Silent, dark,with smiles pasted on our faces.

The Spaniards brought the first enslaved Africans to what would be known as Florida in the early sixteenth century.[1] But Virginia was the first *English* colony to begin importing slaves, and maybe—if you've read a lot—you learned about the Africans who disembarked from the *White Lion* in late summer of 1619, referenced in the letter by John Rolfe, the man who married the kidnapped Indigenous Algonquin girl Metoaka, also known as Pocahontas: "About the latter end of August, a Dutch man of Warr of about 160 tunes arriued at Point-Comfort, the Comandors name Capt Jope . . . He brought not any thing but 20 and odd Negroes."[2]

In fact there were African people already living in Virginia by the time the *White Lion* landed. A Virginia census (called a "muster") was taken in the spring of 1619; this census lists thirty-two Africans, seventeen women and fifteen men.[3] By 1624 the Virginia census recorded only twenty-one Africans, including a family enslaved by Captain William Tucker of Elizabeth City: "ANTONEY Negro: ISABELL Negro: and WILLIAM theire Child Baptised."[4] It is not known when Isabell and Antoney arrived, but most assume that it was on the *White Lion*.[5]

The English were Christians, and their Bible was their sourcebook for all they accomplished. For example, they believed that by settling the land—actually, *stealing*, though that's not how your teacher put it—that belonged to the Indigenous inhabitants, the English were committing anointed acts that the former would eventually thank them for: "Planting . . . may well be divided into two sorts, when Christians by the good liking and willing assent of the salvadges, are admitted by them to quiet possession. . . . Harke, harke, the earth is the Lord's, and all that is therein."[6] To justify their taking, their victims had to be made non-Christian. Indigenous peoples were "salvadges," and the Africans they sold into slavery were, too. For example, in that spring 1619 Virginia census, the "negroes" were labeled "not Christians."[7]

Initially, not all Africans in Virginia had to fear perpetual slavery.[8] That kind of bondage occurred gradually in Virginia, recalling the tale of the frog in increasingly heated water, until the poor creature is finally boiled.[9] The House of Burgesses in Virginia, the colonial legislative body, began passing laws that constricted the lives of the enslaved Africans brought over on the ships—that's when the water grew hotter.

And in October 1629 Virginia passed a law making a contrast between African women's and Englishwomen's labor.[10]

And if an Englishman lay with an African woman, he polluted his body: On September 17, 1630, an Englishman, Hugh Davis, was punished for having sex with an African woman: "Hugh Davis to be soundly whipped, before an assembly of Negroes and others for abusing himself to the dishonor of God and shame of Christians, by defiling his body in lying with a negro; which fault he is to acknowledge next Sabbath day."[11]

And in January 1640, a legal contrast was made between African and White men, concerning the right to bear arms: "ALL persons except negroes to be provided with arms and ammunition or be fined at pleasure of the Governor and Council."[12]

And in March 1643, the English owners of African women and girls were taxed—what the Virginias deemed as "tithing"—for the enslaved females that they held in bondage: "Be it also enacted and confirmed That there be tenn pounds of tob'o. per poll & a bushell of corne per poll paid to the ministers within the severall parishes of the collony for all tithable persons . . . as also for all negro women at the age of sixteen years."[13]

❧

Early writings on the categories that we now view as "racial" emphasized differences between Africans and Europeans, usually in derogatory terms (for Africans). The seventeenth-century French explorer François Bernier, in his essay "Nouvelle Division de la Terre" ("A New Division of the Earth"), enumerates what made "a different species of Africans, these are 1. Their big lips and their flat noses, there are very few among them who have aquiline noses and lips of a moderate size. The blackness which is essential to them and whose cause is not the heat of the Sun, as some have thought; since if one transports a black man and a black woman from Africa to a cold country, their children and further descendants do not cease to be black until they marry white women."[14]

English religious interpretations would point to Africans' inequality in the sight of God, because Virginia's colonizers believed God marked African peoples like Ham in the Bible—or was it Cain? The Virginians waffled back and forth between these two justifications for Blackness, as English minister Morgan Godwyn wrote in 1680, after a visit to Virginia: "They strain hard to derive our Negro's from a stock different from Adam's: but [conversely] they bespeak them as descendents from Cain and to carry his Mark: and yet, by the last, as if condemned to contradictions, they make them the Posterity of that unhappy Son of Noah who, they say, was, together with his whole Family and Race, cursed by his Father. Of which Curse 'tis worth the observing what blessed use they to themselves do make, and what variety of advantages they thereby reap."[15]

This supposed curse argued by Anglo-Virginians, Godwyn continued, gave them the justification to keep Africans in bondage, to deny them rights as full Christians, and eventually, to conflate "slave" with "Negro."[16] And increasingly, Whiteness—also an evolving concept—became conflated with "Christian," rendering all Black people incapable of God's favor, at least in the sight of White Virginians.[17]

For an Anglo-Virginian, a White woman was the most desirable mate—that is, if she did not toil in the field, and was not a sex worker or a woman of ill repute—a wench.[18] The ideal woman was a wife and mother, the mistress of her household. Even if she wielded a whip, she was delicate, beautiful, worthy of patriarchal protection. In the seventeenth century, supporters of indenture—unfree servitude contracted for a set time—assured poor Englishwomen from across the ocean that if they came to the New World as indentured servants, they would not be forced to work the fields.[19] For example, in *Leah and Rachel, or The Two Fruitfull Sisters Virginia and Mary-land*, John Hammond emphasized that female indentured servants were meant to work on light tasks inside the home, while their husbands provided more difficult labor: "The Women are not (as is reported) put into the ground to worke, but occupie such domestique imployments and houswifery as in England, that is dressing victuals, righting up the house, milking, imployed about dayries, washing, sowing, . . . yet som wenches that are nasty, beastly and not fit to be so imployed are put into the ground."[20]

To Anglo-Virginians, however, African women were different: They were not made to be mistresses of the house. Examining public writings by (male) English travelers, Jennifer L. Morgan found ideas about African women's difference—in negative descriptions.[21] This kind of belittling of African women was circulated in early travelogues that were published while slavery was gaining a foothold in the Americas. For example, in *True and Exact History of Barbados*, Richard Ligon pruriently expresses his fascination—and then disgust—with the naked bodies of African women: "These women are faulty."[22] Early Anglo-Virginians also believed that African women were lascivious, and by the eighteenth century the term *wench*, connoting loose morals as well as hard labor, became increasingly applied to woman of African descent.[23] By the nineteenth century, *wench* in America would *always* apply to Black women, at least according to Noah Webster in his 1828 dictionary.[24]

Like that liberty that Thomas Jefferson explored in the eighteenth century—that which would spark an actual revolution in North America—harmful seventeenth-century ideas about Black women were already regarded as self-evident. Ideas about cultural differences are *shaped*, however; they aren't truly natural. When Anglo-Virginians compared African women to White women, of course, they would find dark women lacking and their own pale women superior. Certainly these attitudes about racial hierarchies—and White male desire for legalized power—would be transformed into laws chipping away at Black women's status.

What we view as racial categories did not evolve until decades after seventeenth-century Virginia, with early "intellectual" thought about Black people, and especially with unashamed examinations of African women's naked bodies. Yet the seventeenth-century legal changes that made formal differences between African women and English women—such as the taxing of the owners of enslaved women— solidified the idea that authentic womanhood was English/White.

This privileging of White women was a foregone conclusion, for you cannot cherish an angel of your own making without troubling a created fiend. An opposite serves as a negative and a definer of the ideal by explaining what that ideal is *not*. If perfection is the only option, soon perfection will become commonplace, and perhaps even flaws will be detected in what was considered pristine. Therefore a defective example must remain in place, to highlight how wonderful its perfect opposite is. This is what happened when the North American definition of womanhood transformed into White womanhood in colonial Virginia. The more lascivious, ugly, supernaturally strong, and maternally unfeeling that Anglo-Virginians made Black women's images and characters, the more delicate, beautiful, moral, weak, and tenderly maternal White women would become.

But in 1658 a woman named Elizabeth Key would challenge these laws and ideas.

Elizabeth was neither a self-contracted indentured servant nor sentenced to slavery for life, but rather someone born in-between. Her mother had been an enslaved Black woman, but her father was Thomas Key, a free Anglo-Virginian. Thomas was an indentured servant who, after the end of his contract, somehow pulled himself up from the ranks—we assume by dint of hard work, and because he was White and not African.[25] When his Anglo-African daughter was born, Thomas contracted Elizabeth—a child named after the first ruling Queen of England—out as an indentured servant to "Humphrey Higginson" for "nine yeares."[26] Higginson wasn't supposed to give or sell Elizabeth's contract to anyone else, but he did anyway, because when another Anglo-Virginian named John Mottrom died, Elizabeth was part of his estate.[27]

Not much is known about Elizabeth's mother, the African woman whom Thomas Key compelled to accept his attentions. The historical record does not memorialize her. We don't even know the circumstances surrounding her pregnancy, other than that one witness recalled that Thomas had been "fined for getting his Negro woman with Childe."[28] Another witness recounted that she saw Elizabeth's mother "goe to bed to her Master many times and that I heard her mother Say that shee was mr. Keyes daughter."[29]

I wish I could step lightly here, but I can't. I must tell you: An unfree person cannot give their consent to intimate contact, even if there is love. I'll be blunt, in case you don't catch my meaning: In this country we call nonconsensual intimacy rape. And so Thomas had raped Elizabeth's mother. You may want to fantasize about love between them, though she was enslaved and Black. Perhaps the mother was directly from the continent, or at most, one or two generations removed. If there was love, Thomas had a strange way of showing it, for instead of taking the child Elizabeth—his daughter, his line, his kin, his flesh—into his home, he gave this baby as an indentured servant to another White man, though he had stipulated that Elizabeth be treated not as a servant but as one of a slightly higher status.[30]

If we think of what James Baldwin called the "innocence" of White folks, how innocent Thomas Key was, to think that the Anglo-African daughter he passed to someone else would be treated better than Thomas treated the child's mother, and then her child.[31] But Thomas was allowed to keep his willful—and *willed*—innocence because he was an Englishman. He could claim opacity when it came to his affectionate responsibility. He ruled a house, even if he'd denied his child entry into that place, though her skin was probably lighter than her mother's. Perhaps her eyes were light—blue or green or gray—instead of brown. Perhaps her hair was curly or waved or straight, instead of kinky.

But if you think you're supposed to have more sympathy for a lighter-skinned daughter—child of a White father—because Elizabeth has traveled further away from "true Blackness," then perhaps you need to examine why your sympathy isn't split between Elizabeth and her mother, a woman whose baby was taken away from her. A mother who didn't even have a name that appeared in court records: No one seems to have cared who she was, not the man who had a child with her, not even her daughter.

Years passed.

Ordinarily, an indenture for an English servant in Virginia lasted between four and seven years.[32] Remember, though, Elizabeth's indenture had been contracted for nine years to Henry Higginson. Though the historical record doesn't say why her indenture was so long, we can assume it was because she was Black, female, and her legal status was morphing—or rather, eroding—in real time in colonial Virginia. Higginson sold or gave Elizabeth away, and gradually, sixteen or seventeen years elapsed: Elizabeth's indenture transformed into seven or eight years beyond what was supposed to be the end of her already-long indenture contract. And now Elizabeth belonged to the "Estate of Col. Jon Mottrom"—and its executors were trying to claim her as *a lifelong slave*. One of the executors did not even call Elizabeth by her birth name. Instead, he called her "a Negro wench named Black Besse."[33] At best, "wench" indicated that he considered Elizabeth as lower-class and meant to serve—at worst, he was calling her a whore.

Let's be clear that at this point what happened to this girl-child-now-woman was trafficking. But Elizabeth found some comfort. She and a fellow indentured servant, William Grinstead, had struck up a relationship. Though he was a White man, their relationship was not rape or compulsion; Elizabeth Key could consent to William, as they had nearly the same status as indentured servants, though not of race or gender. At the time of her freedom suit, William's indenture was over: He and Elizabeth had a son together. But then I think I can safely make a leap: An anxiety must have hovered over Elizabeth, the way it had over her unnamed mother about her own child. What about Elizabeth's son? William had been set free, his indenture term honored, but Elizabeth was still in bondage, and the new possessor of her indenture had no intention of letting her go. Would Elizabeth's son be free or not?

Maybe William had promised that he'd always take care of Elizabeth and her children, no matter her status. But why would Elizabeth trust this, when her own married (to a White woman) father had cast her out of his home? Whatever occurred between Elizabeth and William in private, when she filed her case, her justification for her freedom was that her father had been free and Christian, and so Elizabeth was the same.

At her first hearing on January 20, 1655, Elizabeth Key won her freedom.[34]

At her second hearing on March 20, 1655, the Mottrom estate appealed the ruling.[35]

At her third hearing on July 21, 1656, Elizabeth was given her final freedom.[36] But because either the owners of Black/African women had to pay taxes on their female enslaved, or free Black women had to pay taxes on themselves, it was ordered that "by the tenth of November next [she must] pay fifty pounds of tobacco to the said overseers [of the Mottrom estate]."[37] In other words, Elizabeth *was forced to pay reparations* to the estate of the Englishman who had kept her unfairly in bondage.

～

After Elizabeth Key Grinstead's freedom case, Virginia lawmakers passed other laws concerning Africans. In March 1661, laws concerning African runaways were passed.[38] A year later, there was another law on the same issue.[39] In 1662, six stingy years after Elizabeth's triumph, the Black mother was made a despised figure. Virginia passed a law that changed the status of her children: *"Negro womens children to serve as the condition of the mother.* WHEREAS some doubts have arrisen whether children got by any Englishman upon a negro woman shall be slave or ffree, *Be it therefore enacted by this present grand assembly*, that all children borne in this country shalbe held bond or free only according to the condition of the mother, *And* that if any christian shall commit ffornication with a negro man or woman, he or she soe offending shall pay double the fines imposed by the former act."[40]

The aftermath of this law was tragic. As Jennifer L. Morgan explains, it created new, enslaved children who would be available for the auction block.[41]

More than that, this law continued the peculiar branding of Black women: Their lives were never truly private, but available to scrutiny by someone who assumed Black women's inferiority. By legally separating the status of Englishwomen's children from that of Black women, the law elevated Englishwomen as preferable mothers—because the latter could contribute to a free lineage.

Thus 1662 was the snake in the Eden that Englishmen believed they had invented—those men who would later call themselves White. They were the creators of a false narrative of splendor, one that concealed the misery they enacted upon dark others. In an odd twist, Black women became creators, too, albeit unwillingly, the authors of other enslaved people: their own children. If the credit for founding this nation has been given to the White man, then the burden of slavery has been assigned to the Black woman.[42] She was the inverse image of Eve, both mother and not-mother, for her children didn't belong to her.

This law also effectively severed Black fathers—whether slave or free— of Black children from patriarchal possibility, for one of the rules of patriarchy is the ability of the father to pass on heritage. The 1662 law created a huge likelihood of enmity between Black men and Black women, like an alternate Adam's resentment toward his mate in the Bible. These two figures were naked in the North American garden, their protective covering snatched off, since patriarchy was no longer available for a Black man—but then, it never *had* been his anyway, for that system only was for White men in America. As for the Black woman, she was despised inside her body, down to her very womb.

Two centuries later, new language would be added to this slave code: *Partus sequitur ventrem*, which translates to "Offspring follows belly," a barnyard term, given to the breeding of horses and cows and pigs and dogs.[43] This is how colonial White men viewed Black women: animals grunting and shitting in a field.

⁊⁊⁊

I can't help it. I keep wondering, whatever happened to Elizabeth Key's mama?

This woman's daughter was free and her grandchild free as well, but at what cost? Elizabeth Key and William Grinstead published their intentions to be married on the day that she won her freedom suit: "William Greensted [*sic*] and Elizabeth Key intends to be joined in the Holy Estate in Matrimony."[44] Further, William accepted patriarchal responsibility for his wife: She was transferred directly from the Mottrom estates to his care.[45] The paper trail of their family shows us that one of the male descendants of Elizabeth and William became a White slave owner.[46] This was the custom of the time, for Englishmen making their ways in colonial Virginia—this was the evolution of the brutality of those who would become White.

Would Elizabeth's grandchildren and great-grandchildren care—or even know about—her mother, that first African ancestor? If these descendants did know about her, how did they reconcile that, absent a trick of fate, they would have been the slave held in bondage, instead of the master?

Don't chide or blame me for detesting the dice game of *house* and *field*. I have a right to my say—and to my mourning, my disbelief that one faint move can alter or ruin someone's life.

Where did Elizabeth's mother go? Was she dead, by the time of her child's Pyrrhic victory? If she was alive, did Elizabeth bring her to the home that William built, or did the daughter turn her back, forgetting the chatter of water?

※

So many years that call to each other, harmonizing in consequence. So much history that won't let me be.

3

Blues for the African Woman Whose Name Has Been Erased

Here is the door. She won't return. Push her through to blues. None of us returned. Push her through to new, accursed speech. Push her to rage and prayer and survival.

The door: no one will return. The path: all of us must question. The water. The stolen girls. The taken women.

The way a woman passed through. The way they forced her to leave. The way her lineage will cling. We will sing her blues. We will chant rememory.[1]

The way I weary of beauty. How I long to stop the blood. How I long to refuse water. How I long for dreams of paintings, instead of nightmares: here is the cell for the taken. Here she will wonder what else. Here she will scream. Here is where she begins poeming. And imagining. And rejecting.

Those ships: too much. I've envisioned her. I've screamed all night. The breath. The imperial succubus. The clutching of medicine bundles, of strong root bags passed down. And God. And questioning. The absence of sun. And blasphemy. And forcing myself to hushed words.

And where were You, her God of mercy? And where were lines of wisdom? And where is true
belief? Oh He/She/They made up of infinity. Oh Ancestors. Oh thunder. Oh cacophony of water.
Oh mother of a continent and pulling me from breasts. Oh mother of lingering. And medicine in my skin. And root bag of my kin.

And women erased from paper. And pleas aboard the ships. And water. And sailors. And traders.
And patriarchs of the Bible.

But mercy: the shackled will love each other. Oh God. We came to love each other. Oh mercy. Oh mother. And door of no return. Oh daughter. And water. And door of no return.

And questions, oh questions: Why did they force her to leave? Why do we women sing rememory?

4

Paper Trail

I've resisted taking a swab to my cheek to find out the ways my African/Black heritage traveled, because my imagination has soothed me, these fifty-plus years. I'm afraid a DNA test might destroy the foundation I've glued together, small rock by tiny pebble. I know that paper guards me from knowing my African past, what might be West or Central Africa.

I began a love affair with the people I will never know, my enslaved African/Black ancestors, because of the missing archival records. When I read the nonfiction book *Roots* as a child, I knew that Alex Haley couldn't have known every detail or feeling of his ancestors. Even then, I could understand that.

Yet there was a documentary trail that Haley located. I felt jealousy that he had found his ancestors—but I felt a kinship, too. When I read the monstrous horrors that these enslaved people had endured, I would think about my father, whom I loved and hated and whose behavior threw me into a cauldron of bewilderment. And some had died still enslaved, but some had made it to freedom. While there was life, always there was hope. If I could simply survive, perhaps I, too, could make it out of my house and into some other place, a promised land of liberty.

This dearth of documentation is protection as well, for it keeps me from locating the true cost of slavery. This erasure hides even *more* erasure: that my Africana/Black ancestors weren't capable of intellectual production. That as their descendant, I wasn't quite whole. The places I have entered in a contemporary era weren't legally marked by segregation, but they rang with dog whistle bells when I crossed the threshold, a silent sound of "Whites only." I can't document a *feeling*, though. Who among my former classmates, professors, and colleagues would admit to making me feel that way—on the record? How could I prove I didn't misinterpret what I felt?

I found solace in historical research and critical analysis because the puzzle of my existence in the United States is easier to solve when there is documentation. There is the proof, I will say, pointing to the gorgeously looped cursive writing of a slave ship ledger of human cargo—my African ancestors. Yet my only true documentation of the African *continent* is my mother: her color, her hair, her nose, her mouth. She is my tie to Africa, but also my tie to a tragic history. The person I love most in the world signifies my documentary lack.

I know so little, and nothing that travels back before 1870. Most African Americans don't either, because on what were called the slave schedules—the pre–Civil War censuses—enslaved people were not recorded by name.[1] Before 1870, Southern Black folks were usually recorded only when causing trouble, commercially useful, or tragic. Saidiya Hartman identifies this archival lack for African/Black peoples as one demanding informed historical imagination: "The intention here isn't anything as miraculous as recovering the lives of the enslaved or redeeming the dead, but rather laboring to paint as full a picture of the lives of the captives as possible. . . . The method guiding this writing practice is best described as critical fabulation. 'Fabula' denotes the basic elements of story, the building blocks of the narrative."[2]

I take Hartman's term—"critical fabulation"—as my text when I leap into the breach between what can be known and what can only be felt through prayer, imagination, vision, love—and duty. I must rely on what I believe the ancestors give me permission to do, as surely as they allowed Hartman.

And I encircle Toni Morrison's theory of rememory, which represents turning off gaslighting's pilot light, rejecting Black/African people's erasure in the master narrative.[3] My Eatonton elders and ancestors may not have been able to read, but they had stories, oral traditions, visions that speak to morsels—or mountains—of truth. When other Black folks and I write about early African Americans, we're not writing our ancestors *into* the narrative of this country. We are only saying, "We've already been here." Just because somebody White didn't see our ancestors—or they *refused* to see those people—doesn't mean those ancestors didn't exist, or that this nation's crimes against humanity did not occur.

⌒⌒

There are few records when it comes to the women of my family, and I only can go back as far as Clarissa, the mother of the woman my mother called Great-Grandma Mandy. Both had a last name—Napier—that my mother pronounced in the French manner: *NAH-pee-ay*.

Mama had always told me a story about Mandy: that the old lady had been born into slavery, and that her first memory of her father was him being sold to Mississippi. I have told this story many times. I have grieved her loss and sent sad prayers her way.

It took me fifty years before I decided to find Mandy's paper trail. This was a decision that I knew would bring heartache, but when my mother faced the end of her life, I wanted to find something to grab, as an old saying of Mama—borrowed from Mandy—advised: "You gotta start out with what you can hold onto."

Don't instigate what you can't finish.

⌒⌒

I began with the 1870 census of Putnam County, Georgia.

Before that year, there would be no census record of Mandy or her family on the 1850 and 1860 slave schedules. Besides the "Slave Owner," the schedules asked for items such as "Age," "Sex," "Color," the possible intellectual and/or physical disability(ies) of each enslaved person, and whether the slave owner had freed any enslaved people or had any escape.[4]

I couldn't find a Mandy, but I did find an Amanda, the only child with this name in the county. Amanda was two years old, which would have meant she was born in 1868—three years after the end of the Civil War.[5] She was the youngest child of Richard Napier, a "farm hand" who was thirty-three years old, and Clarissa Napier, who was twenty-nine; no profession was given for Clarissa.

The designation of "farm hand" given for Richard means that he didn't own his own land. He probably worked the fields of a White man, or once worked them before the Civil War; field hand was usually the most taxing physical job for an enslaved person. This knowledge hurts me, more than a little bit.

The ages of Amanda's parents indicate that they had been enslaved—probably born enslaved—and they might not have had a marriage ceremony, if they had decided to join their lives before the Civil War. However, since this census took place after 1865, if Richard and Clarissa had been living together, their cohabitation would be deemed a legal marriage.[6]

They were probably owned by a White man named S. Napier, of Putnam County, Georgia. S. Napier's signature appears in the *Returns of Qualified Voters and Reconstruction Oath Books, 1867–1869*, which every White man who wanted to vote had to sign, certifying that he hadn't fought against the Union in the Civil War.[7] There were other prominent (White) Napiers throughout the state of Georgia, those who could trace their lineage to "Norman French descent" as well as veterans of the American Revolution.[8]

I'm most interested in that 1860 slave schedule, however: S. Napier appears as "slave owner," along with the age and "sex"—there were only two acknowledged genders on this census—of S. Napier's 134 enslaved African Americans.[9] Richard would have been twenty-three and Clarissa would have been nineteen, and I begin to count the number of males and females in their age ranges, give or take five years. I'm desperate, hoping there is only one in each category, so that I can look at an anonymous record and tell myself, "This is Richard" or "This is Clarissa," but there are too many. Besides the twenty enslaved men/boys in their late teens/early-to-mid-twenties, and seven girls/ women from their late teens to early twenties, there are forty-three "mulattoes"—biracial Black folks—on S. Napier's list, twenty-one males and twenty-two females. I wonder who their White fathers were.

Someone might say that these fragments of knowledge should be a victory, but I'm greedy for what I'm owed: my entire history.

⌖

There is a whispered urging: Despite the proof of history, give White men the benefit of the doubt. They didn't mean to erase us. They were only thinking of themselves, and that is selfish, but not malevolent.

And yet they erased us.

I return to the slave ship, and the story of John Newton, the man who wrote "Amazing Grace." Such a sweet story, isn't it? That Newton found God, was horrified by what he had done—trading enslaved Africans—and then repented and wrote a song to God called "Amazing Grace."[10]

But before trading in slaves, Newton had *already* become a Christian. "Amazing Grace" would be written later; thankfully he finally abandoned slave trading, but not because of his Christianity—he suffered a seizure, for which no cause could be found, and was forced to give up sailing.[11] Before that seizure, Newton kept loading human beings onto ships for six years after accepting Christianity, laying them in the bottom like moldy bread on shelves approximately eighteen inches high, and sometimes half crouching. That's like lying in your coffin alive—did you know that? Have you ever tried to breathe in the space between your chest and a wooden board a few inches from your face? Every time I imagine it, I experience panic.

Why do we keep giving these White men so much credit for the barest humanity? We give them praise after they committed uncivilized acts—we celebrate a few years of self-interrogation after a lifetime of ignoring what was right.

Are we so forgiving because the documentation usually doesn't exist? And why *would* it exist? Why *wouldn't* men like John Newton delete the details of the harms they committed—on purpose, so that willful deniers of humanity's horrors could insist that the Middle Passage wasn't so bad?

Does civilization require ruthlessness as its brethren, a Cain to its Abel?

❧

On the 1880 census of Putnam County, Amanda Napier is twelve. Her parents are the same as a decade before, Richard and Clarissa.[12]

The 1890 Georgia census records were destroyed by fire, so there are no extant records for Mandy and her family.[13]

The 1900 census of Putnam County, Georgia, lists a woman named "Mandy Napier" as "black," as the "head of household," and gives her profession as "cook." Her marital status is listed as "Wd," which I take to mean "widowed." The census states that she is thirty years old and was born in April 1870, and lists her three children—two boys, fourteen-year-old Jenkins and four-year-old Albert, and a little girl, one-year-old Easter, all of whom went by the last name Napier.[14] The birth year is different by two years for Mandy Napier and Amanda Napier—1870 versus 1868.

But I'm in surer territory: Jenkins was the first name of my mother's maternal grandfather.

On the next census—1910—I'm leaning toward a belief that Mandy and Amanda are the same person, for Mandy's birth year is listed as 1868 again.[15] Her name is spelled "Mandie," but everyone in her household carries the last name Napier. She is listed as a farm laborer and head of her household. Mandy still identifies herself as a "widow," though now, in addition to Jenkins—called Jinks on the census—she is mother to two other sons, thirteen-year-old Albert and six-year-old Dave. Mandy has three daughters now, the thirteen-year-old Annie—perhaps a twin to Albert, eight-year-old Ethel, and three-year-old Lizzie. The name Easter does not appear for a child in this census, but the information for Mandy/Mandie states that she has six children, and all her children are living. Since Annie is thirteen, I'm wondering if Annie might have been named Easter formally but decided to give another name to the census taker; or maybe it's a middle name.

By 1910 Mandy has become a grandmother to the baby girl Florence and the three-year-old boy Crofford, who I know are the children of Jenkins/Jinks—my grandmother Florence was Jenkins' oldest daughter. (According to family history, Crofford's name was spelled "Crawford.") There is some confusion, though, as nineteen-year-old Lou—whom I assume is Luvenia, my mother's grandmother—is listed both as "widowed" and Mandy's "daughter-in-law." (Or at least it appears so; the census taker's handwriting is unclear.) In addition, Jenkins is listed as "single"—but he is married by then, for there is a Baldwin County marriage certificate for Jenks Pascher and a Lavenia Thomas, dated May 25, 1907; Baldwin and Putnam Counties are only twenty or so miles apart.[16] It doesn't alarm me that Jenks is not a Napier, for Grandma Florence's maiden name was Paschal, which is quite close to Pascher—but there was a reason that Jenkins changed his last name.

※

In Genesis, after Cain killed Abel, he didn't express remorse. When his brother's blood told God a story, pushing up from the soil, Cain didn't fall on his knees, saying, "I am a bad person! I'll strive to do better!"

Cain justified himself as not his brother's keeper, because he wasn't truly sorry, but for some reason God allowed him to live. What was that reason? So that Cain could remember his transgression for the rest of his life, and so for centuries, White men of the cloth—preachers and ministers—could accuse Cain of passing down his murderous blood to Africans—*to my people*?

From behind pulpits these holy White men insisted Cain's punishment was dark flesh.[17] These holy men would believe their paleness meant they had been washed clean, that little color was proof of the favor of God.

This is how slavery was considered acceptable, at least to a Christian deity.

And Black men were called brutes.

And Black women were deemed unmotherly, lustful, and built for hard labor, not at all delicate like White women.

And the children of Black women would be considered unworthy, too, of freedom and a lineage sung in the national square.

❧

On the 1920 census, some of Mandy's children had left her home, including her oldest, Jenkins/Jenks. Last names have changed for some of Mandy's children—Dave is no longer a Napier; on this report, his last name is Cartwright, though Mandy's last name remains Napier— she no longer claims that she is a widow; she is now "single." She has three more grandchildren, with last names that I don't recognize, though fifteen-year-old Luvenia Huff clearly is named for the elder Luvenia Napier, the wife of Jenkins.[18]

On the 1930 census, Dave Cartwright is still living with his mother.[19] Six years later, Dave is gone from pneumonia: His mother, Amanda Napier, and his father, Will Cartright, are listed on the death certificate.[20] Dave's brother, Jinks Paschal, is the informant for the death.

I wonder if this is the first of Mandy's children to die, in this time before vaccines and widespread availability of medical care in rural Georgia—especially medical care for African Americans.

I am certain that Mandy grieved.

❧

If Mama ever told me how long Mandy lived, I cannot remember. Neither could I locate a death certificate for Mandy, only a last census report. In 1940 Mandy is seventy years old—if this is *my* Mandy. I don't recognize any of the children listed, but a last name of distant relative is familiar:: "Waller."[21]

Mandy is still single and still head of her household, but there is a shift that excites me: While on the 1930 report, Mandy said that she could not read and write, ten years later she informed the census taker that she had "elementary education," which might mean that she could read and write. I hope this was true, and if so, I am so proud of her.

∾

A separate 1930 census report for Jinks Napier lists him as head of his family.[22] At the time, he is forty-five years old and seven years older than his wife, Luvenia. Since Jinks reports that he was twenty-three when he married, Luvenia was only a teenager. There are eleven children in the house, including my grandmother Florence, who is twenty, and the baby, Oris. The oldest brother Crawford is not on the report. My mother insisted that teenage Crawford ran away because of Jinks's cruelty and never was heard from again.

By the 1940 census, Jinks is living in Putnam Country with Luvenia and their children in a separate residence—Mandy and Jinks's other siblings are living elsewhere.[23] On this report, there are two items of interest: Several of Jenkins's fifteen children have left home—my grandmother married in 1933. And Jenkins has permanently changed his last name from Napier to Paschal. His children will change their names, too, even those who have lived through adulthood with a previous surname; my grandmother Florence always gave her maiden name as Paschal.

The census report was not the first time that Jenkins had been documented as having tried on a different name. There was that variation of Paschal on his marriage certificate, but it took thirty-three years to make a permanent change—and to declare his paternity, for Jenkins took the last name of his father, a White man named Ambrose Hutchinson Paschal, born in 1859.[24]

Ambrose was the son of William Paschal, who appears on the same 1860 slave schedule where I encountered S. Napier, the (probable) former master of Mandy's parents. On that slave schedule, William Paschal (the father) owned seventy-nine enslaved people. Twenty-one of these enslaved Black folks were "mulatto"; twelve of those were female, and nine were male.

On the "Find a Grave" page for Ambrose Hutchinson Paschal, a commenter disputes that he fathered at least two biracial children.[25] It appears that this objection was left by a White descendant of Ambrose, but in a later comment, the same descendant seems to have finally accepted that Paschal had biracial descendants. (I haven't reached out to her to inquire why she was adamant that Ambrose couldn't have slept with Black women, and then became convinced that he had.)

What I do know is that my mother recollected that a well-dressed White man and his wife regularly came to Sunday dinner at the house where Jenkins lived with Luvenia—the "Lou" from the 1910 census. Mama maintained that this White man was Jenkin's father, but he couldn't have been; Ambrose Hutchinson Paschal died in the 1920s, before Mama was born. So who was this man who came to dinner? A brother? A cousin?

Mama said that there was a general store, too, one she frequented as a little girl. This store was owned by White males with the last name Paschal—there, the owners would call her "Jenks' granddaughter" and give Mama free candy.

In the only picture of Jenkins Napier Paschal that I've seen, he looks like a White man. (At least two of his children with Luvenia looked White, too.) Thus, even if Ambrose Hutchinson Paschal wasn't Jenkins's father, *some* White man had crossed a racial—and sexual—boundary and fathered a child with Mandy.

Even though I am a skeptical person, I look at names in my family, how they repeat over generations. For example, Crawford and Ambrose were the names of two of Jenkins's sons, and on that "Find a Grave" page for Ambrose Hutchinson Paschal, someone named "Crawford Waller" is identified as *another* of the White man's biracial children—a very nice coincidence.

❧

I remember Grandma Florence's brother, Great-Uncle Ambrose, for he traveled from California to Eatonton the summer I was a teenager, to attend the funeral of Luvenia, his mother. (Black) Ambrose was a kind soul—very sweet, because that summer, I lost my manners, went nosing without permission through his luggage, found a T-shirt I liked, and wore it! The memory truly embarrasses me, these forty-plus years later, though Ambrose didn't even complain. He only said mildly, "Just ask me the next time, baby."

☙

The paternity of Mandy's firstborn son leads me back to what would have been her transgression at the time: At the age of around sixteen, she had a baby by a White man. She was unmarried at the time, and to my mother's knowledge, she never married. Naturally, I wonder if Mandy's liaison with Ambrose Hutchinson Paschal was voluntary or forced. Of course I do.

Either way, at least one of Mandy's children—her biracial child Jenkins—would have been a sign that she was an outcast, or at best, an outlier. She was listed as the head of her household on every one of the census reports. Mandy might have told the first census taker she was a widow, but that probably was to avoid his rude remarks about her being single with a house full of children.

My mother never criticized Mandy or seemed ashamed of her actions, instead speaking glowingly of her as a Black woman who'd looked out for herself and her family. Through Mandy's relationship with a well-off White man, she'd secured a better economic situation for herself and her family—and it seems, a *protected* situation—in the years when White supremacist oppression reconfigured from slavery to the Black Codes and then to Jim Crows laws, with constant extra-legal racial terrorism.

But the mystery remains, concerning my mother's story about Mandy: that she had seen her father sold farther south during slavery. What really happened?

Mandy's age on those census reports means that she was born free. Her father Richard is listed on both the 1870 and 1880 censuses as the head of his household. Richard was present in his daughter's life—so who exactly *was* that man Mandy remembers being sold to Mississippi? Did Mandy make up this story? Or was my mother's "rememory" wrong, though she fiercely clung to her version?

I'm certain *somebody's* family in Eatonton's Black community had a male forebear who was sold away—the separation of family members was a regular event in the antebellum South. Or perhaps the man was Mandy's uncle or other close kin, who was sold to Mississippi before the Civil War, and she heard the story from her parents. Maybe the man who was sold was a grandfather, the sire of Clarissa or Richard Napier.

Or instead of Mandy's relative being sold into the bondage that most of us know about—pre–Civil War chattel slavery—that relative might have been snatched off a country road and unjustly imprisoned due to the Black Code laws passed in Georgia in 1865 and 1866, after President Andrew Johnson, sympathetic to the defeated Confederates, entered the White House. Mississippi passed the first Black Codes concerning African American freed people.[26] Other Southern states—like Georgia—quickly followed.

When reading about racist laws in post–Civil War Georgia, I observed so many parallels to today. What I find interesting is that in 1865, Southern states were just as enraged as today's conservatives about immigration, with restrictions on movement for those who were not considered US citizens. (In this case, Black folks.)[27] In addition to issues of immigration, Black Codes controlled "vagrancy," which meant that a Black person—usually a man—who couldn't prove he was employed by a White person could be subject to imprisonment.[28] Exploitation of the labor of unfree, incarcerated people continues to this day in the United States.[29] Further, when considering issues surrounding power against those who were deemed vagrants, I'm reminded of the racist history informing *currently* proposed ordinances against the unhoused in the United States.[30] And until the Peonage Abolition Act of 1867, Black folks (and others, too) could be held in bondage to work off their debts—the same way that today, people can be kept in prison without trials if they owe court costs.[31]

Though this Black male relative of Mandy might not have been sold to Mississippi before 1865, after that date he might have been traded through vagrancy laws to another county. In the late 1800s it took about two hours by horse to travel twenty miles. If Mandy's relative had been rented to a farm three or four counties over from Putnam, that would have been a long distance for a little girl to imagine. Naming Mississippi as this relative's landing place might have been Mandy's way of measuring untraversable distances of grief, ancestry, and bewilderment.

☙

Oh Mandy. Oh absence. Oh door of no return. Oh Mandy and red dirt and emptiness of paper.

What is the reason our blood must leave us? Why must we daughters keep singing rememory?

5

A Brief Note Concerning Womanist Identity

Let's be clear about what a "womanist" is.

Let me drop some science on you. (I'm not really a scientist. I barely passed biology and chemistry in high school. "Drop some science" is an African American vernacular reference from the 1980s, when I was a young girl. It means: I have a bit of wisdom to share.)

Are you ready? Then, let's proceed.

The first use of the term *womanist* is attributed to the poet, novelist, and essayist Alice Walker, who defined it in her 1983 essay collection, *In Search of Our Mothers' Gardens: Womanist Prose.*

To be a womanist, you must care about Black people, and about other communities of color—and you must understand that there is a global majority of people of color. You should care about the well-being of families and racism and oppression of *all* genders in those communities of color—and certainly this includes the welfare of men, though it does not include the dominance of men. You must want justice. You must want love. You must want children to inherit a better world.

And you must be a feminist to be a womanist. Walker writes that into her definition: "A black feminist or feminist of color."[1]

To be a feminist, you can't believe in patriarchy. You can't believe that it's okay for men to rule the world—or even to rule your individual household. If you are regularly reading the Book of Ephesians in the Bible and nodding your head in agreement with Paul—agreeing that a wife should submit to her husband—please stop calling yourself a womanist.

As a womanist, you don't have to be strong all the time—none of us are—but you must have courage, because claiming the political identity of womanist means that you can't live one way in your home and another way outside on the curb. You can't say things like "Let the Black man speak or eat, or lead *first* because the Black man has it harder." You should understand that Black men, Black women, and Black nonbinary people *all* have it hard, just in different ways. This isn't a contest to see who suffers the most.

And if you want to be a womanist, you must be a feminist. I beg of you, please stop misreading Walker's definition of "womanist" on purpose to make your life easier. Nobody ever said this life would be easy. That's not the promise of womanism.

I know that it's difficult—especially for an African American woman, who is expected to prop up everybody but herself—to say, "I am a womanist, which means I am a Black feminist," because you're afraid you will suffer consequences. You're afraid you will be shunned in your Black community. If you like to sleep with a man, you're afraid you won't be able to keep that man.

But if you're a Black woman, you're already suffering. Look around in this country— do you really want to keep a man by throwing your equal rights by the side of the road? Wouldn't you like to suffer in service of something, rather than suffer because you have no rights?

And yes, sister, you can still sleep with men if you're a womanist. You can ride or be ridden, whichever you choose. Do you, girlfriend, because I sleep with men too, and I like it. Oh, I like it very, very much. But I like—no, *I love*—being a womanist, a Black feminist, because I love the rights that feminism gave me and other Black women. I love those rights more than I love sleeping with men.

I don't assume that those rights spontaneously assembled in the ether and then drifted upon my shoulders—that I only have the rights that men gave to me because I'm so *pretty* and *special*. I know that other women fought to give me these rights through their battles and sacrifices.

Here are just a few of my favorite things that feminism *legally gave me* and other women (of all cultural backgrounds) in this country: being able to have my own bank account in my own name. Being able to buy a home, and not need my daddy to cosign for me—or have the home in my husband's name. Having my own credit card.[2]

I love knowing that I don't have to get married to survive economically as a woman in this country, because I have a great job that pays well. But most Black women have always worked outside the home—recall that we toiled during slavery, and in low-wage, domestic jobs afterward.[3] (This, along with the sacred pursuit of literacy, probably was the reason schoolteachers were historically revered in African American communities.) The image of the female housewife who looks out the window of her kitchen, longing for the privilege of working for her own wages, was not the usual reality for a Black woman.

I love that there have been laws passed saying, if a woman gets pregnant, she legally can't be fired. I don't want my own children, but I worry about other women, because I'm a feminist.[4]

When I still had periods and could make a baby with my body, I loved that I could use birth control legally, without having to worry about going to prison.[5] Until *Roe v. Wade* was overturned by the Supreme Court of the United States in 2022, via the *Dobbs v. Jackson Women's Health Organization* case, I loved knowing that if my birth control failed me, I could legally seek an abortion in all fifty of the United States.

And though I never called the police on that young man who forced me to have sex—yes, I am a rape survivor, I am sad to say—I loved that if I could have collected my courage, the next time I was forced, I *could* call the police, unlike in the nineteenth century, when the state of Mississippi decided in the case of *George v. State* that the rape of an enslaved African American woman or girl was not a crime.[6]

Before feminist activism, I didn't have many rights, and that's why, when I encounter a woman who repudiates feminist identity—or I meet a Black woman who tries to carve feminist out of Walker's womanist definition—I must work very hard not to judge her.

I love being able to vote, though that wasn't a right actually enshrined into national law for Black women until 1965. I know you've read that "women" got the right to vote with the Nineteenth Amendment because of suffragist activism, but that only counted (mostly) for White women.[7] I continue to be a feminist despite the White supremacy of first-wave feminists like Susan B. Anthony and Elizabeth Cady Stanton, women my Southern Black mother would have called Miss Anne types.[8] These White women didn't care about whether non-White women got the vote. They only cared about themselves. These days we call those types of White women Beckys or Karens instead of Miss Annes—but whatever their names, women like that have been walking around the North American continent for centuries.

You thought I didn't know about the White supremacist tendencies of early White feminists, didn't you? Oh, I do. Yet though this history is concerning, I continue to identify as a feminist. Do you know how irrational it would be to give up the rights that feminism gave me and other Black women in this country—or for me to stop identifying as a feminist—simply because a few pale ladies were racist?

Alice Walker, the founder of womanism, wasn't perfect herself, either; no human being is perfect. But Walker's books are enduringly important to at least two generations of Black women. (And I love this lady so very much. As my granny might say, I wouldn't trade Miss Alice for "nothing in the world.")

Let me enter the sturdy house of logic. I'll hold your hand and bring you across the threshold with me.

As a Black woman, am I supposed to give up what the civil rights movement gave me—the Voting Rights Act, integrated schools, the desegregation of public spaces—just because there were plenty Black male misogynists and homophobes in *that* movement? Am I going to repudiate the works of Martin Luther King Jr. because he ultimately rejected Bayard Rustin, the gay brother who organized the March on Washington for Jobs and Freedom?[9] Am I going to deny Malcolm X's antiracist activism because of his sexist ideology of Black women's subservience in *The Autobiography of Malcolm X*?[10]

Movements have flaws, like the people who start them. I'm not dismissing those flaws—and yes, I despair over the fact that some of my heroes and heroines weren't nice people or didn't give a damn about Black women. But should only White women's prejudiced attitudes and actions matter, when it comes to political history, while Black men's sexism and homophobia always get a pass?

Come on now.

As for me, I'm grateful to the civil rights movement, the same way I'm grateful to the mainstream/White feminist movement. But I'm especially grateful to Black women feminists who understood that gender equality and antipatriarchy should be ongoing projects within our African American communities. Those problems and prejudices of the civil rights movement and the mainstream feminist movement led to Black women formally starting their own vehicle for activism: Black feminism. One example is the Combahee River Collective, founded in 1977.[11] A few years later there were feminist writings by other Black women, such as the 1983 anthology *All the Women Are White, All the Blacks Are Men, But Some of Us Are Brave*, edited by Akasha T. Hull, Patricia Bell-Scott, and Barbara Smith, who was also a member of the Combahee Collective. A year after *But Some of Us Are Brave*, Alice Walker published *In Search of Our Mothers' Gardens* and defined "womanist" for us.

The activism of these Black women is why I identify not only as a feminist but also as a womanist—but again, *you must be a feminist to be a womanist.*

If you haven't read Alice Walker's book, go find a copy. You need to know what the lady wrote instead of what you deliberately refuse to accept. You need to stop saying things like "I'm a womanist but I'm not a feminist." Such contrived semantics make you look foolish—and like you've never acquired adult reading comprehension.

I know you're scared to embrace what many view as a radical political identity, but it's okay. I'll wait for you, my sister, because others waited for me. I was frightened myself not too long ago. I won't pretend that I've always been strong.

6

In Search of Our Mothers' Crossroads

Every summer Mama would drive me and my two sisters, Val and Sisi, down from Durham, North Carolina, to Eatonton, Georgia, her hometown. We'd turn off Interstate 20 and hit Highway 441. If you followed that road past town—which frequently Mama did—there was a fruit stand. Without fail, Mama would stop and buy fresh produce—peaches, watermelons. No need to purchase anything preserved: When we arrived at the house of my grandmother Florence, there would be plenty of glass jars filled with wonderful things, including one of my eternal favorites, Brunswick stew. These days, as a vegetarian, I don't eat meat unless somebody sets some barbecued ribs or Brunswick stew in front of me. Then, I cannot be held responsible for my actions.

The summers in Eatonton sweltered. I'd walk down Concord Avenue—now Martin Luther King Jr. Drive—with the children of my grandmother's neighborhood. We'd wave politely at the old ladies sitting on their porches, using fans from Mr. Rice's funeral home to swat away the flies. Sometimes those elders would call me over to their rocking chairs.

They'd ask, "I know you? Who your people? Who's your mama, child?" Meaning: Who was my family? Who raised me? Who taught me how to behave among the members of my community?

I would respond, "I'm Trellie Lee's baby," and they would smile in recognition.

"Oh, all right now! I know your mama. She used to be a school-teacher, down to Butler Baker."

"Yes, ma'am," I'd say. I was polite, as if I didn't already know what my own mother's profession was.

I tolerated the questions of the elders—Who was I? Who were my people?—because I thought I had no choice. I loved the landscape like an exotic oasis. But those women—country women—embarrassed me. Their slanted grammar, their sudden memories that returned to a terrible past of oppression, clawed at me. They knew history that challenged the beauty of the Georgia landscape. These women-elders, some my actual kin, some near strangers, told stories about their ancestors, dead people who seemed so removed from me.

Like my mother's great-grandmother Mandy, a woman she had adored. She'd laugh when the old lady ordered her to sit down and listen to her talk, that she needed to remember. Mama was a little girl, so only listened halfway, squirming on the floor of the former slave shack where she had been born. Mama only wanted to escape, to go outside and play.

☙❧

I imagine two narrow throughways in Eatonton, one slicing the other: the crossroads where my grandmother Florence lived, in the house on Concord Avenue.

That crossroads was the blood power contained in my grandmother, too. She was African, European, and, she claimed, part Native American, though she had no documentary proof. Her only proof was oral tradition, as for many other Indigenous people who are acknowledged in their cultures but don't have a paper trail to prove their heritage. Grandma wasn't ashamed of being Black, though. She always called herself "colored," her generation's polite label for an African American: She was born in 1909.

I can still hear Grandma singing the spirituals in a reedy voice in her house on Concord Avenue. Those holy songs—those paeans to God—were the sacred equivalent of the blues.

In African/Black cultures, the crossroads represents a location of difficulty *and* possibility, a boundary between the divine and the human. In the Yoruba religion of West Africa, the orisha Esu appears at crossroads that humans encounter.[1] Although Esu is many times depicted as a man, in some renderings Esu is a dual-gendered figure, both (cisgender) male and female.[2] Across the Atlantic, where African peoples were enslaved, the crossroads were transformed—as all cultural symbols are, when pulled away from their original source. In its literal sense, the crossroads remain in a geographical location, meaning where one causeway traverses another. But in its spiritual sense, the crossroads morphed in North America from the place where you met Esu to a place where trouble meets hope. A blues place, the spot where Robert Johnson insisted that he met the devil and traded his soul for greater musical ability. Some believe that this story is an extension of the Esu/Legba tale of the crossroads; that at his crossroads, Johnson received the "root" (as my grandmother would call it) that gave him power.[3]

I want to laugh and say that Brother Robert was telling a "got-that-wrong" (we old-school Black folks try never to call somebody a liar in the South). You must be ready to fight when the word *lie* comes out your mouth. But can I doubt Brother Robert, when I hear him on that guitar? As the descendant of Southern Black women who carried their figurative root bags—and as the inheritor of an invisible root bag of my own—I know what is *not* seen can hold power.

Robert Johnson didn't own the blues, though: Women sang those twelve-bar laments, too. Bessie Smith, Ma Rainey, Billie Holiday. Who walked through the folks' adoration in a juke joint or a tent in deep woods, stood on a messianic stage, sang and brought solace to the people.

In contemporary times, Kimberlé Crenshaw has gestured to the crossroads to describe the unique position of Black women, a space less mythic than logical conclusion. As a Black feminist legal scholar, Crenshaw writes about how American feminisms ignored the collective significance of Black women's race *and* gender in the law, naming this Black and female combination "intersectionality."[4] Though Crenshaw's field is legal scholarship, in this one word—*intersectionality*—she captures centuries of struggle and a universe of beauty, seeing and uttering the lives of African American women: We are not only a race, and not only a gender, but both. The problem is, not many folks other than African American women can concentrate on more than one issue at a time.

There are those who still talk about "women and Blacks," as if these can't be overlapping identities. Perhaps Crenshaw was fighting this refusal to see the simultaneity of race and gender when she coined the term: Intersectionality was not something that she *created*, but rather something she *recognized*. As a legal scholar, she was familiar with how English and American lawmakers fashioned injustice, when they brought enslaved females from Africa, then set about legally *unmaking* them.

❦

When I return to Eatonton—in my spirit, for it's been a long time since I physically traveled there—I think not only of my mama but also of another woman: the poet, novelist, and essayist Alice Walker. As a child, I recalled Mama referencing Walker, but it took me until my twenties to connect the "Alice" she referred to—her former student—with the famous woman who wrote books.[5] Walker's very early books continue to be of paramount importance to many Black women, and certainly to me.

I started reading Walker in earnest not out of intellectual curiosity but out of the need to commune with *someone*, even just on the page. I'd been in two other graduate programs before then. One was in journalism at the University of North Carolina—I tanked in that program, but dropped out before I received the official correspondence that essentially told me, "Look, heifer, your grades are trash. Leave here and don't come back." I'm grateful that, even though I never finished that degree, I encountered the historical archives in person for the first time at the university's Southern Historical Collection.

The second graduate program was in English at Clark Atlanta University, which I entered in 1992. I already had read the works of many Black people, and Alice Walker's early novels. Though I earned good grades, by the end of my second year, I knew I didn't want to continue to a doctorate. I left before I earned my master's, transferring some of my credits to a master of fine arts in creative writing at the University of Alabama. I'd finally claimed my title of "poet."

I cannot linger on my experiences at the University of Alabama for more than a few moments—the racist bullying I endured, the intellectual and creative diminishment of my writing—without bursting into tears. One might think that my experience with racism was expected because this university was in the South—but, ironically, most of my White classmates were from other geographical locations in the United States. The only other Black poet had left after the first semester. There was one Black fiction writer who stayed, but that was it, and, based upon my conversations with her, I believe I can say with confidence that both of us were frequently miserable.

I was a young woman who doubted myself in the creative classes I attended—of course I was the only Black person in those rooms—and while workshopping my not-very-good poems. But none of us were polished writers then: The whole point of a creative writing program is to find a voice, shape it, and believe in it. Our apprentice status didn't stop the bullying, though. My intelligence was constantly questioned by most of my White classmates, even when I tried to prove myself. I would read and write long into the early mornings, pushing sleep aside with the help of chocolate-covered espresso beans. (At the end of those three years, I graduated with a perfect 4.0 grade point average. I have the transcripts to prove it. However, as of this writing, I am not listed as an alumnus on the departmental website of that creative writing program, though I rank among their most renowned alums of any racial/cultural background.)

In graduate school I frequently contemplated suicide, and it is a wondrous realization that I was held aloft by something greater than myself, that I was fragile yet contained endurance. I encountered God and the ancestors—or perhaps they found me—and during those moments when I longed to kill myself by cutting or swallowing something, an invisible collective would speak to me and tell me, "If you just hold on, there will be peace."

I didn't believe that collective for one moment, however. I believed in God but had no strong spiritual faith and no practice of ancestral reverence—that would come much, much later. It was reading Alice Walker that opened a world of Black feminist possibility—and survival. Her book of essays *In Search of Our Mothers' Gardens* felt like Scripture to me. I'd kept a copy that I cribbed from my mother, but like many of the books in my small library, I hadn't yet read it. I hate to say that pain drove me to Walker, but I'd be lying if I didn't acknowledge it.

Alice Walker was a woman who (like me) was raised by Black women from Eatonton, Georgia. My mother and she loved each other. Her essays pointed me to a new consideration of women in African American history, and in those moments when I wanted to kill myself, when I would set down that razor or put those pills back into my medicine cabinet—or vomit up the pills I'd swallowed—I didn't do it for myself. I survived for those Black women who had gone before me. I was determined to live for them, because I knew they had prayed me into being, long before I was conceived. Alice Walker gave those women to me.

I'm a poet, so timing is everything, and at this point in my life I'm a deeply faithful woman, though I don't attend church anymore. The old folks in my grandma's community had a saying: "Our time is not God's time." I was in my late twenties when I saw the beauty of Black women—deep in the country of Eatonton, Georgia. When I understood their wisdom. It was a divine time, and a maternal time: Alice Walker helped me see that.

When I reread Walker's *In Search of Our Mothers' Gardens*—as I have, every other year since my turbulent twenties—she opened the possibility for me of the crossroads of Black and woman. From Walker I learned about womanism, our own brand of feminism—*Black* feminism—that acknowledges how African American women continue to resist White supremacy. That we reject the male domination of patriarchy—even from our own Black men. That we love our Black people, sometimes even—bewilderingly—those who have harmed us. That we hold a duty to make our communities and this nation better before we die.

In the 1990s Alice Walker's work sent me searching, and I returned to the matrilineal history of my family and America with fresh eyes. In turn, I saw myself, who I'd always been and was meant to become. I was no activist. I did not march. I wrote no rage-filled declarations. But I could speak on the page.

∿

Power can be found in the past, even in a painful time: I can reach back to before Eatonton, dreaming of that African woman who was captured or sold in her homeland and forced onto a boat. I will never know her name. I will never know her language, lost on that transatlantic journey—more than a *trip*, an *entering*. Someplace in the middle of an ocean is where she became something else, not African anymore, but not yet American.

There is power in her crossroads: I could take one of four journeys, and then turn back around to where she started and begin again.

I can call out her two identities—Black or woman—and each would be correct.

It is a remembered place that my ancestors gave me, one I recall in spirit or dream. It is a lost place, and maybe I *should* want to leave that place behind. But I cannot leave these women, and I never will: I've never had that choice.

7

Altar Call

This is what you need to know about me: I am my mother's child, though for years, I pretended otherwise. Like Mama, I am a storyteller. I can paint a journey until you surrender and curl in the palm of my hand. I can bend a rhythm and make it holler. Sure enough, I'll whisper a word into submission.

What else you should know is that my entire maternal line is from Eatonton, Georgia, a place of red dirt, slavery, Jim Crow—and Indigenous echoes.

I have a father that I knew. He lived in my household, and I carry his last name—but I was truly raised by Trellie Lee James Jeffers, a woman who grew up in tangled country woods. I'm strong-backed, with big roach-stomping feet and plenty meat jiggling on my frame. In Mama's hometown, they used to call me "big-bone-ded."

When summers arrived, my mother would drive my sisters and me south from Durham, North Carolina. In Eatonton, I would walk the cramped street of my grandma's neighborhood, what used to be Concord Avenue. Men and boys would say I was pretty and fine. And I, a teenager who'd spent years in the Black bourgeoisie, a place where darker skin and fleshy arms and big thighs were viewed as crimes, would slow my walk in the heat. I courted that adoration. I'd had so little beauty in my life, so I drank every sweetness. I let it paint my tongue.

It was in Eatonton that I learned the down-home grandeur and complicated wisdom of my family's women, how they embraced community yet regularly misbehaved. I saw—or heard tell of—those women building up a man with charm. How they fed these men heavy, seasoned food, laundered and pressed shirts until the "cat faces" disappeared, smiled at their bullish compliments.

But when angered or capricious, these women—*my* women—could cut the meat from bones with dangerous words. Sever men's feelings out of their souls. Let them know it didn't matter what the world thought outside of Georgia. It didn't matter how the world was wrought: Down in the red dirt, a Black woman held the true power. She just loaned it to a man for a while.

These are the names of the women of my line, starting with my mother. Reaching back, until history refuses paper: Trellie Lee. Florence. Luvenia. Mandy. Clarissa.

Yet my words are for all my sisters, and when I say sisters, I mean those Black women who are trans, cisgender, nonbinary, straight, lesbian, stud, stemme and femme. You are my kindred, and we are a crossroads. In our bodies, we holler aberrance and ecstasy.

For you, my sisters, I will descend into history. I will conjure my own life as Black and woman-child. Sometimes, I have lived what our people call the blues, though I'm no Robert Johnson. I didn't give up my soul when I arrived at the crossroads, the spot of my making. I can't call the devil by name, and for that I am truly glad.

But I made the acquaintance of a different kind of spirit: Kneeling in the red dirt, I laid my head on a dark mother's belly.

II

A DAUGHTER'S THEORY

Rememory as in recollecting and remembering
as in reassembling the members of the body,
the family, the population of the past.

—TONI MORRISON

they ask me to remember
but they want me to remember
their memories
and I keep on remembering
mine

—LUCILLE CLIFTON,
"WHY SOME PEOPLE BE MAD AT ME SOMETIMES"

Three Sisters: A Fairy Tale

1.

These are the little girls who live in the green house on the slight hill, trapped inside Weaver Street in a place called North Carolina. There are flowers in the yard and books in every room—and a sad mama and a mean daddy whose mouth is screaming, always opened wide.

Val is the oldest and the rebel of the family. Sisi is the middle child, the good girl who behaves. Honi is the baby and the fattest, though she is cute.

These three girls wear labels like the pinafores that their mama sewed for them, their socks pulled up the legs that are never ashy but greased and clean. These are the girls reminded to keep quiet secrets. Don't ever tell about what their daddy does to them.

2.

Val is the one who loves rock music, loud and unapologetically mad: Led Zeppelin, Mother's Finest, anything with an electric guitar.

Sisi likes the sweetness: Frankie Beverly and Anita Baker, with a bit of Luther thrown in.

Honi is the weird one, for a Black child: She likes Olivia Newton-John and Lawrence Welk and Buck Owens from *Hee-Haw*. She reads all the time and tries to act like the boys who are characters in her books: This is why she has no friends.

3.

Val is the fighter and the smartest—the college girl who is a genius. She goes off far away, to Atlanta. Whenever she comes back to her family's green house, only her ghost seems to return.

Sis is the charming and popular one, the protector of crying Mama. Daddy is afraid of Sisi, after he drops to the floor, clutching his chest. Sisi stands over him, laughing, threatening, until she picks up the telephone to call 911: "I will kill you. I will kill you," Sisi croons, as he opens his mouth and begs, until the ambulance arrives.

Honi is the recluse, the one who won't stop eating. The one who has no friends. She tugs on Mama's sleeve—"Don't leave me with Daddy. I don't want to be here with him. Take me, Mama. Take me with you"—and sometimes Mama complies.

4.

Val is the one who marries at nineteen and drops out of college, disappointing Mama with her cast-off hopes. Val arrives a year later with a growing belly, triumphant that she has escaped.

Sisi is the hard worker, who finds job after job at fifteen. She makes her own money and kisses many boys. She comes and goes from the green house, however she likes.

Honi is the freak who won't understand that she's a girl: She must learn to be nice. She must stop always speaking her mind.

5.

Val has a second baby, then her husband leaves her. She begins to drink. She abandons her children. She can't stop eating meals of rage. She disappears. She reappears. She disappears. She reappears. Val becomes the story that no one ever knows.

Daddy dies. The sisters cry at his funeral, but secretly, they all dance. That man is gone, he's in the ground—rejoice, rejoice, the villain has flown.

Sisi becomes the lawyer, the successful one who makes Mama proud. One day she crosses the street without looking, and then Sisi's mind changes forever: Sisi is not Sisi anymore.

Honi is the rebel now, who turns her back on her family. Like Val, she fills her plate with rage, but Honi and her sister will never again share a meal.

6.

Val is finally sober, but no one will forgive her. They wash her face in the past, they remind her of stolen purses—she has sinned. She's a bad girl. See her marked in the town square?

Sisi is the sister who used to be pretty, but the car that hit her stole her looks. She can't remember anything but Daddy. She has to keep telling her story. She can't be quiet, and Mama and her family turn their backs.

Honi is the writer and the college professor, living in a town that frightens her. She is Black. She is a woman—nobody wants to see her face. She rarely leaves her house except on the page. Honi thinks of death all the time.

7.

Val becomes a writer, but she won't stop smoking cigarettes. She coughs and rattles between her seething rants. She ignores everyone's advice.

Sisi is the first little girl to close her eyes. Gone sister, may she have all the sweet-and-sour pork she asks for in heaven. May they play Frankie Beverly on repeat.

Honi pretends to herself that her sister isn't dead, that she didn't abandon Sisi. Honi smiles at her new husband, increasingly despising him. She dreams of spitting in that motherfucker's rice.

8.

Val is the second sister who goes to meet glory. May there be forgiveness and a rock concert with loud guitars and singing above.

Sisi is the one who appears in Honi's dreams, urging, "Stay alive, baby sister. Mama needs you—baby, go visit Mama. Baby, don't forget about her, please."

Honi is the last sister living, the one who finds a guilty peace. If she prays very hard, she'll be little once more. There'll be Val and Sisi up in heaven, if she promises not to forget: that once there were three girls in a car with Mama driving, far, far away from constantly screaming Daddy. They are headed down to Georgia, to Grandma Florence's house. They are laughing and they are brown and they are talking through sunlight.

9

Things Ain't Always Gone Be This Way

My mother never told any hard-luck stories about Jim Crow in Georgia. She talked to me about the brutality, the racism, but she always had a way of framing herself as a heroine. Once, when I spoke to her about a mass lynching that had taken place in Walton County in 1946[1]—I'd read about it in a book—Mama said casually, "Oh yes, I remember that. That happened right up the road from me."

"You were a young girl then, weren't you, Mama?"

"That's right. Only thirteen."

I let some moments pass.

Then: "How did that make you feel, Mama?"

A dangerous question, for my mother wasn't one to dwell on feelings. With rare exception, she had a way of understating her early life, the pain, the trauma. When pressed on this personal history, she'd slow to silence, or abruptly move on, for as she once told me, if she started crying, she might not ever stop.

"I was angry," she said. "I kept expecting the Black men in Walton County to do something, but they never did. I promised myself, when I grew up, I wasn't going to take that kind of abuse. Like my daddy used to say, things ain't always gone be this way."

Predictably, she changed the subject, this time to when a White man had cursed in her daddy's face, on the land Grandpa Charlie rented as a tenant farmer. As the White man kept shouting—"cutting a jig," as Mama called it—Grandpa ordered one of my mother's brothers to get his shotgun, and the White man jumped in his car and drove away. My grandfather sat on the porch all night with the gun, waiting for the White man to return—perhaps with the Ku Klux Klan—but nothing ever happened.

Mama had a way of circumventing, until what was left was her father's anger, his courage in the face of a disrespectful, racist White man. Other Black folks in Georgia were murdered, but not Charlie James. My grandfather was a farmer who never owned land or even finished grade school, but Mama cast him always as the victor, not the victim.

There were many of my mother's stories about her father's moxie. It took me years to clarify the ways that Mama canted her father's suffering in the segregated Deep South. By focusing on his individual courage, she drew attention away from his oppression. She made his resistance possible—his everyday acts extraordinary.

But there was that day when she talked to me about the first time she voted. She insisted that the Black people in her hometown of Eatonton could vote. They weren't truly disenfranchised. Every time there was an election, she repeated this, stressing that she'd always voted.

I'd grown up watching documentaries of civil rights protests on public television, seeing the limp, bleeding bodies of teenagers and young adults dressed in neat church clothes, pulled from the streets where they politely demanded their rights and beaten by hard-faced White police officers. I was amazed that my mother had exercised her right to vote, without drama or broken bones.

"For real?" I asked.

"Oh, sure," she said.

"Your parents, too?"

"Well, no. Your grandma didn't read that well, and Daddy, he couldn't read or write at all. And you had to be literate to vote in those days."

About ten years ago, while doing genealogical research, I'd found the marriage certificate of my maternal grandparents, Florence (Napier) Paschal and Charlie James. I saw their neat signatures, which confused me. If my grandfather couldn't read or write, who had signed his name?

Grandpa Charlie had signed his own name, my mother told me; that's all he knew how to do, because he hadn't finished elementary school. The White man who had owned the land that Grandpa's family lived on would require the African American children to work during planting and harvest season. This had constantly interrupted their education, which was bare-bones to begin with for African American children in the early twentieth century. That's why—somehow—when Grandpa became an adult, he found a more liberal White man to rent land from, a nice Jewish man. And Grandpa wasn't a "sharecropper," either. He was a tenant farmer, allowed to keep whatever crops he grew for himself. He had promised himself that nobody was going to come to the schoolhouse and interrupt his children's learning and make them work in the fields.

I knew enough not to question my mother about why Grandpa never learned to read, or how he felt. We don't talk about pain in my family. We only talk about what you must do to walk around it. A few seconds after informing me of her father's illiteracy—though she never called it that—my mother moved our discussion away from her father's disenfranchisement to his insistence that his children finish high school. He would demand that all his progeny "get their lesson out," so they'd have their education.

She told me how proud Grandpa had been when she graduated from Spelman College, and when she came back to Eatonton to teach at Butler Baker, the new, segregated high school for Negroes. How he'd bragged on her to anybody who would listen. So proud that when he used to drive her to the town's segregated dime store, he'd dress up in his church suit and tie and wear the good shoes that pinched his corns.

I'm embarrassed that this conversation about voting took place at least twenty years ago, and all during that time, I didn't have the curiosity to question my mother further. I'm not a politician or an activist:

I'm a poet and writer, and even though I study history, the twentieth century isn't my wheelhouse. It was only while finishing up the first draft of this essay that I decided to look up the details of voter suppression.

Certainly I already knew that in the American South the history of keeping Black folks from voting goes back to the nineteenth century. Before the end of the Civil War, and the end of slavery, African Americans legally couldn't vote in the South. After the passage of the Fifteenth Amendment in 1870, Black men should have been able to vote. (Not until 1920 and the passage of the Nineteenth Amendment would *White* women be given that right.) But Southern states found myriad ways to work around federal laws. For example, on August 21, 1907, Governor Hoke Smith approved a literacy test for any Georgia male who wanted to vote.[2] The next year—on October 7, 1908—an amendment to the Georgia constitution changed even more requirements to vote, and these changes applied almost exclusively to Black men.[3] The concept of the "grandfather clause" in Georgia (and around the South) began with voting rights legislation: For a Black man to vote in Georgia in 1908, he needed to have been eligible to vote by January 1, 1867, or his father or grandfather needed to have been eligible to vote on that date.[4] An editorial in *The Atlanta Journal*, "Disfranchisement Completes Program," made the racial bias of the 1908 act obvious:

> But the one great reform to which the administration [of Georgia] was committed and which will be remembered in years to come as belonging most distinctly to this era was the disfranchisement of the ignorant and vicious negro. . . . The negro as the balance of power, who has to be bought at every election, is a thing of the past, and we are grateful in the realization that such is the case now in Georgia as well as the other states of the south . . . This is the white man's Georgia from now on.[5]

In 1951, the year that she enrolled at Spelman College, my mother left Eatonton and moved to Atlanta. When she graduated from Spelman, she returned home to teach at Butler Baker; it was her responsibility, she told me. She wanted to give something back to her hometown.

By the 1950s, women had the right to vote in the United States. However, in 1958—the year before my parents were married—a new law was passed, the New Registration Act of Georgia.[6] A literacy test had already been required to vote, but in 1958 White lawmakers approved a more difficult test, reiterating their urgency to only franchise the "well-educated."[7] Here are fifteen of the questions from the 1958 literacy test:

1. What is a republican form of government?

2. What are the names of the three branches of the United States government?

3. In what State Senatorial District do you live and what are the names of the county or counties in such District?

4. What is the name of the State Judicial Circuit in which you live and what are the names of the counties or county in such Circuit?

5. What is the definition of a felony in Georgia?

6. How many Representatives are there in the Georgia House of Representatives and how does the Constitution of Georgia provide that that be apportioned among the several counties?

7. What does the Constitution of Georgia prescribe as the qualifications of Representatives in the Georgia House of Representatives?

8. How does the Constitution of the United States provide that it may be amended?

9. Who is the Chief Justice of the Supreme Court of Georgia and who is the Presiding Justice of that Court?

10. Who may grant pardons and paroles in Georgia?

11. Who is the Solicitor General of the state judicial circuit in which you live and who is the judge of such circuit? (If such circuit has more than one judge, name them all.)

12. If the Governor of Georgia dies who exercises the executive power, and if both the Governor and the person who succeeds him dies, who exercises the executive power?

    a.) What does the Constitution of the United States provide regarding the suspension of the privilege of the writ of Habeas Corpus?

    b.) What does the Constitution of Georgia provide regarding the suspension of the writ of Habeas Corpus?

13. What are the names of the persons who occupy the following state offices in Georgia?

    1. Governor

    2. Lieutenant Governor

    3. Secretary of State

    4. Attorney General

    5. Comptroller General

    6. State Treasurer

    7. Commissioner of Agriculture

    8. State School Superintendent

    9. Commissioner of Labor

14. How many congressional districts in Georgia are there and in which one do you live?[8]

For this new Georgia literacy test, there were no agreed-upon responses to each of the thirty questions.[9] The discernible implication is that each county registrar—who was always White—would decide subjectively whether the answers to the test were correct. In Terrell County, Georgia, there were different—segregated—color-coded test forms for voter registration, according to the race of the person seeking to register.[10] Variations of these literacy tests existed throughout the

South until 1965, when President Lyndon Johnson signed the Voting Rights Act.[11]

As I looked at the list of questions on the Georgia test, I thought of how my mother had beaten so many odds. She'd been able to finish high school, unlike her parents—even after losing one of her eyes in a tragic childhood accident. Unlike Grandpa Charlie, she'd been able read and had the reading comprehension—and high school civics, even with her segregated education in Georgia—to understand this humiliating, internecine questionnaire.

Mama had been so matter-of-fact about the literacy test, but as I looked at the questions—how much detail one had to remember, how much reading comprehension was required—I thought of how she'd set aside her suffering, once again.

I don't remember when Mama became a community activist in the city of Durham, North Carolina, the place where she and my father moved our family in 1973. I didn't even know what an activist was.

I just remember that at some point, my mother had acquired a lot of very loud friends. Some of her friends were "bourgie"—light-skinned and "proper" speaking. Others were "of the people," with large Afros and African-style garb. But they came together to meet at our home church, St. Joseph African Methodist Episcopal, and she always took me with her. (I was the baby, and my big sisters refused to babysit.) She'd remind me to bring my books, because she knew I'd get bored, but I loved to read.

I'd sit in the corner of the church fellowship hall, scanning the pages of my book, but I'd eavesdrop on the meetings. Mama was a passionate speaker, and sometime, her friends would chuckle, saying, "All right now, Trellie. Calm down." They aired complaints of the Black folks in the city. How the laws had changed, but White folks had not. How the school board in Durham didn't spend the same amount of money on the schools or roads on the African American side of town—though we didn't have the term *African American* in the 1970s; we were "Black" with a big B.

When I became an adult, my mother would tell me, her friends weren't just meeting to talk loudly. They belonged to an organization called the Durham Committee on the Affairs of Black People. The committee had been formed in 1935 (originally as the Durham Committee on Negro Affairs) by a group of prominent Black male citizens.[12] These men had been some of the most successful African Americans in Durham. For example, there was Charles Clinton Spaulding, head of the North Carolina Mutual Insurance Company, and James E. Shephard, who had founded a college for Blacks in Durham, which later became North Carolina Central University—when I was a little girl, my mother worked as an adjunct professor at this institution. In addition to teaching, Mama did extensive volunteer work in educational affairs and community service—she did so much that I didn't even know about, until I became an adult and started researching her life.[13]

In 1976, when Jimmy Carter ran as the Democratic nominee for president of the United States, my mother and her activist friends were concerned about Black voters in Durham. Because of the ways that White people had kept African Americans from voting before 1965, not enough were registered to vote. In the eleven years since the Voting Rights Act had been signed into law, there had been a deflation of excitement about voting in our city. That meant Jimmy Carter might not win North Carolina, and even worse, the other candidates "down ballot"—the local candidates that had Black folks' best interest at heart—might not win, either. But Mama and the Committee on the Affairs of Black People planned to do something about that: They were going to get more African Americans registered.

☙

That year I was nine years old, and Mama took me canvassing with her. She greased and brushed my hair into two ponytails, decorated them with yarn ribbons, and adorned me in a cute dress and ankle socks with my comfortable shoes. She explained what our job would be. We had to walk around the Black neighborhoods—for Durham was still de facto segregated—and get as many Black people to register to vote for the presidential election as possible. We had to tell them about the best candidates for local positions, too. Some of those local candidates weren't Black, but they were friends to our communities, and we had to support them.

It wasn't enough to vote for president of the United States. You had to vote for the mayor of your town or city, the members of the city council, and the board of education. You had to vote every time an election came around. And Black folks had literally died to secure our right to vote. So voting wasn't just about rights, Mama told me. It was about the fact that we needed to honor the Black folks who had come before us, the ones who weren't here anymore.

She spoke to me as if I knew what she meant about politics. I didn't know at all, but I nodded gravely in response. Fortunately, I didn't have to memorize that information, because when Mama knocked on the door, she already had her speech prepared: She was registering Black folks to vote, because Gerald Ford had been Richard Nixon's right-hand man during his presidential administration, and Nixon had lied when he said he hadn't been a crook. And now, Ford—she never called him "President Ford"—had pardoned Nixon, and that ought to tell us what we needed to know. Mama talked about the other, local candidates, too, those who were friends to the Black community in Durham.

There was one home we stopped by, small and neat with a short stack of steps and a few flowers in the yard. That day, the lady who answered the door was light-skinned and maybe forty-five, though again, I was nine, so she probably seemed ancient to me. Her face was apathetic, and she sighed in a bored way as she explained that it didn't matter who somebody voted for for president, because these White folks were going to do whatever they wanted.

I expected my mother to correct the light-skinned lady—maybe even start shouting, because Mama wasn't known for holding her tongue. Instead she nudged me toward the lady, asking, was her message of futility what we wanted to send to our children? That they didn't have any power? That they couldn't ever change their circumstances? Mama's voice had turned "proper," the accent of a schoolteacher who had graduated from Spelman College and had a master's degree from another university as well.

I thought the lady would close the door on us, but she looked at me and smiled. Told me I sure had some pretty, long hair, and Mama nudged me again.

"Tell the nice lady who you want to be president, baby."

On cue, I said, "I'm voting for Jimmy Carter!"

Mama held out the registration clipboard and pen to the lady, and after some hesitation, the lady took both and wrote down her information.

On Election Day that year, Mama picked me up after school and drove us to the polls. She told me she had a very important job for me to do. But first, she needed to remind me of how I was reared, how I should remember to respect my elders.

She explained that I would take the hand of each old Black person she would send my way. These would be people who couldn't read. They knew the candidates they wanted to vote for, but because they couldn't recognize the names on the ballot, they needed me to call out all the names for them, and then they'd tell me which of those names they wanted to vote for. Mama lectured me: Under no circumstances was I to laugh or ask these old people any rude questions about why they couldn't read. If I did, I would hurt their feelings, like those children hurt me at school when they teased me for being chubby, and I didn't want to make anybody cry, did I?

I don't remember how many old Black folks I helped at the polls that day, only that when I stood in the booth with them, I did what my mother had asked. I called out the names, and they'd tell me who they wanted to vote for. Then, very carefully, I put my finger by each name they'd chosen. I watched as they filled out the ballot. And I'd beam as each old person heaped praise on me, telling me how smart I was, how sweet. What a good little girl my mother had raised me to be.

When I'd come out the booth, I'd call, "Mama, I voted!"

"You sure did, baby!" she'd say. "And don't you feel good?"

Then she'd point another old, Black person my way.

10

Blues for Roe

M y mama once told me . . ."
This is the phrase that describes so much of what I know about real history, not simply what I read in books or encountered in the archives. And when I think of the word *abortion*—before I ever heard of *Roe v. Wade*—I think of Mama's stories.

When these lessons began, I'd started my first period some weeks before. The day Mama decided to talk to me about pregnancy, I do know we were sitting in the Dodge Dart. The car she'd purchased with her own money, because my father didn't believe in buying a new automobile until the current one that he owned was broke-down and set him by the side of the road.

Mama began quizzing me about what I already knew concerning how a girl or woman became pregnant.

❧

Forgive me. Forgive my mother.

It was the 1970s. We didn't have the vocabulary back then to describe people who weren't girls or women, but who still could carry a pregnancy.

We didn't yet have that *knowing* that I wish that we'd possessed. It would have saved me a lot of pain and stupidity through the years. It would have made me kinder, as a child and adult. The times are what I think about, these days, when the past comes back around, frightening me.

I blame the times because it's too painful to blame myself.

～

Such an embarrassing conversation with my mother, and I huffed, letting her know that I already knew the specifics about sex, but being careful not to go into details. Such as, I was an avid reader of Judy Blume's books, and I was an expert eavesdropper. I'd learned about what was called "grown folks' business" by sitting quietly when Mama and her women friends—or her sisters—talked.

"Yes, Mama!" I said. "I know! Dang."

She said something like "All right, if you ever get in trouble with a boy, I've always got money for an abortion." Her tone was very calm.

When I'd look up *abortion* in the dictionary, though, I couldn't quite get a handle on the meaning. I can't say I was curious, not until I fully entered adolescence.

Over the course of weeks, Mama began to share other cautionary tales.

Like the story of her great-grandmother Mandy, who'd had a child by a White man at the age of around sixteen or seventeen; Mandy named the son Jenkins. Of course, under Georgia law back then, Mandy and this White man couldn't have married. The *Loving v. Virginia* Supreme Court case making interracial marriage legal wouldn't occur for another hundred years, in 1967. And besides, Mama never talked about any abiding affection between Mandy and the father of her child.

There was another relative, Mama's grandmother Luvenia, who'd married Jenkins. We called Luvenia "Ma Sweet" in our family, though she'd been anything but nice. Though Ma Sweet had been married, she too had given birth to her first child in her teens. She went on to have many more children—fifteen live births in all, and one stillbirth. "Way too many kids," is how my mother termed it.

Ma Sweet was born in 1891. Her oldest daughter—Grandma Florence—took care of her until she died. I have only a few memories of Ma Sweet, none of them pleasant. I think about the old lady who sat staring at the television, her gaze resentful, even of Bob Barker, the friendly man who gave away loot on *The Price Is Right*. Ma Sweet mostly ignored me, but whenever she talked to me or my mother, she wasn't kind.

There was a story that Mama told me several times, about when she had gone to see Ma Sweet, when she and Jenkins—Great-Grandma Mandy's oldest son—lived on a large farm. Ma Sweet had a large sack of sweet potatoes. Her granddaughter—Mama—asked her for some, and the woman pulled out the three of the smallest tubers. She handed them over to Mama and said, "Take these, and don't ever ask me for anything else."

As a grown woman, I can collect some understanding syllables, whenever I think of my great-grandmother. Mama swears that Ma Sweet was lowdown to her darker-skinned grandchildren because she was color-struck, even though she was a deeply brown woman. I can't argue with that—colorism runs rampant through my family—but I do wonder if Ma Sweet was mean to Mama in particular because of jealousy, too. My mother was a precocious child who had entered school at four years old. Even after a childhood accident stole an eye from her, when she returned to school, she quickly ascended to first in her class. She found her way from Eatonton, Georgia, to Atlanta's Spelman College, and became the first college graduate and schoolteacher in her family.

I wonder how my mother's educational success made Ma Sweet feel. I never remember seeing the old woman read. I don't even know if she *could* read. What might have been Ma Sweet's dreams as a young girl, before she married (or was married off to) Jenkins Paschal as a teenage bride, a girl whose first child was born soon after her marriage? Maybe she had wanted to become a teacher as well, and to attend Spelman College, which had been founded to educate African American women ten years before her birth. Ma Sweet's marriage and motherhood would have made that dream impossible, though, for married ladies weren't allowed to matriculate at Spelman at the turn of the twentieth century.

Instead of going to one of the historically Black colleges founded to educate the children of freed enslaved people, Ma Sweet had married as a near-child herself and birthed many children, some of whom she didn't want, if the family stories were correct. There were three decades between her first and last child. She'd lived her life as a bitter farmer's wife, her journey only different from other Black women in Eatonton because Ma Sweet and Jenkins Paschal weren't sharecroppers. Instead they were tenant farmers, and Jenkins was on friendly terms with his White relatives, which provided some protection from the violence directed toward Black people at that time.

༻⁕༺

During an argument I'd overhear between my mother and father, I'd learn that she'd considered having an abortion when she learned she was pregnant with my oldest sister, Valjeanne, who was born in 1959. Convinced by my father that he couldn't get her pregnant—that he'd been told by an army doctor during World War II that his sperm count was too low—Mama had stopped using her diaphragm. She'd secured her contraception through a Black doctor in Atlanta, one who pretended all his African American female patients were married when he prescribed birth control.

He might have been the same physician whose name rode the whisper network among Spelman College students and graduates, one who performed safe abortions for $500, the equivalent of around $5,000 these days.

Mama said that when Daddy begged her to have his baby, he didn't judge her or call her a murderer. Though deeply flawed—and sometimes truly disturbed—my father was a modern man who viewed abortion as a woman's right. He came from a family of pro-choice men, like his grandfather George A. Flippin, a physician and the first Black football player at the University of Nebraska.[1] George's father, Charles A. Flippin—also known as "C.A. Flippin"—was a physician, too, as well as a Civil War veteran who had served in the US Colored Troops.[2] Charles had been an infamous abortionist in Nebraska. White women—yes, *White*—had flocked to his practice to terminate their pregnancies; perhaps they trusted Charles because he had married at least one White woman.[3] (At times Charles—the biracial son of a White slaveholder and a Black enslaved woman—would insist that he was White, too, a "mixture of Spanish and Irish, his mother having been a Spaniard and his father an Irishman.")[4]

It was only after a young woman died that Charles was prosecuted, eventually losing his medical license.[5] To me, it's a miracle that in the early twentieth century, Charles wasn't lynched for even touching a White woman, much less performing an illegal operation on her.

❧

Those days in the Dodge Dart, Mama would provide other stories about friends and relatives who'd been forced to marry grown men after they became pregnant. A beautiful girl Mama had gone to high school with, a dear friend. At the age of fourteen, a grown man had impregnated her; her family had forced her to marry him, but then the girl died in childbirth.

There are stories like this throughout the South—probably even all over the country. There's a reason the term *child bride* entered the national vocabulary, although not many folks recall its origin. So many states in our union allowed—or forced—children to marry the predators who would assault them, with the permission of the children's parents, or even their compulsion. Marriage was the custom back then, if a girl was supposedly lucky enough for the father of her child to do the so-called right thing. If luck held, hopefully, that girl wouldn't die in childbirth, as so many people do, even in the twenty-first century, especially Black women.

But that's why Mama had been terrified of becoming pregnant and had avoided boys and men at all costs. Abortion was not only prohibitively expensive; in some cases, it was deadly. Only luck and God had protected her from a fate like Mandy's, Ma Sweet's, and the fate of that beautiful girl with whom she'd gone to school. I understood that, didn't I? she'd ask. Fear had propelled her to relative success as a schoolteacher. Fear should keep me careful, because no one could trust a man.

But like any blues, Mama's bitter mélange offered morsels of humor: She never raged or wept as she laughingly instructed me about contraception—"You know what they call people who use withdrawal for birth control? *Parents!*"—and what it meant to be Black or a woman or both. But she did teach me how hard life had been when she was a girl, that compared to the lives she had witnessed, my own life was so easy.

Birth control was legal, she reminded me. I didn't have to obtain permission from my husband to use it, not like Mama had when she was first married to my daddy. Abortion was legal, too—and safe—and always would be. I didn't have to be scared anymore, like she had been. Like a girl or woman, back in the day, if a man assaulted her, or even if she married the wrong one. The law had changed, and women had their rights. Women were finally free. And I should thank God for that.

All these years later, I awaken to my mother's secondhand terrors. I hold on to the memory of our conversations: My mother was warning me that things could change in an instant.

I knew she was a dreaming woman. Had she foreseen what would happen in her lifetime? That the law would change *again*—that the symbolic declaration of *Roe v. Wade* would become a curse instead of a joyful exhortation? That people who could get pregnant would lose the rights over their bodies, and experience what Mama and the women of her family had gone through—what other Black women in this country had gone through, when White men had control over the issue of their bodies?

11

In Search of Our Mothers' Justifications

My daddy went off to work in the morning three times a week to teach at North Carolina State University, the mostly White university in the next town over from Durham. Sometimes he would kiss each of our hands before going. If the clouds spoke kindly, my father would be in the best of moods, whistling jazz tunes.

Those good days in Durham, we competed to take care of Daddy. My sisters and I poured his juice and hugged his sandpaper cheek he couldn't seem to shave smooth enough. My mother smiled wanly at his ribald humor that hinted of their bedroom activities. And Daddy laughed at our hovering and called his daughters by our special nicknames, from songs he had composed. Mine was from an old poem by Paul Laurence Dunbar that Daddy had put to music, "Little Brown Baby."[1]

We were so hopeful! Yet my six-year-old mind couldn't understand the alchemy that transformed my father from the charming man who first declared he loved only us—he was the sweetest man in the world, the smartest man—and then changed into the danger he presented to our house, when the thin shell of his goodwill peeled away.

On other mornings, Daddy would be vicious—and always, in the evenings, when he returned from teaching. He would be hard to us: my mother, my two older sisters, me. He'd snatch food from our plates with his unwashed fingers and dare us to say anything. He'd forget the sweetness of the songs he composed to show us how much he loved us—the love poems he wrote for my mother—and would call us other ugly words that made us know he hated us for not taking away his unhappiness.

No more kissing of our small hands. He knew our fears well.

"You know, you're too fat," he'd say to me, ignoring his own girth. "No wonder you have no friends. You're never going to be as pretty as your sisters when you grow up, no matter how hard you try."

"Now this one"—this to my middle sister, Sisi—"you're pretty. In fact, you're too pretty, too yellow, and not at all smart. I hope you can find a husband. You're not good for much else."

Or to my mother, "You think I don't know why you married me?" A question, but never with an answer.

Some evenings, Mama tried never to leave him alone with us. She knew he became more vicious when he didn't have her as an audience. She'd hover in the background nearby, her eyes aware, then step between him and us, deflecting the blows of his words. "Go upstairs, sugar, go on, now," she'd say to us, and we would run, run, even as he ordered us back. "You have not been excused. Come back here, I said! Do you hear me? I am the man here. I am!" And at first she would speak his name like the soothing of oil. "Lance, Lance. Baby, stop it now."

Then there would be the shouting between them, which would go on into the night, drifting upstairs to me and my sisters, where we listened at the heating vents leading to the rooms below us. The crying of my father, exposed, like that of a very small child.

The next morning my father would sleep late, and when I came home from school, his office door would be closed, and he was typing his poems, his mood ruined, no matter how much we tried to make things better for him.

When I became a woman, after my father died, I would remember that living in the house with my father meant fear of those Whites in the place my father went during the day. Whatever happened when my mother and sisters and I tried to make him happy, my father would not know he was worthy.

Who were these White people who kept me from making him happy? They must have been different from my teacher at my own school, who smiled at me and gave me extra snacks after lunch. My teacher's face flushed pink in pleasure at the high marks on my papers. She stroked my hair when she walked through the aisles of children. Who were these *other* White people my father saw three times a week? Whoever they were, I thought I should have protected him from them. If he was cruel, I needed to know how to change that cruelty into goodness. I could never become angry at him or fight back because first I needed to take care of him, to shield him from what confused him.

The color of my mother confused him, the shades of meaning in the skin of a *black* Black woman walking among the yellow idols of my father's family. These light-skinned kin believed their own truth: God did not forgive certain sins like the Blackness of my mother. She could breathe when every one of them was dead. She could ask me, her brown daughter, for advice and never have to look again over her shoulder at her in-laws who expected her to fail.

～

Other long-ago evenings, Mama would sit at the kitchen table, eyes glazed over. This is when I knew she was elsewhere. I would complain to her about Daddy, and her smile would be vague. She'd be glancing into the distance. Where had she taken herself, to escape my father and his strident humiliations?

After Mama's death, while pondering whether she'd lied all those years, saying that she didn't remember my calling to her in the night during one of my father's visits to my bedroom, another snippet of memory came to me, a burgeoning, like one of the orchids a friend would bring me after Mama's funeral: the prescription bottles of Valium in her bathroom.

I waver in telling this: Which version of the truth will indict my mother further—which one will save her legacy? Is it a worse betrayal to say that Mama lied, or that she *truly* didn't remember, because of the pills she had swallowed? To say that she suffered from depression caused by my father's emotional and sometimes physical abuse—I can recognize it from my own depressive symptoms in my twenties, thirties, and forties—and her doctor had prescribed her Valium, as he probably had for so many other middle-class women who were trying to survive their own difficulties? I know what my father did to me, how he humiliated me and harmed me for years. The memories haunted me even after his death. How terrible must it have been for Mama, to be married to a man like that and bear his children?

We left my father for good when I was fourteen, moving south to Georgia, where all but one of my mother's siblings lived, along with Grandma Florence. Without my father's income, our financial circumstances and social standing changed greatly. No longer was I the middle-class girl who had public pride of place in the bourgeois Black enclave of Durham, North Carolina—even though, secretly, my family had been a dysfunctional mess. After leaving Daddy, Mama moved us first to one low-income apartment complex in DeKalb County, Georgia, and then a house in the West End of Atlanta—then an apartment in what's known (now) as SWATS, the dangerous (at that time) neighborhood—"Southwest Atlanta, too strong."

I was angry over these changes, while relieved we'd left my father behind. I was always surging from one emotion to the next, and the insensitive—and mean-spirited—teenager that I became started taunting my mother with her Valium.

"You're a junkie," I shouted at her one evening during an argument—there were so many arguments.

Mama's face crumpled, then quickly reassembled into her usual stoic expression.

But with no notice, one day, she threw the Valium in the garbage, never to renew the prescription.

A decade later, after she'd quit smoking cold turkey, too, Mama would thank me for my meanness: "You were a lowdown little thing," she'd say, laughing. "But child, I needed that wake-up call! If you hadn't said anything to me, I'd still be popping those pills right now."

❧

I learned in unspoken ways, after my daddy was dead, that when I tell any stories, I should not forget my mother's life. Her life was full before she met him, before my sisters and I came along. I should not forget to talk about the red clay of her home and the slave shack where she was born, the cabin that used to stand on the now-vacant ground. I should not forget the stripes and flowers of her brothers' and sisters' clothes, made from cheap fabric remnants or sometimes flour sacking. I should not forget the picking of peaches, plums, and cotton when she was young, earning money for her store-bought underwear and sanitary napkins; nor the newness of the books she read in college—"*brand new!*"— and how they felt in her already roughened hands. There was no marking of "colored" in the front of these books, and no one prepared her for this joy. And I should not forget her first sight of a real bathtub when she was in college at Spelman, and how she began to bathe so many times a day that she rubbed her skin raw.

She went against the advice of her own mother, who said she had the gift for hair, could start a real beauty shop, not stand for six hours over someone else's hot plate or the gas eye of someone else's stove. Instead she could make a life as a Black businesswoman in Eatonton, Georgia (maybe the first one; my mother doesn't know), not a life of scrubbing a White somebody's drawers for the rest of her life and pretending to smile while doing it. Scrubbing drawers or wiping little white noses, or both, was the only job a poor Black woman—"a *black* Black woman"—could get when my mother was a young girl.

My mother says that from the beginning, her mother was never proud of her. She was too dark, her nose too broad, her hair too kinky. (When Mama was a little girl, my grandmother would permanently damage Mama's past-shoulder-length hair by pressing it too often and with too much heat. I understand that this, too, was abuse.)

Grandma found no pleasure in being the mother of a foolish dark girl who wanted to waste her time on college. Why should my mother need to go to college, only to return after four years, to work the same job as every other Black woman? Better for her to work for herself than to face that day, surely down the line, when one of those factory women's husbands would ask her to take an extra dollar a week for a little "night labor"—sexual favors. And surely down the line would come the day she might meet a moist gaze and gently pry little pink fingers from her own darker ones, go home, and be forced to solve the problem of her children's hunger. Or surely would come the day when she might come home late, bringing sweet-and-sour candy for her dark children to suck, turn her back to her husband in bed, ignoring his confusion.

In college, my mother held books during the week, a straightening comb on Friday nights and all day Saturday through those four years, charging fifty cents from the moneyed and lighter, more "acceptable" Spelman women who were middle class, whose fathers were doctors, lawyers, insurance salesman, Pullman porters, whose mothers—of course, at that time, probably even lighter than the fathers—were teachers, social workers, housewives. Fifty cents for a regular or hard press with the metal heated comb. First the oil to protect the scalp and hair, then the hot comb, then the round irons clicking between my mother's fingers as she stood over a hot plate in her room and made beauty. Always the sound and smell of heat.

I should not forget my mother standing next to the hot plate, talking to her customers in a deadly, cheerful voice. I should not forget how she ignored her own mother and went to college anyway, met and married my fair-skinned father, the progeny of almost-never slaves. My father thought her exotic, a dark woman raised in that old slave shack, so he took her across the country to meet his parents. I should not forget that my father was a man who had never put his fingers in a woman's hair and come away with grease coating his nails.

❧

My father insisted there was not much of a story to his family. Just a simple cliché: miscegenation. Convenience or rape more likely, in those unions between the Black female enslaved and their White mas-

ters. Their consequential children were pushed into freedom long before Mister Lincoln came along. The lucky and mostly pale ones.

Decades later came the important details: my mother and father
meeting on the coolness of academic grass in the Atlanta University
Center, where they read books together in English or French. Nothing else, not really. What was he ashamed to say to my mother and
his three daughters, especially me, the darkest child? That those who
looked like my mother, his wife, had worked the fields right until Ju-
bilee, and sometimes for years afterward, if their masters weren't kind
enough to inform them of their manumission?

The details about Daddy's family were few; he told my sisters and
me the basics about his pale mother, Dorothy, and her equally pale
husband, Forest, my father's stepfather.[2] (He hated them both.) Before
Forest, Dorothy had been married (for how long we don't know) to a
darker man, Henry Nelson, my father's father. (We met Henry when
I was three. We rode in a car for what seemed like months, to a state
where it was cold, and the trees were outlined in gray. Henry took me
on his lap and kissed me and said I was a pretty, pretty baby girl.)

Henry had married Dorothy when she became pregnant, and they
lived in a small flat, one room or two. Dorothy's own father, George
Flippin, a doctor married to a White woman, came to take Dorothy's
only child away. She followed and stayed with her child for a little
while, then left him behind in Nebraska.

The one memory given freely by my father, worn smooth in his
mind from constant use, was of Mertina, his grandfather George's
White wife.[3] Sometimes my father would speak adoringly of her on
those days he returned from teaching. A courageous woman, going
against the racist and lawful tide to marry her Black doctor, a woman
smelling cool and of flowers that did not grow in the Nebraska wilder-
ness. The kindest woman on earth, my father claimed. A nurse, working with his grandfather, the only doctor in Stromsburg, Nebraska.

Mertina holds my father, a toddler, in a picture I will see after his
death; in another picture, she guides the huge horse he rides on.

In college, the weekend of Mother's Day, I tried calling my grandmother Dorothy, who had never evidenced any interest in having a relationship with me. I sat waiting on the phone for nearly twenty minutes. The housekeeper told me, "Mrs. Jeffers not here," and put down the phone. I waited and checked my watch as the time passed. Finally, I heard Forest, my step-grandfather, over ninety himself, walking heavily down the stairs to tell me that Dorothy had died two weeks before. There was a cremation, no ceremony, and he "didn't want to bother us." My mother hovered in the background until I hung up in tears. She wanted me to call back. There had to be some mistake—but I refused.

A week later pictures arrived from California, pasted onto the thick black paper of old albums, a triangle at each corner of the photographs. My grandparents bequeathed all the rest of their belongings and money to their nephew, the son of Dorothy's brother. Only the pictures were left, and Mama wanted to give them to me. She asked how she should preserve the photographs, printed on delicate paper nearly a century ago. "Your sisters don't want them; do you?" she asks. "I would think you should want them. If they were my family . . ."

I was startled at images of Dorothy as a child, or together with Daddy's stepfather as a young couple in stiff, stylized poses. In every picture Dorothy looked light enough to pass for White, her hair waving only so slightly away from her forehead, the lashes long and thick on the slanted eyes. She was identical to my sister Sisi, whose face would wrinkle in tears, pink underneath the buttermilk, whenever we argued. Sisi, who would get mad enough to fight if you called her "high yellow" or even "light skinned."

Mama tapped another picture of Dorothy, this time as a young girl wearing long, lace-edged bloomers and a camisole, a strange image that at the time was nearly pornographic—who had taken this picture? (I still wonder. And I'm still disturbed by my unanswered question.)

"Ain't Sisi the spit of her?" Mama asked. "When she was a baby, folks used to ask me was she my own. I told them, 'No, I'm just carrying around this big ole child, hurting my back cause I'm crazy.' Now you? You were a pretty, brown thing. I used to call you 'Mommy's little representative.' I didn't have to prove to anybody that you were mine."

Mama carefully flipped the pictures over when she was done looking at each one so as not to tear the thin paper. After all, they would be mine soon. She stopped and made a noise of deep satisfaction—*Umph*—when she saw a face that didn't match the others at all.

This was a woman much darker, with curly hair like me. On the back of her picture, her name is printed in block letters, GEORGIA LELA.[4] This was not Mertina, the White woman whom my father adored, who taunted convention to marry a Black man. This was *another* woman, George's first wife, an African American woman who looked just like what she was. Behind her stood a fair-skinned little girl with long hair brushed into curls: Dorothy, who carried my sister Sisi's face. Dorothy rested her hand on Georgia's shoulder. Sitting at the mother's feet and leaning his head in her lap was a much darker boy with neatly brushed, kinky hair: Dorothy's brother, Robert Browning Flippin, so named for the English poet, one who was rumored to carry African heritage.

Georgia's husband, George, left her for Mertina, who watched my father so carefully in those other, fragile pictures, who supposedly loved my daddy so dearly, who promised George that she would take care of my daddy until he became a man. Yet according to my mother—who told this story after Daddy died—Mertina waited until her George was dead, buried under hard Nebraska dirt. She waited until George's will was probated and the land and house and respectability belonged to her. Then she placed a tag around the wrist of the child who would become my father and mailed him on a train back to Dorothy, the pale mother who would say to Daddy—her only child—that if his hair wasn't so nappy, he wouldn't be a nigger.

Mertina waited and then peeled away my father's nine-year-old heart. She peeled his heart away, layer by layer, and left the cold inside for my mother, my sisters, and me.

≈≈≈

When I was a baby, my parents visited San Francisco, where Daddy's mother and stepfather lived. Mama would sit on the couch in the living room of my father's parents' house, feeling the chill of their dogged politeness to her. The only sweetness that my mother recalls is that Forest, Daddy's stepfather, was taken with me. He constantly talked about what a pretty child I was: this, despite my darkness.

By that visit, Daddy's name had been changed for a third time. He was born Lance Henry Nelson, the son of Henry, whom Dorothy divorced a short time after they were both recorded on an Iowa census, in 1920; mother, father, and baby are listed as "Mulatto."[5] Then Daddy became Lance Flippin, after Dorothy left him with her own father, George Flippin, the doctor who had settled in Stromsburg, Nebraska. Finally my father would be Lance Flippin Jeffers, having been sent back to his mother in California. By that time Dorothy had married Forest Jeffers, a man my father would praise in print but despise privately—how familiar that custom is to me. Dorothy, Forest, and little Lance would live with a grandmother, Georgia Lela Flippin. (Again, I'd only find this out by checking census records.)

I had believed there were few people in Daddy's family: all appropriately pale; no children for color-struck Negroes who were terrified that the blood from across the water might show up again, a freakish joke of the Creator. Then I learned that my father's family tree had begun with a dark matriarch, his great-great grandmother Veta, who was coerced or assaulted by her slave master, Hugh Flippin. Veta gave birth to Charles Albert, who would join the Colored Union Troops; this woman's son became a doctor who sired a doctor. Who begot who begot. Veta can be forgiven, for her line would grow paler with each generation.

⌘

In those pictures that Forest would send us after Dorothy's death, all Daddy's childhood friends are White. It was only after he moved to San Francisco that he found Black boys to play with.

Is that why Daddy wrote about his "Blackness" so much in his poems, when his skin was buttermilk-colored? Did something in his spirit remember the African American mothers whose legacies were erased?

There was Veta Denipplif, the enslaved, second great-grandmother who my father never talked about, the mother of Charles (C. A.) Flippin, my father's great-grandfather.[6]

There was Mahala, Charles's wife, who was maybe Native American—the name has an Indigenous origin—or maybe "mulatto," because the oral history my father gave to my mother would change (and I only located scant documentation.)[7]

There was Georgia Lela, my father's grandmother.

There was Daddy's mother, Dorothy, whom my father hated and feared so much that a simple letter from her would send him spiraling—and punishing his wife and daughters—for weeks at a time.

Did my father see all these women in the face of my dark mother? Did he love them? Did he hate them? Is that why he never seemed to decide whether to cherish or abuse his wife and daughters?

I should not forget the color of my mother, or of my father, or of his people, or of her people—all of whom are *my* people. At the end of this story—at the beginning of my own—will I talk about the hue of my skin, about the wriggling tail of color showing through history? And at what point should I say there will be dark women looking at me, always, their lips pressed together in a constant warning?

12

Going to Meet Mr. Baldwin

ATLANTA, SOMETIME IN THE EARLY-TO-MID-1980S

This was before James Baldwin became a god to some, before that short Black man would become a prophet. Before people—of all shades and cultural backgrounds—who had ignored him, or didn't know who he was, would share his words on their blogs, articles, and social media timelines, as if he'd always been loved. As if he'd always been worshipped, when he had not.

I wish I could remember the year or even the month that I met him. I can prove Mr. Baldwin was in Atlanta at the time, because he was researching the missing and murdered Black children of that city, which at the time was nothing but a big country town.[1]

I was a teenager who constantly courted death, laughing when my mama told me, "Be careful out there. They're killing Black children."

"They" were a mystery. "They" are still an unknown.

Ever since we left my father and moved from North Carolina to Georgia, I'd ignored that somebody in Atlanta was stalking young folks who looked like me. I was unafraid of Death. I set out plates at a cozy table for Mr. Square Toes and asked him to take me on a never-ending vacation. I hitchhiked once, getting in the car with a White man more than twice my age. I walked into dark corners with Black boys who would hurt me. I took the bus and roamed downtown Atlanta with girls my age.

Death was my friend, keeping me company from a distance. I was reckless, in those years, coming home way after dark. In the news, the pictures of the missing and murdered showed hopeful smiles and brown skin. *This is what youth looks like,* those images told us. *This is how you'll remember us before we are broken by cynicism or cracked apart by weapons.*

❧

Some of the young folks who were killed seemed reckless as well, though I want to think of them as free. The young should be free. A child should be free. I insist upon that freedom: Perhaps someone else's childhood won't be like mine, a time I consider as bondage.

These days, Death is no longer my friend, though anxiety is. I've grown fond of living. Whenever Death comes knocking, I tell him, you're no longer welcome here: "Nigger get back: Go find somebody else's house."

❧

"Where were you?" Mama would ask the adolescent-me of the 1980s. She spoke through tears and anger, her voice ascending in panic.

"Just around," I'd say. Her own anxiety couldn't touch me. I hated her or I loved her—I couldn't decide which.

The kids at my high school, Booker T. Washington, said they found one of the murdered boys in the bleachers behind the school. Student of the historical archives that I am, I've never conducted research to make sure that was true. I'm afraid to go looking for the proof that obsessed Mr. Baldwin in his book about those children, *Evidence of Things Not Seen.* I don't want to see the names. I don't want to think of each of them gone—how I could have been gone myself.

I don't know why Mama brought me to see Mr. Baldwin that evening. Was it to make me happy or to watch me, to keep me from becoming one of those dead children spoken about on the news? She wanted to bring a book for Mr. Baldwin to sign. I wished I hadn't insisted that we didn't, that it would be tacky to do that. Though my own cynicism had taken root, I remember the books by Mr. Baldwin, the first ones that made me feel as if he were my friend: *If Beale Street Could Talk* and *Go Tell It on the Mountain*. Those books made me suspect that Mr. Baldwin loved Black women and Black girls when I'd seen so little love of us in my young life.

I loved Mr. Baldwin back, though I didn't know him—but I wasn't going to tell Mama of my affection, of course. I wasn't going to give her any satisfaction. I was lost in a tangle of self-destruction and depression that she couldn't understand. Be strong, she would urge me.

"Don't be weak," she hissed one night, standing in the doorway of our apartment in the 'hood. "Stop crying! Get yourself together," as I lay in my twin bed. I didn't answer her, I only cried for no reason that I could remember—or for every reason that I can remember.

There is miserable justification when you are a girl-child who has been abused by your father, the man your mother dearly loved, though she sold wolf tickets about him. She insisted she'd put two states between us and my father. We were never going back. We had left him for good, but that didn't matter. Most days, it seemed that my father and Death had struck up a bargain: Daddy had destroyed me, and Death would take the spoils. Sometimes, though, I rallied: I would live. I *would*. My desires were unpredictable.

Now that my mother is dead, years after Mr. Baldwin died, too, I wonder about that evening when she brought me to his lecture. I've tried to find evidence in old newspapers—where *was* Mr. Baldwin's lecture, during those years I was a teenager? Was it at Spelman College? Was it at Emory University? Was it at Georgia State or Georgia Tech? But I know it happened. I know there is *evidence* somewhere, and over the years I have stalked the internet, looking for the date. I know Mr. Baldwin came and went from Atlanta during the trial of Wayne Williams—the Black man believed to be responsible for the child murders from 1981 to early 1982—so maybe I met Mr. Baldwin during *those* months?

Williams was the Black man tried and convicted for the murders of two young Black men, but nobody has ever gone to prison for the murders of over twenty others, most of whom were children.[2]

⁓

I can't remember the details of Mr. Baldwin's talk, only that he spoke about racism in America. He spoke about how things should be, but they weren't there yet—how things in our country just weren't right. I noticed that he was elegant and angry, and before that night, I hadn't known you could be both of those simultaneously.

During the question-and-answer portion, a White man rose and began with a statement, "As a gay man in America . . . ," and I saw Mr. Baldwin shift his body. The atmosphere in the room changed: The audience was no longer warm. I realized that Mr. Baldwin was uncomfortable.

This was Atlanta in the 1980s. There was no acceptance of Queer Black people forty-plus years ago—there's barely any acceptance now—and I felt protective of Mr. Baldwin. I wasn't gay, but I was different. I knew what it meant to live without the permission to fully be myself. And I felt so tender toward Mr. Baldwin, because even though I didn't know him—I had only read his words—I had witnessed his tenderness toward Black women and girls through his work. He cherished us and wanted us to be safe, and in turn, I wanted to cover him with safety.

⁓

Two decades after Mr. Baldwin passed, I'd read what Toni Morrison wrote about him in *The New York Times* when he died in 1987—the depth of her grief—and I'd known I had been right about Mr. Baldwin's kindness.[3] Professor Morrison couldn't have such a profound love for Mr. Baldwin unless she had been loved in return—she spoke of his "tenderness." Professor Morrison did not call Mr. Baldwin a gay man—but as a writer myself, I see there is a defiance wrapped around her grief, that she *names* the beauty of his sexuality everywhere in her piece. She demands that we see him, and she is a Black woman writer who has witnessed the homophobia of the community—and the church—that made Mr. Baldwin.

I am an older woman, not a young girl of misery—and I must say this, in joy: I have been loved in the way that Mr. Baldwin loved Professor Morrison. I have been cherished by a man who did not touch me to harm, who did not search my flesh in any longing—*frightening*—way, but rather, acknowledged that a woman's meat was no less than his own.

I have loved a man who was not my lover, and in the loss of this man—after his death—I, too, have been stricken by the comprehension of his devotion to me. That man was named James as well, a word written down in the Bible that I both cherish and reject.

I had a sweet nickname for him: I called him "Big Poppa."

Somehow the uncomfortable moment passed: The Q & A after Mr. Baldwin's talk was over. Mama gathered her purse—I didn't carry one back then—and said we would go to meet Mr. Baldwin. We walked to the reception area. We stood in line, inching forward, and I thought about what I would say to him. But when we finally were before him, I was quiet. After over forty years, I know that I suffered from what is called social anxiety, but at the time I considered myself stupid.

Mama introduced herself to Mr. Baldwin as Lance Jeffers's wife. It seemed an odd thing to do—who cared who she was married to?—but then Mr. Baldwin asked, "And how is Lance?" There was a lit cigarette between his fingers, and he moved his hand in the most beautiful way.

I wanted to bathe in the glow of that familiarity: Mr. Baldwin knew my father! That made me special. But I couldn't tell him that the man he was animatedly discussing with Mama was so very cruel. Daddy had abused my mother. He had abused my sisters and me. He had crawled into my bed at night.

I was silent. I didn't talk about Daddy, or anything at all. I didn't say, "Mr. Baldwin, I love you back. I admire you so much. I want to be a writer like you one day."

As Mr. Baldwin talked with Mama, a young man came behind him and draped a fur-collared tan coat around his shoulders. Mr. Baldwin pulled the coat closer, then kept talking. He waved his cigarette elegantly and ignored the long line of others waiting to talk to him: I could see that he liked Mama, and I adored her in that moment—she had captured the attention of *this* man.

I never said a word to Mr. Baldwin—I was a southern Black child among my elders, silent as I had been taught—but every few seconds, he would turn and smile at me.

～

I'm more than a decade older than my mother was that evening.

I never thought I'd write these words—never thought I'd survive to this age, when too many children in Atlanta did not make it. I am alive because my mother wanted to save me. Mama was flawed—as I am flawed—but somewhere inside her she marshaled love, if only in scattered moments. The kind of love that draped her Black girl-child in protection.

That evening Mama was victorious: She insisted on taking me to meet Mr. Baldwin, that tender man who cared about Black women and children. It was a miracle he performed that evening. Though he wasn't a god, I believe that I am alive, too, because of Mr. Baldwin. How, with only a few looks, he made a silent, hurting girl feel as if one day she could speak—how he tossed back his head and laughed in our small circle, not like a prophet, but just a regular brother who was right at home with his family.

13

Ode to SWATS (All Day)

Ode to the MARTA, when I rode the 86 Lithonia bus out to where I once lived in Decatur. Ode to the other bus—sorry, I forgot the number—that I rode when Mama moved us to SWATS, away from my daddy.

Ode to every manner of vehicle I rode in when I was trying not to kill myself and get grown. When I lived in the ghettos of Atlanta and its surrounding nigger-villes, while my mama lied and tried to tell me that despite the roaches and the pinto beans with cornbread and them good-good government cheese grilled sandwiches, we weren't living in poverty.

Ode to them boys on Campbellton Road, on Martin Luther King Jr. Drive, on Panther Road, and all the way out to Bankhead, boys that sat in the classrooms with me at Clark College. Thema boys who liked to fight too much, swag-walking through Greenbriar Mall. Skinny boys trying to figure out how to unhook a bra in between singing on corners, rapping on corners, slanging on corners to pay for tuition, running when the police drove by, trying not to get arrested, trying not to get shot. Them boys who ended up in county jail, then state prison, then the same old thing. *Ain't no thing, baby,* them boys told me. But it was a thing. It really, truly was.

Ode to me and all the Black girls trying to heal from the touching hands of dirty old men who didn't have no business around us, girls trying to find a tenor-high, red velvet cake, Luther Vandross love, girls ignoring our mothers' hot-comb-with-blue-grease warnings, "Leave them boys alone, all you need is an education." Girls with their pretty, brown, big-leg selves.

Ode to my first sister, dead. Ode to my second sister, dead now as well.

Ode to my mama with them growing hands working magic on my hair with a marcel iron—who hung on so she could speak the name of my lowdown, good-hair daddy like he was a good man, like he was her personal Jesus who she moved the Rock for, just so Daddy could ignore her like Jesus did Mary Magdalene. I was Black and my mama was Black and my sisters were Black so I learned I must still dig in the dirt to grow some understanding like Mama grew those tall collards in the garden of that green house before she packed us up in Durham and drove us down to Atlanta, where we all tried but failed to leave Daddy behind.

Ode to me on this Sunday past my double nickel year, living four states over from Georgia, driving the interstate in the hipster hybrid that barely burns gas, listening to Scarface and Outkast and Al Green and Aretha and Luther and Anita Baker. Ode to this day when here I am all alone in this Midwest former sundown town, wishing I could conjure up another Georgia backyard fish fry, another thick-n-thin-sock barbecue, another moment in Grandma Florence's church in the country, ninety minutes from SWATS.

Ode to when I still believed in church. Ode to another ride in the long gas-guzzler car with them boys whose names I remember: Black Boy and Scut and Junior, who would grow up to disappoint their ma-mas, to disappoint their baby-mamas, to deny what *Ebony* and *Jet Magazine* told them a Black man was supposed to be to the grown Black woman who loved him, the woman who used to get their hair pressed and curled or burned with a relaxer so one day her prince would show up kind and rich or at least paying bills or bringing a gallon of milk and some diapers.

I miss them boys. I miss my sisters when they were my sisters. I miss when I thought Mama would stop loving Daddy—and oh, this ode to them rides in a 'Lac winding through SWATS, smoking somebody's weed, winding to the interstate, the hot air through the rolled-down window, the inevitable mosquito bites, and I'm so lonely this morning for my disappeared blood.

14

Trellie Lee's Baby[1]

1.

I was five years old when my mother separated from my father for the first time. We had been living in Maryland, where my father, a poet, was teaching at Bowie State University. Mama moved me and my sisters Valjeanne and Sidonie—Val and Sisi, I called them—down to Eatonton. For a long time, it was the happiest interval of my life. There were months away from my roaring, abusive father, whose moods were becoming increasingly unpredictable.

I have snippets I can recall, before then. I know I spent the ages between one and four in Long Beach, California, but that is hazy. After California, there was Silver Spring, Maryland, but most memories before Eatonton, I've pushed over a bridge into a swiftly moving water.

Here was serenity: The drive on I-20 East. The turning off the exit, taking the right onto Highway 441, past the dairy farm. Past the building where the Dairy Queen used to be, through the town square, and down Concord Avenue, before it was renamed. My beloved fruit stand with the sign announcing "Peches." (The word is misspelled either way. If English, it's missing an *a*. If French—for there were French in what is now Georgia during the eighteenth century— it's missing a circumflex over the first *e*.)

Mama settled the four of us in one large room in a yellow house down the street from her own mother, on Concord Avenue. When my sisters and I walked to Grandma Florence's house, we passed the residences of our relatives: Aunt Iola, my grandmother's younger sister who lived across from Mr. Rice's Funeral Home. Further down the road was the house of Aunt Iola's son. We children knew never to act up in daylight: My mother allowed us to be verbally chastised by every adult through those four blocks on Concord, though she didn't let anybody (but my father, I suppose) hit us.

That year, my oldest sister Val taught me to read from *Dick and Jane*. My middle sister Sisi braided my hair in complicated cornrows, even though my mother fussed at her: It took too long to take all my hair down. There was no fear in Eatonton, though I should have been afraid. It was the 1970s, and danger lurked for African Americans in Georgia, and girls have always been unsafe around boys and men.

But my grandmother was formidable; she was known—and seemingly feared—by everyone in that tiny town's Black community. Her name was a passport through any dicey situation. Then, too, my mother was a graduate of Spelman College, and that fact alone made her close to a god to every Black person that I encountered in that town. I'm sure I was an arrogant little girl, surrounded by that kind of female power.

After a few months in the yellow duplex house—the memory is hazy after more than fifty years—we moved to another rented house made of brick about a mile away. Across the nearby road that led deeper into the country, there was a jail. There was nothing else to do in Eatonton back then except walk around. When my sisters and cousins and unrelated playmates passed by the jail's fence, I'd wave wide, though I knew that my mother would have disapproved. Dark men would call from a distance, from behind those bars.

I think of those brothers as real-life versions of Bruh Rabbit and his archnemesis Bruh Fox from a folktale I've considered so many times, "The Wonderful Tar-Baby Story," as transcribed by journalist Joel Chandler Harris.[2] As the tale goes, a doll made of a sticky substance sits in the road where Bruh Fox has placed her, in hopes of trapping his ever-enemy, Bruh Rabbit. Bruh Rabbit says something to Tar Baby, but the doll doesn't reply, of course. Then the doll is punched and kicked by Bruh Rabbit, who is angry at the lack of greeting.

And I think of the road as red dirt. I think of those brothers in the jail—and those creature-brothers in Harris's tales. I think of the frustration of both sets of brothers, that they can't take out their rage on the man who owns the lands on which they walked—or cavorted and hopped on. Surely that owner is White, as the land in the Deep South was stolen from the Indigenous folks and given to the descendants of Europeans.

2.

I turned six, and that fall Mama, my sisters, and I moved from Eatonton, and my childhood drastically changed. My parents reconciled, and my father relocated to Durham, North Carolina; after what seemed to be a period of insecure unemployment, he was hired as a tenure-track professor (with a great salary) at the mostly White institution in Raleigh, North Carolina State University.

Durham was so different from Eatonton. It was a small city, we had no relatives there, and I couldn't play in the dark in my neighborhood anymore; I had to come inside when the streetlights flickered on. Though Durham was still de facto segregated—meaning, segregated by custom, if not by law—there were twenty-five Black millionaires in the city, including the CEO of the Black-owned insurance company North Carolina Mutual. My parents' huge, fancy church, St. Joseph African Methodist Episcopal, was one of the jewels of the Black religious community. There was a Black-owned bank, Mechanics and Farmers, where my parents kept their checking and savings account.

Among the members of the Black bourgeoisie there were pushy Black folks in Durham, ones who waged battles against segregation. My mother became one of those activists, sitting on the Durham Committee on the Affairs of Black People. My parents' friends—also activists and sometimes artists—were highly educated African Americans who had earned (at least) college educations. They spoke in perfectly elocuted English, with subjects and verbs that matched.

❧

I missed Eatonton so much, and lived for the summers when we would return. The only joy I had in Durham was working alongside my mother in one of the three garden spaces she kept. One was a tiny plot behind our house on Weaver Street. The other spaces were rented: a second, larger plot beside a barbecue joint across town, next to the Durham County line, and a third in Chapel Hill, a longer drive to a large clearing in the forest, where strangely dressed yet friendly White folks—Mama called them hippies when only she and I were together— dug in the earth. Once a year, she preserved what she'd grown. (There was a dill pickle recipe that she never wrote down, now lost forever.) Regularly, my sister Sisi's boyfriend would come to Chapel Hill with us, to kill the rats that tried to take over the clearing.

Memories of working in the garden have been transformed into a larger history for me: I learned that when I helped Mama to cook collards or turnips, those verdant leaves, when she stirred hot water corncakes, we were continuing foodways traditions of centuries. This was the same cuisine that my enslaved Southern ancestors ate to supplement the meager weekly rations apportioned them by their White slave masters. My reading short chapter books (before I somehow leaped into Alex Haley's *Roots*) to Mama at bedtime becomes a backward trajectory, in which my life connected to Black folks who defied eighteenth- and nineteenth-century antiliteracy laws that denied them the ability to read and write.[3]

❧

When I was around eight, my mother somehow secured the piano teacher most renowned among the children of what Mama called "the best Black families" of Durham.[4] This was the legendary Mrs. Barbara Logan Cooke, a former professor of music who had attended Fisk University and Juilliard and a woman dedicated to service in the Black community—she was a member of The Links, Inc., *and* Alpha Kappa Alpha Sorority, Inc. Every Black adult whom I'd encountered in Durham knew Mrs. Cooke and worshipped her, and though my family wasn't wealthy, I was proud that I was one of her handpicked piano students.[5]

How I adored Mrs. Cooke! She was a strict piano teacher—"Watch those fingers, Honorée! You know where they should go!" "I'm sorry, Mrs. Cooke—I'll do better!"—but so warm and loving, a calm port in my chaotic childhood. At Christmastime Mrs. Cooke gave her piano students musically themed gifts, and at this big age, I grieve the loss of a triple-clef bodice pin. (I loved that pin; I wish I knew where I misplaced it.) Her big house had a marble foyer and an actual working soda shoppe in the basement. Mama told me that Mrs. Cooke probably had that soda shoppe built because her children had come of age during segregation: Neither they nor their Black friends could sit in Durham's drugstores and enjoy refreshments.

Mrs. Cooke's house was directly across the street from North Carolina Central University, the historically African American institution where my mother had started working as an adjunct instructor. My parents would take my sisters and me to listen to lectures in the auditorium at NCCU, or to watch an opera or piano recital. During these cultural adventures my father was charming, and he was greatly respected in our community. A fellow artist, Mrs. Cooke seemed to adore Daddy almost as much as I adored her. I was certain that she wouldn't have believed me if I told her that he turned into a shouting, frightening man at home. I wasn't going to tell her or anybody else; in Durham I had learned what shame was, not only about my father but about the working-class origins I'd inherited from Mama.

When I played with the children of Durham intellectuals, I neglected to mention anything about Eatonton—that from June through late July, I lived with my cousins and two sisters in Grandma's house, across the railroad tracks. I would have been horrified to tell my friends in Durham that Grandma didn't buy her vegetables from the grocery store because she kept a large garden out back. She didn't purchase bacon at the grocery store, either. Every morning she fried something called "streak-a-lean," an odd pork variant bought from a farmer she knew.

It didn't matter that Grandma Florence's own lawn was manicured like those in my middle-class neighborhood in Durham. That one of my uncles would mow Grandma's lawn in Eatonton. I didn't care that Grandma cultivated red and pink roses in her front yard. To me, those Eatonton flowers weren't as pretty as Durham flowers. Grandma's sun didn't shine as bright as the one up in my city. I was confused by my feelings toward her. The way Grandma Florence turned her phrases in English shamed me. Her speech didn't adhere to formal grammar rules. Her rough hands and feet weren't manicured and soft. And she only had about an eighth-grade education—but at the same time, I admired how she didn't "take no junk."

Mama presented similar contradictions, ones that I neglected to discuss with my classmates as well. (Not that I had any real friends at school.) A "proper lady" sometimes, a growling adversary at others, she ached to belong to what she called "the authentic Black bourgeoisie" but made fun of them in private: their colorism and their pretensions, the dark-skinned husbands who had married the lightest of wives but propositioned my chocolate-colored mama when the wives' backs were turned. (She'd tell me this in my twenties.) She joined the Spelman College alumni chapter in Durham but rarely attended the meetings.

We lived in a reasonably nice middle-class neighborhood, but Mama was the one who cut our grass and tended the flowers, while my father, the (lazy) poet, sat in his office and typed up his books.

I didn't know *what* Mama was, but I knew she didn't belong among the middle-class Black people in Durham. She was different but refused to change, to adhere to what I learned was respectable behavior for Black women and girls. She was educated and married to my Columbia University–educated father, but she fit right in with her loud, country kin farther south, her misbehaving maternal line. Surely my mother wasn't a member of the snooty Black bourgeoisie. If that was the case, as her daughter, neither was I.

But hadn't Mama sought out Mrs. Barbara Cooke to be my piano teacher? And hadn't my dark-skinned mother married my privileged light-skinned father, a man who was Ivy League educated? Though Mama never said she married my father precisely because of his skin tone, I couldn't count the number of times she'd proclaimed, "I would have died before I'd ever lie down next to a nigger who split verbs!" Yet she viciously criticized those she saw as "color-struck" in our Durham community.

I saw complications in so many ways in Mama's public behavior: the way she fought for the rights of poor African American school-children in our community; her voting rights activism, knocking on the doors of poor and working-class Black folks, urging them to vote. In Durham she corrected my grammar, yet she code-switched to the country vernacular of her childhood when she was home in Eatonton.

And then, there was her gardening. She didn't just tend flowers. Like her own mother, she kept a vegetable garden and "put up" preserves. I concealed these facts at school, for already my classmates made fun of my "mammy made" lunches—sandwiches on thick home-made whole wheat bread—and the clothes that Mama sewed for me. I didn't report that every summer she left my father behind and drove her daughters down south to stay at her rough-talking mother's house.

3.

On the voyage to womanhood, I left my mother and Eatonton behind. A tall barrier of memory—my father's intimate abuse of me—and resentment had arisen between Mama and me. There are so many other reasons, too, so many small and large moments that added up to that decades-long acrimony.

I refused to visit Mama or attend the family reunion: a hoodoo interval of abandonment. I'd become a faithless daughter, violating the biblical commandment I'd learned as a child: "Honor thy father and thy mother: that thy days may be long upon the land which the Lord thy God giveth thee."

It seemed even worse, even more of a filial betrayal, that Mama had granted me a French name that translated as "the honored one." She'd insisted that the day I was born, she held me and saw greatness etched upon my small face.

In the last years of my mother's life, I began to lie to people. When they asked, "How is your mama doing?" I'd answer, "Oh, she's doing just fine!"

I talked about traveling back home, but I didn't say, sure, I visited the South regularly. But while I was there, I avoided the personal homes of my family members, and especially I avoided my mother.

There were friends I lost because they believed me to be a cold person; they couldn't understand my cutting off contact with Mama. In Black communities, that's not even conceivable, abandoning your mother. When I was married, my former husband told me that only a horrible person did something like that.

So I lied, because I didn't want to seem like a monster. I lied because I loved my mother, and I continued to feel loyal to her—I would never tolerate someone criticizing her in my presence. I lied because I didn't want to explain in detail why I'd made this painful decision. I lied because I didn't want to seem weak and say, I stopped seeing my mother because I experienced mental and/or physical breakdowns every time I visited. I lied because the shame was overwhelming. I lied because I was supposed to be a strong Black woman, but I wasn't strong. I was always close to breaking, and every time I was in my mother's physical presence, it took me months to recover emotionally, to stop craving never-ending sleep.

My refusal to visit my family or attend reunions—or to call my mother—was criticized within the family as well. There was a lot of talk about "forgiveness" and "letting go of the past," but not so much about what might be done to get me to those two existential locations.

≈≈≈

As soon as I could, I left the South. I moved from Alabama to Illinois, eventually settling on the flat prairie of Oklahoma. I came to that state, where cowboys claim to be Southern, for a job, but I found that I can't trust people who wear boots all four seasons of the year. I couldn't love a place where the trees don't grow tall, where beauty seemed absent. There was nothing in Oklahoma to console me when I remembered the violence that formed this state. Violence had made this place, like a body embroidered in the womb.

I'd long known about the violence of the South. My Georgia elders made sure I knew about that history, but as the years passed, I understood that those folks hadn't meant to frighten me. They only wanted me to carry pieces of them forward. To remember a past that went beyond the beauty I idealized. I never succeeded in rejecting my history, for one day my Georgia origins reclaimed me. My tongue surrendered, and a drawl emerged from my lips. My voice had absorbed history, the places where the women of my family worked. The yards where these women had chopped wood. The gardens where they grew their own food. The White folks' kitchens where they'd dreamed of different lives for their children, something other than working as servants. Those Black women: enduring the night until the morning's vowels cracked the darkness.

Oklahoma was a place that made me shudder, for it could never be home, and the ugly landscape couldn't justify the spilled blood of the Trail of Tears and Death. I can't defend my Deep South origins too much: Truly, there is horror sown in the red dirt land of Georgia, screams that only those of us who have been chosen to tend altars still hear. But the beauty of the Deep South! The tall trees, the overgrown flora that hides snakes and creatures that frighten me in other places, but that I wave away as "nature" when I think of my home. There is none of that in central Oklahoma, though to be fair, I haven't tried to explore the eastern side of the state, where residents insist beauty is present.

I think of the original inhabitants of Georgia, how they were forced from their homes to the flat prairie where I lived and worked. I think of the grief of these people, the Creek and the Cherokee, how they must have howled when they knew they would never return. Such rememory—the words that ancestors whisper to me—slices me clean whenever I think of Georgia, my true home.

~∿~

And then I began to speak in the parables and proverbs of my maternal line. I pulled my Bible from its hiding place and traced the words. I greeted the days with the songs of my grandmother: *Guide my feet while I run this race.* I remembered Grandma Florence and Mama bookending me on a church pew at Flat Rock Primitive Baptist. They'd been so sure of the mercy of God.

Every now and then I'd drive back south, to the place that conjured glory and ruins in my imagination. I'd offer gratitude because I truly missed this place. Oh, how I missed my home! (Headed toward my sixth decade, I've become unafraid of my sentimentality.)

The journey on the interstate east was long, and after some hours in my car, I'd anxiously search for the highway sign: WELCOME TO MISSISSIPPI. That state's not where my maternal people live, yet the sign told me, if I was patient, I'd see Georgia soon. I'd return to the cotton fields sprinkled with white (if the season permits). To the church where the people sang spirituals. To the fruit stand beside the road. To the red clay of indelible stains. To a history I both created and inherited.

4.

In my fifties, Mama began coming to me in dreams. I come from a line of seers, women who believed in "roots," who insisted that God spoke to them directly while they were sleeping, and sometimes, rarely, when they were awake. I tried to ignore the messages, but they only became stronger.

In those dreams, my elderly mother was trapped in a debilitated house. I was trying to rescue her before the structure deflated and trapped her inside. Termites ate through the walls, and I could see the tails of rats as they scurried away. I'd call to Mama, "Give me your hand!" But I never could touch her.

I had this same dream for months, until I couldn't take it anymore, the constant awakening with tears and a thundering heart. I called two friends—both former students of Mama from her days teaching at Talladega College in Alabama—and told them I was troubled. I had a real, real bad feeling. My friends encouraged me to go see Mama, but I was afraid. Every time I visited her, the old disagreements would come back—the old pain—and things would be worse than before. My friends assured me they would be praying for me daily, and though I hadn't been to church in over four years, I was comforted by the old ways.

THE MORNING AFTER my fifty-sixth birthday, I flew into the Birmingham Shuttlesworth Airport in Alabama, the state where Mama lived. It seemed there were good signs from the moment I touched down: the warmth of the African Americans. The way the older Black men called me "young lady," and the younger ones called me "ma'am." I had reserved a car that I considered affordable, but when she heard that I had flown to Alabama to see my eighty-nine-year-old mama, the sweet young sister at the rental car counter upgraded me to a Mercedes for the same price.

I was in a conservative "red" state, but even the White folks seemed kind. Unlike in Oklahoma, there was no instant interracial hostility, the twist of pale faces that communicated, "You don't belong here." As I placed my bags in the trunk of my fancy rental, I reasoned, the public niceness of White folks in Alabama must come from that ingrained, renowned Southern hospitality that acted as a surface buffer to history—as long as you didn't go too deep.

My fear didn't return until the next day, when I awoke early in my hotel room, then prepared to drive to the hospital in Anniston, Alabama, where a relative had told me Mama had been admitted. As I drove on the highway, the beauty of the landscape pierced me. I prayed, "Be with me, Lord. Please."

In the hospital parking lot, I sat in the car, panic taking me over.

I couldn't take one more argument with Mama. One more denial of what had happened to me as a little girl. I was too fragile.

I prayed once again and opened the car door. At the entrance to the hospital, an older Black gentleman told me "Have a blessed day."

When I walked into my mother's hospital room, I saw a very old woman, not the indestructible matriarch that I'd remembered. One of her shoulders listed to the left side of the narrow bed. Her gray hair was sparse and braided in cornrows.

From the doorway, I called, "Mama?"

She lifted her head, peering in confusion.

"It's me, Honi. It's your baby girl."

She smiled. "Honi? Is that you? Hey darling!"

There was joy that I heard in her voice. A whispered song. She called my name again, reaching for me, and I folded Mama into my arms.

III

RED DIRT: INTERLUDE

I swallowed mountains, even as I fought.

—TRELLIE JAMES JEFFERS,
  "THE BLACK BLACK WOMAN AND THE MIDDLE CLASS"

From the old slave shack I chose my lady
from the harsh garden of the South . . .

—LANCE JEFFERS,
  "WHEN I KNOW THE POWER OF MY BLACK HAND"

15

from the Old Slave Shack: Memoirs of a Teacher[1]

BY TRELLIE JAMES JEFFERS

By the time I entered high school, I was convinced that I was a very bright girl. I had been told this by my elementary teacher, Mrs. Roland, when I began attending Flat Rock Elementary School at the age of four. Mrs. Roland was a heavyset lady with piercing gray eyes. She had the reputation for being mean. Her reputation was well deserved: she was the only teacher who spanked me throughout my elementary school days. Yet she praised me for already knowing the alphabet; my numbers from one to ten; and how to write all the names, with correct spellings, of my immediate family members.

From the first grade through the third grade, I was my elementary school's spelling champion as well as the oratorical champion; I tutored my classmates in math; I could recite every verse of Longfellow's poem "The Psalm of Life" as well as Gray's "Elegy Written in a Country Church-yard" and Paul Laurence Dunbar's "In the Morning." I learned every line and every cue of any play that was presented at either school, whether I was in the play or not; and I set the curve for all my high school math and science classes at a perfect one hundred points.

My teachers and people in the community who attended school functions had given me standing ovations each time I performed in a play or recited a poem or sang a song. Their ovations were further proof to me that I was smart; therefore, there was no doubt in my mind as I approached high school graduation that the goal of beautician, on which I had set my sights, was firmly within my reach.

~⁓~

Throughout my school years, I had compared my life to many of my classmates: and that comparison had taught me the undisputed fact that I was poor. I knew by the way children poked fun at my clothes made of colorfully printed feed sacks left over from the food bought for the pigs and cows, at the way I had put those flowers and stripes together for my outfits. My lunches sometimes consisted simply of biscuits with homemade peach or pear preserves or a single slice of fried salt pork.

Another sense of shame in high school was that I lived in a literal slave shack; my classmates constantly reminded me of this. Some of their parents had purchased their own homes. In fact, there was a section of town called Pleasant Grove (we poor students jokingly called it "Buzzard Roost") where the "better off" black families lived. Some of these families had fathers who were former veterans of World War II and who worked at skilled professions as barbers or brick masons. Other families had mothers who were beauticians or teachers. There were also two black morticians in town.

Where I lived was an old weather-beaten hut without windowpanes with a tin roof that sounded like bullets exploding during a hard rain. I don't remember any insulation; in winter, the house was bitterly cold and in summer it was unbearably hot. In the summer months, we had to wait until ten or eleven o'clock at night when the shack had cooled down before going to bed. We didn't have electricity; therefore, we did not have any way to cool the place. There was no grass, and so the soil had eroded so that flowers would rarely grow in the yard.

Another problem we had was overcrowding. Nine months before my tenth birthday, my mother had given birth to her sixth child, my brother Charlie Jr., in a two-room shack. That December, shortly after my tenth birthday, we moved onto the Wood Place plantation, where my father became the manager. The owner of the plantation was Mr. Frank Brinfield, a Jewish gentleman. We still lived in a slave shack, but this one was bigger, since it had three small bedrooms and a kitchen. The kitchen and the back bedroom had been added on and ran the length of the original house, and then that addition had been divided into two rooms. At first there was more space, but then we became nine instead of eight when my uncle Jinks, my mother's brother, was evicted by my grandfather for assaulting him with a pistol. My grandfather had snatched the cover from Jinks one cold morning at four thirty a.m., and my uncle refused to get up. So Uncle Jinks came to live with us.

On the Wood Place plantation we had access to more and richer land that we could use without penalty. Mr. Brinfield gave my father resources to buy livestock, and the plantation became filled with horses, goats, pigs, and cows. To these my mother added turkeys, ducks, and laying hens. My mother kept frying chickens: when the first chicks reached maturity, she would order another hundred baby chicks. She always kept chickens of all sizes.

We grew all of our food, both meat and vegetables. My father, Uncle Jinks, and the two oldest brothers, Thedwron and Alvester, would slaughter goats, pigs, turkeys, chickens, and young bulls any time there was a special occasion.

Mr. Brinfield gave my father permission to use any and all of the farm animals and land for his own purposes. This seemed like a wonderful idea to my parents, but to my brothers and me, the work seemed insurmountable. I was ten; my brothers were eight and nine. My brothers helped my father with the farm animals, with planting and harvesting the crops, and I helped my mother with childcare, cleaning, washing, and cooking.

We children had little or no childhood. In spring we went to school, came home, and worked until dark. In summer we gathered fruits and vegetables for canning and other preservation. In the fall we picked cotton, pulled corn to store for bread and for food for animals. In the winter, we also attended school, tended to the animals, and found wood for fire. My father and Uncle Jinks worked as hired hands in winter. This meant that we children had to assume their chores. I was often so exhausted during my elementary and high school years that I felt half alive.

For all the eleven years of my school time, I would return home from the four miles' journey to and from school and cook. I had to cook supper after gathering dry chips that would quickly ignite a fire in the wood-burning stove. Whatever I cooked, we always had corn bread for supper. It was made from the corn we grew and then ground by an old white gentleman who owned a mill near the river. I would always try to make a treat for the family who I felt had worked so hard during the day. One treat was sweet potato pudding; others were peach or blackberry cobbler from canned fruits, gingerbread or tea cakes. Other times, there was butter to be churned or family wash to be completed.

Despite my new sense of plenty at Wood Place, at school I learned that I was still poor, but also, I learned I was ridiculed perhaps not so much for my poverty, but because I dared to be smarter than my other classmates and be poor at the same time. I was even resented by some of the parents who might not have been middle-class, but were certainly better off than my own parents. I overheard these parents complaining that their children should have received more attention in school than I did.

Once when my mother's father found out I was receiving an honor for scholarship, he remarked, "Poor, hungry children work much harder than those who have plenty."

❧

When I reached the age of twelve or thirteen, we began selling eggs. My brothers and I would carry a basket of eggs on our way to school in the morning to Old Man Willie Waller's country store, that was located about a hundred feet from our schoolhouse. I used this money to keep my hair "fixed," and on my regular trips every other Saturday to my hairdresser, Dot, I watched her stuff money in the greasy pocket of her smock. So I knew that the hot, sweaty task of moving the Marcel irons from the slow-burning gas flame to transform a wild mass of tangled hair into a smooth, easy-to-manage condition brought great monetary rewards. I knew that what I needed to do after high school was to find a way to make money, and lots of it. One day when I watched Dot, I realized that I had stumbled upon the way to annihilate my poverty.

Dot seemed to get great satisfaction with the transformation of her clients. At the end of each task, she often smiled and then advised her customers on how to maintain her finished product until their next visit. After watching Dot at her craft for two or three years, I approached her and discussed with her the procedure for entering training for what I had concluded to be a rather lucrative profession. Impressed with my ambition, Dot went to great trouble to supply me with information on how to secure enrollment to the Madam C. J. Walker School of Cosmetology in Atlanta, the school that she had attended.

During this time I often felt the weight of my entire family on my back, and though no one told me, because I was the eldest child, I intuitively sensed that I was expected to stamp out my family's poverty; from an early age, I saw nothing in my parents that would remove the stains of poverty from our lives. Though my mother was very keen on our attending school, rain or shine, and insistent on our making excellent grades, she could only do work that yielded minimum wages; the same was the case for my father. We barely survived, even with everyone doing his/her best in the situation. Both parents had very little education, though my mother had ambition for us. I became aware that our way of life was far below the standard that I wished to live, and I felt that there was a complacency in our condition that only I could change, by studying hard, graduating, and then attending beauty school.

~•~

As a little girl, I walked four miles round trip to Flat Rock Elementary School, an ancient wooden schoolhouse with an outhouse for a toilet, and a battered potbelly stove in the middle of one room for heat in the winter. The boys had to go in the forest behind the school to gather wood for fire in the winter when the parents had not brought wood for the stove. We had to get our water from a spring about one quarter of a mile away. This was another task for the boys.

We had small wooden benches and tables that were often too high for the small children. We could hear the rats in the closet while we were having class, and we could smell their urine when and if we opened the closet door. We could not use the closets because the rats would chew up our books and gnawed holes in our winter coats as they had done on several occasions.

However, the white children were bussed to a big brick building, the consolidated elementary and high schools. Their buses would pass us on cold winter mornings as we hurried, sometimes in the rain, to an even colder building. Our books were cast off from the white schools, with names already written in the books, and we often recognized the names of the white children whose parents operated grocery or department stores.

Although we had another building for high school, the conditions didn't change much. For example, in chemistry, we had one test tube. There were never any experiments for lack of equipment. Despite all of this, it was drilled into our heads by our principal, Mr. W. N. Mc-Glockton (who was lovingly called "Mr. Mack") and the science and math teacher, Mr. Odell Owens, that an education was the only escape.

Though the constant ridiculing from my classmates throughout the years had made me insecure, I kept studying hard, learned French for its own sake (since I never thought there would be a situation where I would need it), and excelled in math and science.

Then, in my eleventh grade, the highest possible grade to obtain at my high school, a woman named Miss Janet Virginia Talley arrived at my school.

She was a quiet, honey-brown, attractive woman with a distinct walk and even more distinct voice. She impressed me, first with her mannerisms, and secondly, with her intellect in English class. When she pointed out to me one day that I had the same last name as Henry James, the writer, and that I had a unique first name, I surmised that she had found something special about me, and I knew that I was going to like her.

In later years, I realized that her pointing out these two qualities concerning my name may have been her way of becoming my ally in warding off the constant hostility and insults that I endured daily from my classmates, both for excelling in my classes and for my "tacky" clothes. In Miss Talley's class I was able to recapture my former intellectual stance where the hostility from my classmates had cracked my confidence. I regained the confidence I once had in my ability to speak and write.

Also my ally, Mr. Mack, was a Morehouse man and had recruited Miss Talley to come to the Eatonton Colored High School to teach English. I had overheard some of the other teachers remark that Miss Talley had a superior air since she had attended Spelman College, but I had no idea where that was or why her coworkers would be concerned about where she had gone to school. Until that day when Miss Talley ordered me to remain with her during my lunch period, no one had ever mentioned the word *college* to me, and it was even more surprising that she would mention a Spelman College and emphatically assure me that I was going to attend it after my pending graduation from high school.

Miss Talley's insistence that I would attend Spelman would run afoul of my plans after high school, of course, but I had great admiration for Miss Talley; consequently, I humored her, for she had expressed belief in my abilities and I liked her class so much. For example, it was in her class that I discovered my passion for Shakespeare's *Hamlet, Prince of Denmark*. Though this had been my third Shakespearean play, preceded by *Julius Caesar* and *Macbeth*, *Hamlet* was my favorite. I had such identification with this young man who had been given an impossible task by his father-ghost. This task included the honor of the whole state of Denmark. I, too, felt that I had been given an impossible task at a very early age of taking care of my younger brothers and sisters, and like Hamlet, I was expected to succeed. Often, my parents had told me that not only should I set good examples for my siblings, but also, I had to protect them from any harm.

I was so saddened by young Hamlet's death, trying to obey his dead father's wishes. I felt the weight of my entire family on my back, and I knew I was expected to stamp out their poverty as well. My tasks, like Hamlet's, were impossible ones. No wonder he went mad, and I was so disappointed and saddened by his downfall. I wanted him to win, for his victory would somehow be victory for me.

I discussed my ideas about Hamlet's fate with great passion in Miss Talley's classroom through the many giggles and the remarks of "girl, you crazy" by those who didn't have a clue of what I was talking about and knew even less about what Shakespeare meant. Miss Talley seemed to know, though, and complimented me for my "fine thinking," to the chagrin of my classmates.

That day when Miss Talley called me to her desk to assist me in writing a letter of application to Spelman College, I had no conception of what going to college would mean. Later, when I foolishly confided to my classmates that I had decided to apply for college, most of them didn't know anything about college in the first place and even less about Spelman. They assured me that I would never be accepted; as a matter of fact, they poked greater fun at me. How could I, with the scar of poverty imprinted so plainly on my forehead, dream of going someplace that they had never heard of? They remarked that while I was smart, surely, I was too poor to attend college.

And so, even as I completed all of the requirements for admission to Spelman, I still had the image of beauty school in the back of my mind.

～

Early that fall, my father's family from Atlanta paid us one of their surprise visits. Since Spelman was in Atlanta, I timidly broached the subject of my having applied to them. When I told them that my English teacher had helped me initiate an application and had recommended me to attend Spelman, they became so intensely excited that I, at that moment, became curious about that place. According to my relatives, everyone in Atlanta knew the reputation Spelman had for educating "colored" women; even I knew that because they lived in the big city, my relatives had more knowledge about their society than country folk did, and I said to myself, I wanted to see that place that caused such great excitement. As if he had read my mind, my father's cousin, Edward, immediately volunteered to come to Eatonton during the Christmas holidays and take me back to Atlanta to visit the campus.

The second day of my Christmas vacation, my young cousin Shirley and I took three buses from Northeast to Southeast Atlanta. We departed the final bus at Northside Drive and entered the main gate of Spelman. Upon entering this gate, I could see on my right what were then Laura Spelman Hall, Morehouse North and South, and further down in the corner of the college, Giles Hall. Almost directly in front of me was Sisters Chapel. The chapel was so magnificent, with its columns, painted a pure white color, and the many stained-glass windows; I don't believe that I had ever seen windows like that in such abundance. And the campus was so well manicured, even for winter. Such a place as this had only been revealed to me in my readings and even then, had never belonged to people who looked like me.

As I stood there, awestruck, it was a revelation to me that Miss Talley could have felt that I could go to school at a place like Spelman. This lady had more respect for me than I had ever imagined possible. Something took hold of me, and I vowed to match the respect that Miss Talley had for me with my own self-respect. I emerged from the gates of Spelman with a new mission: Miss Talley would never regret that she had put her faith in me.

From that day, the thoughts of attending a school of cosmetology never again crossed my mind. I went back to school in January to complete my final semester with a superior attitude toward my classmates. Whenever they made some insulting remark to me, I hissed at them and replied with my own tart comments. And in the history class, when Mr. Mack asked us, what was the highest degree in education we wanted to achieve, I said that I intended to pursue a doctorate degree. I had seen this degree listed next to the names of faculty members in the Spelman catalog that I had recently received. (Back then, I thought that Spelman issued this degree.) The students laughed so loudly at my response, but Mr. Mack replied, "Let them laugh, Trellie; he who laughs last, laughs best!"

After working all summer as a ten-dollar-a-week babysitter to buy needed items for college, I arrived at Spelman in late August of 1951 for freshman week with very few of the items on the list of college necessities that I had been mailed. The list seemed endless: raincoat, galoshes, a white dress, hat, bag, gloves, church clothes, pens, notebooks, and textbooks.

My poor folks had no money to give to me, except for the dime that my little sister Edna slipped to me. It was all of the money that she had left after purchasing the Parker 51 pen for my graduation present.

∾≈∾

For some reason I don't remember (after all these years), I never told Dot that I was not going to the Madam C. J. Walker School of Cosmetology. Perhaps I thought that she would have been offended that I had decided not to attend after she went to all of that trouble to help me learn about the school.

Though I was grateful for Dot's kindness, through the years I never regretted my decision to attend Spelman College, not after my college graduation when I returned home to Eatonton to teach, as Miss Talley had, at the Eatonton Colored High School, and to help all my brothers and sisters out of poverty; my little sister Edna became a high school teacher as well. When I left Eatonton, I married and had children, but also, I earned both master's and doctorate degrees. Certainly, I didn't regret my decision to enter Spelman when I was invited back to Eatonton in February 2001 to receive an Outstanding Achievement Award from an African American communications organization. A former student of mine greeted me in French and then introduced me as "Dr. Jeffers." As I mounted the stage amid the standing ovation and loud applause, I thought to myself, "Mr. Mack, I *do* have the last laugh."

And in 1995, I made preparations to attend the fiftieth-reunion celebration of Mrs. Janet Virginia Talley Bone's graduation from Spelman College.

I arrived at Spelman the day before the main event, when the "Golden Girls" (as the fifty-year celebrants are called) were presented in an elaborate banquet. I searched all day for her among her classmates without success. The night of the banquet, when I still had not seen her, but had been assured by one of the women who knew her well that she would be there, I sat near the entrance where the Golden Girls would stand before marching in and then sitting down at their special table reserved for them. Finally, the moderator came out and began announcing each lady, who was then escorted in by a very young man. The women were listed by their maiden names and so hers was among the final names called.

When I heard her name, I immediately began to think about how to keep my composure, wondering just how Miss Talley (now Mrs. Talley Bone) would expect me to act. When I finally gathered the nerve to approach her table, I was almost in tears. I'm sure my voice cracked when I addressed her.

"Miss Talley," I said, barely above a whisper.

She looked up at me with a puzzled look, a look that said, "Who in the world is this?"

I continued, "I am Trellie James from Eatonton, Georgia, and I want you to know that you not only changed my life, but by changing my life, you changed the lives of my whole family, and I just want to thank you."

By now all of the ladies at her table began to look admiringly at her. I don't know how my remarks struck her; she remained silent, and I did not want to intrude further upon her time with her classmates. But I shook her hand and made sure I said, "Thank you," one more time before I walked away.

IV

OF POWER AND OTHER INNOVATIONS

Great-Grandma Mandy used to say, when
you see the master stepping through the quarters
and smiling, watch out: He's getting ready to sell
one of your children.

—MAMA'S SAYINGS

I, too, am the afterlife of slavery.

—SAIDIYA HARTMAN,
*Lose Your Mother: A Journey Along the Atlantic Slave
Route*

16

Offspring Follows Belly

Virginia, 1662

A barnyard law   Birth
of the erasure

Partus Sequitur Ventrem
Ergo

Mules have four legs
Mulattos have two

Ergo
Bright-skinned children

have no fathers
White men can change

the rules to suit
or please   Remembering

the past is a peculiar
Black disease

but
now

I can be a full-blood
nigger if someone forces me

Juba
Ship's deck

Young girls made to dance
Sailors' breath

Pass around the cargo
Auction block

Plantation or city house
Legislate the screams:

Mixed-breed
Father unknown

Mother servant
That means

Mama's baby
Daddy's maybe

17

History Is a Trigger Warning

During the weeks and months leading up to the publication of my novel *The Love Songs of W. E. B. Du Bois*, I descended into anxiety. I wasn't so much afraid of the anticipated critical reception of the book as convinced that it would be a commercial flop. Who would buy, let along read, a nearly eight-hundred-page novel?

After my novel was selected by *the* Oprah Winfrey for her eponymous book club, I no longer had to worry about sales, but another issue concerned me: Readers began posting reviews online with trigger warnings about my book. There were postings on Goodreads, Netgalley, and Instagram. At the latter site, readers of my novel would tag me on their reviews about the emotional difficulty they had with the portions on childhood sexual abuse. I took no issue with that charge; I suspected that I'd suffered even more writing those scenes than anyone reading them had. But privately—silently—I disputed charges of graphic depictions of childhood abuse. Though there were a couple of adult assault scenes, I had hoped that I'd taken care to talk "around" actual acts toward children, mostly by implying them.

But the trigger warnings did surprise me: Did anyone picking up my book really expect a breezy, amusing read? The description on the back cover should have given them hints: Slavery was a tough subject, and I refused to sugarcoat that. And I was confused why sexual abuse was considered more triggering than the other kinds of physical violence I'd read in other books, and seen depicted in movies.

The truth is that, when it comes to the United States, the actual history of my ancestors is a trigger warning.

In subsequent interviews about my novel, interlocutors would raise the issue of childhood abuse and I'd try to find explanations for why I'd included it. Instead of "This is what really happened during slavery," I took a different tack: I said that I'd written about abuse because I wanted my readers to consider the trauma reverberating throughout generations in African America. But what I failed to mention is that the monster predator, the White slaveholder depicted in my novel, was loosely based upon Thomas Jefferson, our nation's third president.

I'm no Jefferson scholar. Sure, I've read a few books about him, but it's not my role to attempt to summarize the work of scholars who have spent decades researching him. I don't revere him, however, probably because as a child, I met so many people that others might have called "geniuses"—James Baldwin, Lucille Clifton, Sonia Sanchez, Alice Walker; the list goes on. Early on, I became inured to extraordinary intellectual or artistic traits in human beings.

My problem was that to directly acknowledge Jefferson as my model for the "monster" passages in my novel, I'd have to address his sexual assault of an enslaved person, Sally Hemings, who was not a grown woman but a child when this abuse first occurred. And if Hemings was a child when Jefferson began what we scholars insist on euphemistically calling "a relationship" with her, then that would make Jefferson a child molester.

We have our cultural stereotypes of what a molester looks like: a poor man living in squalor. Someone uneducated who probably can't read. Also, he must be conventionally ugly, perhaps missing teeth. He's a drug addict or an alcoholic. He's given to fits of rage, wherein he passes out slaps and punches. When he speaks, spittle flies from his mouth. Definitely a bad dresser.

What I've described above is the real-life equivalent of a villain from a fairy tale, a story read to children, despite these tales' tendencies to discriminate against disabled persons and use physiognomy to assign good and evil attributes to characters. A villain or a monster in a fairy tale is capable of, say, asking a hunter to kill and carve out the heart of a beautiful, sweet (and certainly White) young girl and place that organ in a box.

Even in this era when reasonable progressive thinkers can appreciate that heavy-handed deduction, they still can't shake this outmoded idea of what a molester looks and acts like. They won't understand that rich, good-looking, brilliant men who are well regarded in their communities—or indeed, well regarded by their nation—also could be child predators. Someone such as Thomas Jefferson, an erudite, conventionally handsome, tall man, who by all accounts was a genius—one has only to look at the architectural designs for Monticello to understand that his intellect was more than prodigious: It was miraculous.

The future African American mother of at least one of Jefferson's biracial children was the half sister of his wife, Martha Wayles Jefferson.[1] Born in 1773, Sally Hemings was the child of Martha's father, John. We have more information on Elizabeth Hemings, the mother of Sally, than for most other early African American women. She would bear six children for her master.[2] At fourteen years old, Sally Hemings accompanied Jefferson's daughter to Paris. Hemings would remain there for two years, and after she returned home to Monticello, she gave birth to a stillborn baby.[3]

In *Thomas Jefferson and Sally Hemings: An American Controversy*, Annette Gordon-Reed crafts a timeline of Sally Hemings's pregnancies, intersecting with Jefferson's presences and absences at Monticello.[4] Reading Gordon-Reed's timeline makes it obvious to anybody—including, as I love to joke, somebody's Southern Black grandma—that Jefferson impregnated Hemings several times.

And we have the oral history of Hemings's son, Easton, who identified Jefferson as his father in a memoir published in 1873.[5] Again, regardless of any affection there might have been between Sally Hemings and Jefferson—her son does not describe any overt affection for his mother or for his mixed-race siblings—this relationship between a master and his enslaved servant was compelled: No enslaved African American legally could say no to sex with a White man. Even if she wanted to engage in a sexual relationship with a White man, her desire was not the point. The White man's desire was.

In Gordon-Reed's second monumental history, *The Hemingses of Monticello*, she provides an insightful history of the African American relatives and descendants of Sally Hemings, allowing us to humanize her Black family as more than mere extensions of Jefferson's life.[6] Gordon-Reed provides details about the preferential treatment of Sally Hemings and her older brother James, who was already in Paris when the younger sister arrived: Thomas Jefferson paid to inoculate Sally Hemings against smallpox;[7] Sally received a stipend;[8] James was trained to cook classic French cuisines.[9]

To someone else, these details might provide proof that there was a loving relationship between Jefferson and the person he impregnated. Instead, what it proves to me is that "predatory grooming of a child" would be a logical descriptor for Jefferson's actions. Here was a powerful, rich forty-four-year-old White man creating a four-thousand-mile-distance between an enslaved child and her Black family—and especially her primary caretaker, her enslaved mother. The child's one present sibling in Paris, her brother James, was *also* enslaved by and beholden to Jefferson for his livelihood and survival.

Sally Hemings had been reared in the same familial community as Jefferson, for one could look at Monticello as its own kinship network. And whenever sexual contact occurs between those reared in either a nuclear or extended family dynamic, that sexual contact is *incest*.

✺

As a little girl, I was tall and fat. I have pictures of that time, but when I look at them, they confuse me. I see a plump, awkward child, not a womanly being, as I'd imagined myself to be, hearing the sexualized remarks men would make about my body.

As a grown woman, I know those remarks were wholly inappropriate, beginning way too early, when I was only nine or ten. Those interactions with grown men make me cringe, as I remember an ugly proverb I've heard more than a few times: "If she's old enough to bleed, then she's old enough to need." These remarks had caused me anxiety: I had to be careful about my behavior those summers in Eatonton, because in that town's Black community, there was a term I wanted to avoid: *fast-tailed gal.*

When I was small, my maternal grandmother and her elderly friends in Eatonton used that term. I could tell when Grandma Florence twisted her mouth that there was something wrong with a fast-tailed gal, and I quickly learned what that meant: a child deemed too sexually precocious. She could be thin or shapely, timid in her manner or bold. The behavioral parameters for a fast-tailed gal constantly changed, like a sexual Mississippi poll tax.

The only qualification for becoming a fast-tailed gal was that someone saw something in you: something vibrant and shameless, whatever your self-awareness—maybe like the titular protagonist from Morrison's *Sula*. It didn't matter how you looked at yourself. It mattered what somebody else thought of you. The person who witnessed that character flaw could be your mother or a sister at church or a teacher or a boy (or man) who targeted you. To become not-fast, on the other hand, you had to pass through a narrow corridor of respectability. Only two entryways opened onto this corridor and allowed for escape: You could get saved by Jesus, or you could get married. Either way, some man—Christ or living sinner—had to wash you clean with his approval.

Behind that vague yet lasting branding as "fast-tailed gal" is a reality called adultification, what happens when a child is viewed as a mature being, though they are still developing.[10]

Adultification has long been a problem facing Black children in North America, due to the slavocracy that depended upon the unfree labor system that had evolved. Enslaved people's purpose in this slavocracy was to alleviate the labor burdens of their White owners: to labor physically, but also, more specifically, to labor in childbirth. In *Stolen Childhood: Slave Youth in Nineteenth-Century America*, Wilma King provides evidence that the labor of enslaved children was not used—exploited—differently from that of adult slaves.[11] Children were worth money and sold for profit, both during the transatlantic slave trade and the later, internal trade in the United States, after the 1808 outlawing of international slavery commerce.[12]

Concurrently, though, White enslavers depicted enslaved African American women and men as having diminished mental capacity.[13] There is an aching irony in characterizing enslaved adults as stupid and childlike, while actual enslaved children were reconfigured as mini adults who didn't require nurturing. In so doing, slaveholders could pretend that they weren't child abusers, that Black children weren't sold on the slave market for purposes of prostitution. (Here, I use "Black" as a descriptor for Afro-Anglo and Afro-Indigenous biracial children, too, since slavery law identified them as such, according to that rule of Black maternal heritage, *partus sequitur ventrem*, established in Virginia eight decades before Jefferson was born.)

Two such sexually exploited Black teenagers—*children*—were Mary Jane and Emily Catherine Edmondson, aged fourteen and sixteen, who would be sold farther South. Did their ages qualify them as women? The recorder of their story, the formerly enslaved James W. C. Pennington, does not think so, for he asks, "But why this enormous sum for two mere children?"[14] Perhaps mindful that oral histories by African Americans (of Pennington's time) do not count as actual documentation—unlike the words of White people—Pennington later quoted from a letter by a slave trader: "Writing from Washington, D. C., September 12th, 1848, this gentleman says . . . 'The truth is, *and is confessed to be, that their destination is prostitution*; of this you would be satisfied on seeing them: they are of elegant form, and fine faces.' "[15]

Harriet Jacobs is another writer who described the sexual exploitations of enslaved Black women and girls in her autobiography, *Incidents in the Life of a Slave Girl*. Using a pseudonym—Linda Brent—Jacobs writes about others' sexual exploitation as well as her own. Her master, "Mr. Finch," sexually harassed her in a relentless fashion, leading her to seek out another slave master, a younger White man who took advantage of her vulnerable position. Though Jacobs frames the latter as a sympathetic character, Jacobs was, like Sally Hemings, around fourteen or fifteen years old—a child—when this older White man began having sex with her.

Considering eighteenth- and nineteenth-century conversation standards for discussions of sexual issues, it's understandable that rape was euphemized. However, in many *contemporary* scholarly treatments of sexual assault of enslaved Black people, the words *rape* and/or *molestation* are rarely used, the same way that *child* is avoided. Instead, much contemporary discussion presents *concubine* as a vague identity for the sexually abused enslaved child. This type of benign presentation switches the blame from powerful White male predators to a *voluntary* choice made by powerless Black female children.

Here are two examples of this muting: on the Thomas Jefferson Foundation website, Sally Hemings is described as a "concubine."[16] And on the Documenting the American South website hosted by the Southern Historical Collections of the University of North Carolina at Chapel Hill, the summary of *Louisa Piquet, the Octoroon, or Inside Views of Southern Domestic Life* represents the rape of Louisa Piquet's mother in passive tense, as if she bore her master's child as a voluntary act.[17] The same summary continues obliquely, characterizing Piquet as the "concubine" of her master John Williams, after the *thirteen-year-old* Piquet was taken from her mother and sold first to one White man, and then to Williams.

This refusal to name what truly happened—what truly wounded—dampens the actual trauma of sexual violence against Black children.

❧

Slavery in the United States references an existing institution that past civilizations practiced, include the West African empires of Mali, Ghana, and Songhai.[18] I am not arguing that slavery was only a US institution, but I do argue that, in antebellum North America, the keeping and exploitation of enslaved Africans created a new *technology*. I don't mean Industrial Age machinery such as Eli Whitney's cotton gin, which allowed for the rapid process of short staple cotton in the southeastern United States, which in turn advanced settler colonialism in southeastern territories. That economic greed led to the US government violently forcing southeastern Indigenous peoples from their homelands on theTrail of Tears and Death.

What I mean by "slavery technology" is that the institution in the United States was a social innovation—a negative one, to be sure—that altered previously held beliefs about acceptable morality, laws, and religion, and thus allowed horrific actions against African Americans to occur within full vision of polite (White) society. These actions appallingly impacted and sometimes destroyed the bodies, psyches, labor, and family structures of enslaved peoples—while Whites concealed the full extent of those actions, using the nebulous language of the time.

Further, I believe that the idea that scholars should be detached, unemotional, and uninvolved when writing about historical violence toward enslaved Black people is a slavery innovation as well.[19] As Ashley Farmer has observed in her courageous essay "Archiving While Black," the hostility toward African Americans conducting research in historical archives keeps the study of American history in the hands of Whites.[20] White scholars *still* overwhelmingly control academic history programs around the country, as chairpersons, faculty members, and students. Yet Black scholars are the ones with a vested ancestral stake in how slavery is depicted in the historical record.

Slavery technology is predicated upon Enlightenment philosophy, which developed alongside the transatlantic slave trade. In the United States, Thomas Jefferson expounds on Immanuel Kant's previous hierarchy of cultures; in "Query XIV" of *Notes on the State of Virginia*, he opines about the inferiority of Black folks. After discussing "laws," Jefferson launches into a strange tangent on African Americans' "physical and moral" attributes, noting that "the first difference which strikes us is that of colour."[21] Then he implies that Black women engage in bestiality with great apes, saying that there is a "preference of the Oranootan for the black women over those of his own species."[22] He continues: "They [Black people] have less hair on the face and body. They secrete less by the kidnies, and more by the glands of the skin, which gives them a very strong and disagreeable odour. . . . They seem to require less sleep."[23] The man's equally weird screed occurs in a chapter titled "The Administration of Justice and Description of the Laws," in which he directly attacks the *art* of the eighteenth-century *poet* Phillis Wheatley (Peters): "Among the blacks is misery enough, God knows, but no poetry. Love is the peculiar estrum of the poet. Their love is ardent, but it kindles the senses only, not the imagination. Religion indeed has produced a Phyllis Whately [*sic*]; but it could not produce a poet. The compositions published under her name are below the dignity of criticism."[24]

Jefferson's White supremacist condemnations draw a direct line of descent from *partus sequitur ventrem*, stripping humanity from Black women—and are shocking, considering that he'd go on to impregnate Sally Hemings several times. Taken alongside Jefferson's virtuous lyricism in the Declaration of Independence, his strange "Query XIV" is a head-scratcher. Just what were Jefferson's views on race and racism—two concepts briskly evolving during the eighteeth century—if he supposedly was such a benevolent slaveholder and a progressive of his time?

As we say in the Deep South, I don't have a dog in the Jefferson fight. I'm not a Jefferson scholar, a Jefferson apologist, or a Jefferson admirer. I *can* read, though, and it doesn't take a genius to see his base, overt White supremacy in "Query XIV." It doesn't take much of a leap to declare that Jefferson engaged in what Négritude writer Aimé Césaire would call *chosification*—in English, "thingification"—in which a colonized person is reduced to a commodity, some*thing* that can be exploited, sold, and despised by the colonizer.[25] And make no mistake, Black folks in America are colonized peoples; despite being brought from Africa to these shores, we were under the purview of White settler colonizers. Human trafficking—slavery—is the parent of slavery technology, and that technology is the parent of thingification.

Jefferson's thingifying of Black people—and Black women—in "Query XIV" does not surprise me, for during his lifetime he owned six hundred human beings.[26] Why, then, would *additional* outrages be considered beyond the pale of Jefferson's slaveholding and "scholarly" thingifying? Why must we euphemize his sexual violence toward the Black child Sally Hemings?

Though notions of adolescence may have changed, biological realities such as pre- and postpuberty have been around since the dawn of humanity. The average age of menarche in eighteenth-century Europe—where Sally Hemings lived from age fourteen to sixteen— was around seventeen years old.[27] Thus sexual maturity occurred much later three centuries ago than it does now. Yet despite most girls' sexual/biological immaturity in the eighteenth and nineteenth centuries, it was acceptable and legal for American men to marry young girls, or even small children. (In the nineteenth century, the age of consent in Delaware was seven years old. This is not a typo.)[28]

In the case of recent Jefferson scholarship, I can see the rationale for not naming him a child molester. An outright public charge (with the research to back it up) of the Jefferson-Hemings connection was probably enough to rock the world of early American studies—though, let's be clear, scholars had known the "true-truth" about that relationship for years. But to go further and name the rest—that it's just goddamned disgusting and creepy for some middle-aged, grown-ass man to groom and rape a child who was *also* the baby sister of his dead wife, a child who was *also* thirty years younger than he was, and a child who *also* might not have even been menstruating yet—well, that would have shut down that whole discussion of the Jefferson-Hemings liaison.

I can understand scholarly silence on that matter, but from my point of view, we cannot justify the Jefferson-Hemings scenario using the excuse of eighteenth-century standards for behavior. There were plenty of appalling standards in the eighteenth century, but it's never a plausible argument that because there weren't solidified notions of adolescence in a particular era, that means that child molestation couldn't have occurred. Or that it wasn't violence because Jefferson spent money on Hemings, and that somehow made it a loving relationship—to draw a comparison, pimps spend money on the people they sex-traffic. Does that make that kind of exploitative relationship *love*? This is not about differing points of view (or how much change Jefferson doled out, in service of his nasty desires): Sally Hemings was around fifteen years old when the forty-five-year-old Jefferson impregnated her—and we don't know that he hadn't assaulted her long before she'd reached that age.

Now, take a deep breath.

We don't know that Jefferson hadn't sexually assaulted *other* enslaved children, either. Why should we believe that a man that molested one child who had no legal power—or moral power, according to the rules of slavery technology—wouldn't have molested other powerless Black children, as well?

It's not realistic to imply that appalling past standards will erase any trauma of a violated child. (See also: those Latinex children *still* currently detained at the southern US border, as of this writing.[29]) There were eighteenth-century standards for, say, drawing and quartering human beings in executions. There were those standards for slave trading and slaveholding. Are we really to believe that simply because a law in any given year says a grave offense was acceptable, that means that those whom that offense impacted did not suffer? That would mean that only a legal standard of traumatic awareness equals the actual trauma of a human being.

And what exactly would that legal standard be? How much Black child-pain and trauma would meet that bar? And who gets to decide what that bar was? In the case of early American studies scholars, it seems as if they decide the standard. By "they," I am referring to the phalanx of White historians marching forward from the nineteenth to the twenty-first centuries.

Further, eighteenth-century legal standards were put in place by powerful White men who wanted to maintain power over White girls, cisgender White women, and Queer White people; Indigenous people of all genders and sexualities; and African American people of all genders and sexualities. Most of these White men did not have a true sense of fairness; they arbitrarily decided what was fair and constantly changed standards—and laws— to suit their needs and desires. That's how slavery technology in North America came into being.

When contemporary scholars offer eighteenth-century laws concerning consent as a moral loophole for Jefferson, they argue that, okay, all right, this eighteenth-century White man was involved in the horrific enterprise of slavery. Jefferson owned enslaved people. He humiliated—*thingified*—African Americans (by name and in general) in print in "Query XIV" in *Notes on the State of Virginia*. He approved of violence done to the enslaved people he owned.[30] And after Jefferson's death, over a hundred enslaved people of Monticello were sold, separating Black families.[31]

Jefferson scholars can accept these outrages.

Yet somehow, in the face of these egregious sins, they can't accept that this same kind of man would sexually abuse a Black child. That's just too much to think about. It's too painful—because if Jefferson was a child molester, then what does that say about the origins of our nation? He wrote the *Declaration of Independence*, arguably our most sacred national text. If a monster wrote those glorious sentences, insisting that "we hold these truths to be self-evident," then what is the evidence about the founding of this country?

When I think of history, I don't consider the improbability of a slaveholding White man becoming a monster. I think about the improbability of him *not* becoming a monster.

How could a man such as Thomas Jefferson become a bad person? Easily: the times sanctioned it. It was easy for a southern White man to commit any crime that he wanted, if his victim was Black. All the laws in his region were working for the maintenance of his power.

I think of Sally Hemings, who is still not protected, 187 years after her death, because scholars are employing euphemisms to excuse what happened to her: she and Thomas Jefferson had "a relationship." Sally Hemings was the "mother of his children," or "Jefferson's mistress," or his "concubine." That's how Jefferson's reputation has been kept intact.

But here's the truth: Sally Hemings was a Black child unprotected by the law, reared with the knowledge that her Black mother had had no legal control over her own body or her progeny, as Heming's Black grandmother had no legal control over her body or progeny, either.

I don't call this child-become-woman "Sally" because she was Black, as many Whites do when they are referring to early African Americans. They'll call White people by their last names—Jefferson, Washington, Adams—but for some reason, Black people don't get this respect.

I call her Sally because I consider her my ancestor. I consider her my own people, and when you are kindred, you think in familiar terms.

Sally was a child when her life would become historical fodder, when she was sent over the Atlantic Ocean, that emotionally resonant water that her African grandmother had been forced over.

Sally was a child sent to Paris to be a servant to coddled White girls, and there abused by the powerful man who was the father of those girls. Thomas Jefferson held the power of life and death—and auction block—over Sally's entire nuclear and extended Black family. This was an enormous responsibility placed on that child's shoulders: What might have happened to her family if she hadn't submitted to Jefferson, who was her master?

When Sally discovered she was expecting a baby, how frightening it must have been, for though Sally was technically free in Paris, how could she have stayed? She would have been pregnant and away from her entire family. She'd have no money, no way to make a living. She could have relied on her brother James Hemings for a while, but soon he would return to Virginia. And so Sally—alone with a small baby—would have no people in a land where the language, culture, and citizens were foreign to her.

What kind of choice would any of us make, as children four thousand miles from home? Could we leave our families for our entire lives?

I think of Sally's brother, James Hemings. The reason behind his alcoholism and death by suicide remains much of a mystery to most historians. If I had to make a guess, I'd wager that James's enslaved status led to at least half of his misery. How many of us would be content to be enslaved? And the other part? That might have been James's guilt about his compelled passivity in the abuse of his younger sister, probably informed at least partly by his addiction. James might have helped convince Sally that she could do worse than their wealthy, White master, so she should just tolerate what happened: *Don't make trouble, baby sister.*

We don't know that, at some point in his life, someone hadn't assaulted James as well.

In Jefferson's house, James might not have said anything at all but just ignored the nighttime sounds. Did his sister cry, did she beg their master, *Please just leave me alone?* I can't believe any reasonable person could believe that Thomas Jefferson would have taken no for an answer, given his already strange desires. This White man's crimes would be excused in the years to come, and maybe that's why James Hemings drank himself to distraction and eventually killed himself. He wanted to forget what so many of us still know: that very few folks care what happens to Black girls.

18

Imaginary Letter to the Now-Dead White Male Poet Who Might Have Given Me the Blues

Dear ___:

A beloved Black woman poet-elder told me to write about you, and what you said to me, the night you took me and several writers to dinner, after my poetry reading.

I was the only Black person and the only woman at the table. I was the youngest person, too. I can't believe I was surprised by what you said that evening, as I cut into my well-done lamb chops, but maybe it's a good thing to be a woman and be surprised by lowdown men.

I'd taken my time to explain to the waiter that I wanted my meat tender but with no streaks of blood. I didn't mind waiting for my food, because lamb needs to be cooked on low to be tender yet well done. I didn't care that supposedly lamb chops should always be rare. I grew up in the South and spent my summers in rural Georgia: Black folks in the country don't eat their meat bleeding at the bone.

My lamb chops were delicious. I tried not to think of what the cute little live animals had looked like, before they were slaughtered.

My mind goes to inappropriate places sometimes.

You said to me—right as I was cutting into the meat—that you loved my southern accent. I was used to this compliment, but it never failed to flatter. I thanked you, but regretted my gratitude immediately when you continued, "Listening to you makes me want to mount you from behind."

This has been twenty years ago, but it's not so long ago that I've forgotten my shame. I felt so dirty, and throughout the years, I asked myself: Why—if you contemplated fucking me—couldn't you have considered missionary position? Why didn't you want to look me in my eyes, if you craved to put your dick inside me? Why wouldn't you want to touch my face tenderly? Or thank me for my time and body?

In the following years, I wondered why you'd thought of me as an animal.

Even though that Black women poet-elder—the one I loved, the one who urged me to write about this—is nearly a foot shorter than I am and probably a hundred pounds lighter, I marveled at her courage. Why wasn't she afraid of White folks, when I was always afraid? What kind of power had she pulled from the air and swallowed? By the time I told her what you'd said to me, you were already dead, but I remained afraid. Every couple of years, I would bring you up to her—what you said to me, how it made me feel—and that elder-poet would get (what I have come to regard as) that Black woman tone.

"My dear sister," she would say, in a stern cadence, "My dear sister, you have to speak on this. You got to, for yourself. You cannot keep giving that man your power. You cannot be afraid."

There was a music to her words—there was a righteous chant—that made me feel strong. I was filled when I spoke to her. But as soon as I hung up the phone, I'd become afraid again. For my career. For my reputation; how many times had my own family treated me as a liar, or called me one outright, for speaking against my father? And my daddy was a Black man. What kind of punishment would I receive for speaking out against a White man?

Not only was I afraid for my career, or afraid of powerful White folks— publishers, other elder writers, people I might need to speak on my behalf in letters of recommendation—but I was also afraid of what other Black people might say. Like, why wouldn't I have known how a table of older White men would treat me? Wasn't I from the South? Didn't I know that I should always be careful of White men? Why would I go out with them anyway?

I was angry that I was still afraid of you. Black women of my generation don't encourage weakness. We think—I think—of fear as weakness. I have a hard time feeling sorry for myself. This doesn't mean I don't feel sorry for myself. It means I feel ashamed when I indulge in self-pity.

When I heard that you had committed suicide, that you had put a shotgun in your mouth and blew out your brains, I didn't think: Good. I wanted to feel happy, to be tough, because I'm tired of singing some Negro spiritual about forgiveness. But I wasn't happy you were dead. I felt sorry for you, because my mother had taught me to feel sorry for people who were cruel to me, starting with my father. That's how my mother reared me.

When I heard you'd killed yourself, I thought about the emotional pain that drove you to commit suicide, instead of my feelings of humiliation that evening at dinner with you and those other White men. They laughed after you talked of mounting me, that night you were still alive.

One of them asked, "What do you think about that, Honorée?"

I replied, "I don't think anything, except these lamb chops are delicious."

I believe (now) that I thought of myself as clever, because I thought I was on the come-up in contemporary American poetry. I thought I'd matrixed past racial danger, but later, when I looked for my name on the poster for visitors to the graduate writing program that you directed, you'd removed me.

There was no proof that I'd been there in that cold, New England town, that I'd limped around for two days in a moonboot, because weeks before I'd broken my ankle and undergone surgery to put the bones back together. My awkwardness, my complicated gestures to maintain my beauty and glamour—I'd wrapped a silk scarf around the moonboot in an attempt at jauntiness—made me even sadder. I'd tried so hard to be a good girl, to suffer through discomfort because I'd been taught by my mother that pain is a matter of the mind. I did all that, only for you to imply I was an animal.

In years to come—before your suicide—I would see you at the annual conference that other creative writers attended. You would meet my eyes and then look away, as if I was no one that you knew. But I knew you recognized me. I started calling your name, in a loud friendly way, to let you know I didn't blame you for shaming me, for comparing me to an animal that was fucked for breeding, with or without its permission. I was tough. I was strong—I was a Strong Black Woman puffed up with my Black Girl Magic. I didn't need to blame anyone except myself.

When you pretended you didn't know me, I felt sorry for myself. Then I'd hate myself for not getting up from the table that night. For not throwing a drink in your face, instead of sitting there, praying that those other White men would stop laughing at me and encouraging you—egging you on. That they would see me as a woman, instead of a chestnut-brown horse immobilized in a pen.

They'd thought I was waiting to be dominated. They thought I was eager for it. I wanted it. Didn't I want it? Of course I did, they told themselves. Of course I wanted to be blessed by this White man choosing me for casual—and if his words were to believed, violent—sex.

It wasn't until I read historical texts detailing how Black women were diminished—that we'd be compared to animals; that slaveholders assumed that we were sexually insatiable, and that's why it was all right to rape us; that we didn't care for our children the same way that White women did; that's why it was fine for slavers to sell our children away from us, because animals don't care the same about their young as true human beings did—it wasn't until I considered all this that I was able to become truly angry and shed aggrieved tears.

What you'd said to me had been repeated to many Black women through centuries. I understood that your phrase had been plucked from the mind of a now-dead philosopher, as you are dead.

And now I am happy you are gone: Your death has blessed me immeasurably.

Sincerely, Honorée

19

A Brief Note Concerning My Late Brother-Friend's Usage of the N-Word as a Verb

My late, dear friend James William Richardson Jr. used to say, "Somebody Black can be niggered at any time." When he would say this, I would giggle, because although this word was invented by White folks to make us Black folks feel bad, I loved to hear James say it. With a hard *r* and a vernacular grunt.

Really, it feels stupid, the way people debate that *nigga* is better than *nigger*. What is truly the difference? And besides, I just loved James's elocution when he explained the verb "to nigger": To be reminded of one's place as a Black person living in a land of White supremacy.

I giggled because, at the time, I didn't believe James's assertion. I believed I was special. I didn't believe racism against Black people—White supremacy—was based on power-driven desires to keep Black people down and/or at bay. As a woman, I was under the impression that I could achieve out of sexism and misogyny. I felt shame whenever I was treated badly by men, but I didn't believe there were power plays; I believed that I was flawed and that I deserved to be treated badly, as a girl and then a woman. I don't say this to assert that my womanhood wasn't a site of oppression, but rather to note that in the Black communities that reared me, nobody ever talked that much about what it meant to be a woman. I learned by example, and then *unlearned* by reading and praying, in that order.

But as a *Black* person—without considering my gender—I felt another way: I knew I was great. I knew I was smart—and I didn't understand why White people couldn't see that—but then I'd remind myself to work harder. That was the key. *Keep your hand on the plow*, as the old Negro spiritual urged. My concerted labor would prove that I was better than racism and White supremacy.[1] I believed in cultural meritocracy. I was a *Jane* Henry—the female counterpart of John—using my hammer in competition with a steam drill: I just knew I could achieve out of the structural inequality designed to oppress me. Bless my stupid little heart.

It took me until my late forties to understand James's theory of niggering, to understand what it meant. It can happen in a department store, when I am followed around by the security guard as if I'm going to steal something when I have my platinum credit card in my wallet. Later, at the checkout, it can happen when I'm waiting to buy several hundred dollars' worth of clothes, and the clerk looks past me to the White person standing behind me and motions them up front. Then I must cause a slight scene—an event that has gotten scarier in these days of unabashed Nazi sympathizers.

"I do believe I was next," I'll say, my voice weary.

It doesn't matter how nice I am; I can always be niggered. Niggering can happen in intellectual settings, such as a faculty meeting, when I raise my hand to ask a question, and White colleagues will smirk and exchange significant glances over my stupidity, despite my earning a perfect research and creative activity score every year on my annual evaluations. Niggering can happen in a classroom, like if a male graduate student in his early twenties writes me a condescending email to instruct me how to conduct a question-and-answer period in class. Niggering can happen when a White scholar uses my research in their essay, or in their book about Phillis Wheatley Peters, and fails to give me credit in a footnote—or condescendingly refers to me as "the poet Honorée Fanonne Jeffers," as if I hadn't spent fifteen years in the historical archives, and presented previously unpublished research in the poetry book I wrote about Wheatley Peters.

There are so many examples of niggering, but the key is that it always happens to a Black person during a self-esteem high, when you are truly feeling great—when you think yourself accomplished or equal to any White person—and then must be brought down a notch. For me, I notice niggering occurs when I don't care how jiggly my belly fat is. When my skin is glowing. When I'm having a good hair day, when my face is beat, and I'm featuring a cute outfit. When I've just been paid more than twenty-five dollars for a new, prestigious publication.

Sometimes niggering involves a small assault to your self-esteem, but sometimes it involves being murdered. You never know how quickly niggering can escalate. The rules when you are Black: Work hard, be kind, don't complain too much. All will be well—even though, statistically, all might *not* be well.

If you are successful, instead of White people telling you how wonderful you are, they will negate everything you do and tell you that you are lazy—or they may tell you this the day after they tell you how wonderful you are. An act of God that you encounter may be an act from someone White who has the self-regard of a god, so that they will make a citizen's arrest, or join with other White people to chase you down to the river's edge.

The point of niggering is to remind you that your Black life's only meaning will be defined by its arbitrariness, the moments where you learn that all the pages of your résumé detailing all you have accomplished will be condensed into one sentence of misspelled words, or ended by a bullet.

Yet do not become angry, nigger. Suffer in silence, nigger, for being labeled as angry and African American is only a tad bit better than being murdered by someone self-righteous and White.

a Black body is somebody[1]

whatever scholar
  you might be

in whatever tortured
  discipline

if you please
  stop saying

the Black body
  stop

arrest yourself
  i'm a person

didn't you hear me
  the first time

i asked
  who

don't you know
  i'm not

what
  i'm a Black human

standing next
  to another

Black human
  we are a riot

a song of humanity
  amassing under

a streetlight
  calling

to our kindred
  join us

we are gathered
  in history's

insistence
  our footprints beckoning

i'm not a theory
  of some

ivory tower
  even in new england

don't call me
  the Black body

as if i were

a dead husk

a container of day-old
  meat

with no brain
  no bejeweled cells

no tongue speckled
  with elder-story

no memory
  no rememory

21

Blues for Moynihan

In 1965, three hundred and three years after Virginia's *partus sequitur ventrem* law, there was another public unmaking for Black women: Daniel Patrick Moynihan's government report "The Negro Family: The Case for National Action."[1]

Like Watergate, "the Moynihan Report" was a phrase I heard often in the decade following its appearance. In junior high school, I asked my mother to explain Watergate to me. It was a short while after I'd inquired about the electoral college; listening to Mama's complicated explanations about Nixon's misdeeds and the US political system, I drew three conclusions: My mother would always be smarter than me; I wasn't that interested in knowing how presidents were elected; and I should forget asking her to explain the Moynihan Report.

In my early thirties, I returned to the report, but that should be credited to another Black woman, Hortense Spillers, who mentioned it in her essay "Mama's Baby, Papa's Maybe: An American Grammar."[2] Spiller's language was so dense; like Mama's explanation of Watergate and the electoral college, it made me keenly feel my intellectual lack. But Spiller's piece kept pulling me back, probably because of the title. I had (and still retain) an affection for traditional spirituals, blues, proverbs, and oh, just the delicious language of Black folks, which flicks a note of recognition. "Mama's baby, papa's maybe"—the African American proverb contained in the title of Spiller's essay—was quite familiar to me. It has a ribald meaning: your mother is free with her love. Put bluntly, she likes to fuck.

To translate Spiller's words, though, I needed to read Moynihan's report for myself.

❧

As assistant secretary of labor under Presidents John F. Kennedy and Lyndon B. Johnson, Moynihan wasn't commissioned to compile his famous report; the idea was his own, and his purpose was to provide reasons and solutions for African American poverty—he hoped to contribute to Johnson's War on Poverty.[3]

Moynihan's is a long text, but with arguments that he revisits: Initially, he identifies a problem with "Negro equality." He admits that Black folks have been oppressed in America. Given that he was a White man writing in 1965, I found that acknowledgment refreshing—until he arrived at his main, other point, which is that "lower class" Black families are completely "damaged" and "broken." And why are our families so bad off? According to Moynihan, the "matriarchal structure" of the Black family hinders Black equality—Black men aren't leading those families, and Moynihan's implication is that a male-headed family is the only avenue to success.

As a nice cherry on top, Moynihan compares "lower class" Black families to those of other communities, and notes that the marriage rates are lower in Black communities, further evidence of the pathology of poor African Americans.

Thus Moynihan's report doesn't just blame Black family problems on past issues of slavery and Jim Crow. It specifically blames our family problems on Black women.[4]

The fallout from the Moynihan Report was immediate but also long-term. Black feminists such as June Jordan and Pauli Murray addressed Moynihan's sexism and patriarchy.[5] But for a long time, Black folks were still talking about Moynihan, including my parents.

Hortense Spiller's essay appeared in 1987, twenty-three years after the appearance of Moynihan's report, and it took me several tries to make it through. It's written in academic language, which is a second—

difficult—language to me. Eventually I picked up threads of outrage in Spiller's work, one borne (I believe, as I cannot read her mind) of a desire to protect the always-beleaguered Black woman.

When discussing Moynihan, Spiller argues that he indicts Black women.[6] This is the "American Grammar" that Spiller references in her essay's title, for grammar signifies the structure of language—and in the seventeenth century, Englishmen in North America created negative opinions about Black women in the social, religious, and scientific spheres that, in turn, were weaponized against this same woman through formal law.

For Spillers, the Black female line is tied to "flesh"—throughout her essay, she mentions flesh several times.[7] I had to sit with that idea a while. Why "flesh" and "kin" and not simply "the Black female body"? I returned to my feelings, which usually seem inappropriate when reading scholarship: to be intellectual to me has always meant that you should sever feelings from research—that you should maintain intellectual sobriety. At least, this is the message I absorbed during my time in academia. But another moment of clarity: Spillers is unafraid in "Mama's Baby" to show her passion, to admit her ancestry. She has literal skin in the game, so, using *body* to reference real people, for her, would indicate dispassion; it would be a distancing term.

While pondering Spillers's idea of flesh, I returned to one of my favorite novels, Toni Morrison's *Beloved*. There, I arrived—again—at Baby Suggs's soul-claiming sermon: " 'Here,' she said, 'in this here place, we flesh; flesh that weeps, laughs. Flesh that dances on bare feet in grass. Love it. Love it hard. Yonder they do not love your flesh. They despise it."[8]

The meaning of this passage that once confounded me comes as clear as the space that Baby Suggs, her friends, and the ancestors occupy: "Flesh" is what it means to live, to be a part of humanity.

It's fascinating that Spillers and Morrison both consider the flesh of African American women, instead of the vague—yet oft-mentioned by African American academics—"Black bodies." Their two texts were published in the same year—but incredibly, they never consulted each other! As both Spillers and Morrison illustrate, in two different genres, these enslaved women are made into objects severed from meaning.

Because of its lack of meaning, a body can be sold, exploited, violated, with no repercussions.

But flesh? Flesh is blood, is ancestry, is kin, is community, is strength, is safety in the arms of a parent or lover.

Flesh is *us*.[9]

~⁓~

When I returned to the Moynihan Report for the second time, I didn't find it as compelling as Spiller's essay or Morrison's *Beloved*. (I suspect there will be no future double-digit readings of Moynihan's report.) I concluded that, as a point of departure, Moynihan started talking underneath Black women's clothes, and then ripped off those garments and left those women naked in the public sphere—a familiar image to me, as someone who's read repeated descriptions of auction-block humiliations.

Though he acknowledges Black oppression, Moynihan's opinions—given as fact—about the "damaged" Black family and the "matriarchal" Black woman are disembodied from that oppression, for he takes a "that was then, this is now" point of view. Sure, Moynihan admits, bad things happened to Black folks, but it's the twentieth century (when he was writing his report). As for Black women, they should step aside and let Black men lead—and because Black women haven't stepped aside, it is their responsibility that Black communities are doing so badly.

What Moynihan failed to acknowledge (or didn't even seem to know) is that he continued the cumulative narrative of Black female aberrance established by Virginia lawmakers in the seventeenth century. In 1662 those White men created an *alternate* patriarchy, one only they could access. Three centuries later, as a champion of patriarchy, Moynihan ignored—or, giving him the benefit of the doubt, didn't know about—that alternate patriarchy.

Moynihan did not acknowledge that patriarchy never had been available to Black people in the United States, but he did believe that patriarchy was a common, natural good. According to Moynihan, Black women should make husbands their heads, their guiding lights. Black women should submit to these husbands, and they should gain satisfaction—pleasure—from looking up adoringly at these men. That is the best to which Black women can aspire. If they don't want that, they are destroying Black communities.

Perhaps most African Americans' inability to trace their origins before a particular year—usually 1870, after the Civil War ended—is why some Black folks can't look at American patriarchy and breathe relief that we dodged all that. Many of us are unable to connect white supremacy and its terroristic actions with patriarchal structures.[10] We Black folks long so much for what we never had that we can't see that patriarchy isn't serving anybody in this country—except straight, cisgender White men.

Yet African American feminists asked an important question of the Moynihan Report, and, really, a still-unanswered question in everyday Black communities: What is so wrong with Black families being headed by females?[11] Why isn't a female-led family an equally respected/respectable structure—especially since most cisgender women of all races (and across the globe) perform the practical daily tasks of child rearing? (For example, how many of us have heard fathers' parental responsibilities referred to as "babysitting"?)

I do understand that many of those African Americans who fetishize patriarchy are wistful about what slavery, Jim Crow, and the US carceral system have denied generations of us: the practice of patriarchy. This is the common message: Who knows what glories our Black people might have achieved if Black men had been allowed to be "real men"—that is, patriarchs? We tell ourselves (and each other) how great our families might have been, even as we protest in public. Our families aren't so bad—*are we truly so bad?*

22

Leaning on the Everlasting
Arms of Respectability

Once I was married, for about five minutes. (Okay, three and a half years.) I met Khalil,[1] a beautiful, tall, coffee-colored man, in Senegal. I'd traveled there for informal research on West African families, in preparation for writing a book of poems on the eighteenth-century poet Phillis Wheatley Peters. Khalil's full lips were so alluring, with a pout that still gives me a naughty quiver whenever I look at his pictures, even though I haven't seen him in person for several years.

When my beloved asked me to marry him, I didn't want to say yes, but I had quickly (and surprisingly) fallen in love with this West African Muslim. And marriage was the thing you did in his culture when you fell in love. A man and a woman could not live together without an official vow.

Six months after we met, Khalil and I were married by a West African imam in an Islamic ceremony in London, where Khalil was attending graduate school. The imam performed the marriage in Wolof, and when my beloved translated the part about me obeying my husband, he quickly said—in English—that I shouldn't pay any attention to that part. A few days later, we married again in a legal ceremony at what I call a British courthouse, in Southwark.

I married when I was forty-five, long past the age of some young bride. Feminist that I was, I nevertheless woke up the next morning and had the urge to scramble eggs and bake biscuits. I used my mother's recipes, learned years before. I used heavy cream to make the biscuits, instead of buttermilk. (Mama always despised the taste of buttermilk.) There were garlic, onions, and sharp cheddar cheese in the eggs, like Mama's, but as a concession to my husband's Senegalese tastes, I chopped up Scotch bonnet peppers. I smiled when my husband thanked me in French, "*Merci, mon amour.*" Then, again in Wolof: "*Jërëjeff, sokhna.*"

After those two ceremonies, I noticed how people treated me. Regardless of their cultural background and with very rare exceptions, when those who'd known me for years found out I'd married, they acted as if I had accomplished something special. At first I thought it was simply their happiness for me, and that seemed so very lovely. But felicitations weren't the end of it: I got the feeling that I was special because I was a Black woman and I had found someone to marry me—finally.

I hadn't been prepared for my marriage allowing me entrance into a particular African American admiration, like I'd won a social lottery. Or as if I'd been inducted into a renowned sorority: I was somebody's wife. The way I'd entered that sorority was not by the selection of other women. A man had to usher me into that sparkling territory: finally, I was covered by patriarchy. I was a respectable Black woman.

⁂

So much depends upon contradictions, like that wheelbarrow William Carlos Williams wrote about in his poem. Somebody painted that thing such a pretty color, only to have it used to cart dirt around.

My entire life has been this way.

When I say I was the quiet child sitting in a corner, that might give you the impression that I was a shy child, and perhaps someone who had a time finding my words. Though I've always described myself as socially awkward—feeling uncomfortable around large groups of people—my quietness in the presence of adults had nothing to do with shyness. It was a matter of home training. I was reared by a Southern Black woman. She might allow violations of age hierarchies in her personal household—but Mama did not play about you embarrassing her in public. You couldn't do it in her presence, or even when she wasn't around. Mama didn't take no shit. She was strong, even in the way she looked. Big hands, big feet. Tall with long legs. Chocolate brown, with a wide nose and an entrancing laugh that you could hear the next county over.

My mama was that legendary "strong Black woman" frequently spoken about in our communities, the one who made everything possible. Yet this same kind of Black woman was supposed to step aside to let her man stand in front—remain silent while he spoke. This was the arrangement that should give every Black woman joy, the reason she worked so hard—so that a Black man could take all the credit.

I blamed my mother for these public and private vacillations, for bragging to her daughters that, as the children of my born-in-privilege father, we were members of the Black bourgeoisie. I didn't know that that term meant, though I'd looked up *bourgeoisie* in the dictionary. But I could tell from her suddenly nasal tone when she said the word that it meant something superior, and though she couldn't claim membership in the bourgeoisie, she told us, her children could. That's why she'd married my father and why she stayed with him, despite his irrationality, his sudden mood shifts. That's why, even though Daddy was mean to his own children, too, we should consider ourselves lucky.

I pretended at school that I was as respectable as my mother believed me to be. No, not as good. Better. And that's why we weren't allowed to play with the children down the road in the housing project, Cornwallis Court—but then Mama didn't say that in public. These were the same children my mother fought for as a community activist, the ones she insisted publicly were worthy of a better education than the de facto desegregation offered in Durham City. It was confusing, even when Mama told us she hadn't accomplished all that she had for us to end up playing with project kids.

But lest we think her needlessly cruel, Mama would launch into a story about her upbringing, to prove she knew what it was like to be poor. More than poor. *Underneath* that category, so that "poor" was the top level of a tall house and Mama had resided in the basement. She'd talk about her birth in a former slave shack. Her losing an eye because of a childhood accident. Her beloved father, Charlie James, who never learned to read or write. The way the light-skinned siblings of her oak-brown mother, Florence Napier Paschal James, had called Mama and her sisters and brothers "Florence's little crows."

This was why she protected her daughters from the children of Cornwallis Court, Mama said. Did we want to slide back to that kind of poverty-stricken existence, when she could testify how horrible that life was? There was no nobility in poverty. It was dirty, it was humiliating, it was dangerous—look at what had happened to her as a child, losing an eye. If her people hadn't been so poor—and if the segregated hospital hadn't been so underfunded, with no skilled doctors—it might have been saved.

There was only escape from poverty, if that was possible. Escape took selfishness and no going back. When you decided to sneak away on that perilous journey, you couldn't be like Harriet Tubman, returning to free the people who lived in slavery. That kind of woman was a saint, and Miss Harriet was wonderful, but a regular Black woman? Mama could only worry about herself and her own kin. She could only leave and not look back.

"Remember that man that Harriet Tubman threatened to shoot, because he didn't want to be free? The one she told, 'Dead men don't jaybird talk'?" Mama asked. "It's always one like that out the bunch. And I'm not risking my life for a nigger like that."

Oh, so many contradictions.

⌒⌒

In my African American community of Durham, North Carolina, and later, when my mother and father separated and Mama moved my middle sister and me to Georgia, I learned that there was more at stake in a marriage between a Black man and woman than romance. More than merely maintaining traditional gender roles.

There was the pressing issue of shoring up a Black man's self-esteem against the White supremacy that he encountered—what a Black woman endured didn't matter as much. Another issue was keeping the image of our community pristine. We could have patriarchy, too, just like the White folks, and wouldn't that be so nice? No, we didn't *like* most White folks, but we wanted them to think we were just as good.

None of it made sense, though it would take me decades to work that out.

In the meantime, despite the prejudice I'd experienced at my majority White junior high school in Chapel Hill, North Carolina, before I transferred to a majority Black school in Durham, and later, at my "half and half," fully integrated high school in DeKalb County, Georgia, I absorbed that my pain wasn't supposed to count, because I was a girl. I was Black and female, so I had it easier than Black boys, my community and family told me. The police weren't shooting at me. That I was molested, and later raped, didn't count because I remained alive after my body had been violated—and I didn't tell anybody about that abuse anyway, not then.

During those community conversations that I'd first listened to as a young girl and then participated in during college, there was a sense of the remarkable. As if these tired debates were the first conversations to have taken place about how Black women and men should interact with each other, how we should live with each other and rear our children together. Sitting in classrooms, or on someone's patio with a blunt between my lips and cheap wine in a red plastic cup, I always took the role of the loud, outspoken radical Black feminist. I'd learned from reading Alice Walker that there was a difference between a mainstream feminist and a Black one. A Black feminist—a womanist—cared about everybody in our community, not just the girls and women. She cared about racial justice for all.

But in my teens and twenties, I did think a lot about getting married. Not because I aspired to the role of wife; my parents' disastrous union made that a frightening prospect. Really, I just wanted to belong to someone. More than that, I wanted another man—any man—to blot out the abuse I'd endured from my father and other men. I thought that belonging to a man would mean that I wasn't dirty. It would mean that I was a good girl.

The messages I absorbed in college instructed me how to climb onto that clean pedestal: I had to fit in with the behavior of other good girls, and pattern myself after them. I needed to dress a particular way, stylishly, but not in a bizarre fashion. I had curly hair, so I needed to either chemically relax it or blow-dry it straight and hot-curl it. (Flat irons came later.) I shouldn't speak too aggressively in front of Black boys (and then Black men). Let the men lead conversations, and don't be winning when playing spades or bid whist, either. If I had sex, I should let the guy think it was his idea and give in reluctantly, after receiving gifts from him and listening to his many sessions of begging. I couldn't initiate any positions or activities that were too bold, like oral sex. If I performed oral sex, I should pretend I didn't know what I was doing and that it was the first time. I shouldn't admit I liked fellatio, and under no circumstance should I swallow. That was just nasty. (Don't laugh. This was middle-class Black culture of the 1980s.)

If my boyfriend raped me, I should pretend it was a misunderstanding. And maybe—but this was at least my choice—I should keep having sex with him to indicate that there were no hard feelings. I complied with that advice: When I was raped at seventeen and eighteen and nineteen, I just acted like it was no big deal. It took a couple decades for the trauma to catch up with me.

There were so many rules to keep track of, and I kept messing up. I found ideas for my clothes from fashion magazines like *Vogue* and *Harper's Bazaar* and tried to emulate those with thrift shop finds. But my outfits were too inspired by punk rockers, not the conservative, preppy clothes that the most popular girls wore. Instead of wearing the 1980s hairstyles of the sisters at my college—a bang with a flip on either side—I shaved off one side of my head, like Cyndi Lauper in the "Girls Just Want to Have Fun" video. When I had sex with a young man, I expected to have orgasms, like I when I was alone. I complained when I didn't have these with a man, and I had the nerve to touch myself during the act. (I had a dude tell me, don't be reaching down there: That was his job.)

But more than my not being a good girl, I was a feminist, and I talked about it. I'd compromised on so much, but my feminism was the one thing I refused to relinquish, no matter how many times I was told to do so by Black men *and* women. They warned me of my ultimate downfall: I couldn't keep quiet. I didn't know to shut up when the brothers were talking, and that's why I couldn't get no man.

Whenever I look at nineteenth-century daguerreotypes on African American women and their families, I always feel proud. Look at how beautiful they were! The stiff grace of their poses. The cleanliness: the brushed hair and pressed clothes. Rarely are there smiles on the faces of the ladies in these images. They are serious about what it takes to keep their families together, but sometimes they tilt toward the beings they love. *We belong together and no one will pull us apart, not anymore.* There is a curated morality in these pictures. These women—these *ladies*—are carefully chiseling a permanent image: *We are good enough, despite what the White masters told us.*

This curation was wise. By the end of the Civil War, two centuries of social and legal messages to Black women had been telling them that they were inferior to White women, who would provide a moral clarion for all other women. An early, extremely popular guide for White women was *Godey's Lady's Book*, founded in 1830 by Louis Godey.[2] The magazine featured fashion images as well as writings by well-known literati of the time. Though the magazine offered lighter fare, behind the scenes, there was a sinister motivation: the editor of *Godey's*, Sarah Josepha Hale, opposed the abolition of slavery and (White) women's voting rights.[3]

Despite Hale's frankly anti-woman politics, for almost seven decades the extremely influential *Godey's* set the tone for female moral behavior. And after the Civil War, free *Black* women received their moral cues from the dominant White patriarchal ideal that Barbara Welter particularizes in her essay "The Cult of Womanhood, 1820–

1860."[4] In the nineteenth century, Welter argues, society dictated that a woman's primary focus should be on her roles as wife and mother, while her husband built the world outside the home—but in Welter's estimation, this woman was a "hostage" in that domestic sphere.[5]

Like so many White feminist scholars of the mid- to late twentieth century, Welter doesn't separate women into racial/cultural categories—there is no analysis of the intersectionality of race and gender. However, in her *Righteous Discontent*, Evelyn Brooks Higginbotham offers the background for Black women's nineteenth-century moral curation, what Higginbotham calls "the politics of respectability."[6] The purpose of this activism was to counteract Whites' negative cultural messaging of African Americans: "The politics of respectability emphasized reform of individual behavior and attitudes both as a goal in itself and as a strategy for reform of the entire structural system of American race relations."[7] Women were assumed to have the greatest influence in the home.[8] If women—wives—were unseemly, immoral, hypersexual, and dirty, what on earth would become of their children?

In the twentieth century these ideas solidified in Black communities. In exchange for adopting the moral strictures of the politics of respectability, the assumed benefit for Black women would be the protection of the kind of Black male that bell hooks called a "benevolent patriarch."[9] This was the African American man who would provide financial support and physical protection and use his patriarchal authority to guide his family in a kind, nonviolent fashion.

Growing up, however, I had witnessed dysfunctional families centered around a benevolent patriarch. As Barbara Welter argued about (assumed White) women, I saw most African American homes as traps, for in exchange for the leadership of this figure, Black women were required to give up their power—and to gamble that the husbands to whom they'd surrendered power would not abuse them.

And I'd seen the hypocritical behavior of the most respected—and the kindest and most nonviolent—patriarchs in my middle- to upper-middle-class Black community of Durham: though these brothers would publicly praise their wives' beauty, morals, and household skills, many of these same men privately cheated on their wives. (Gossip was rife in Durham.) By requiring their wives to stay at home instead of working for money outside the home—the former was considered a great privilege in my Black community—these benevolent patriarchs subverted their wives' career ambitions. There was plenty *unpaid* labor, though: raising children, keeping a clean house, engaging in community service, and actively laboring in the church. These women were exhausted but didn't make their own money. Yet they were supposed to be grateful for not "having to work"—though if they divorced their husbands, they would end up outside the circle of respectable African American society—and broke, like my mother when she left my father.

I'd never be foolish enough to call my father "benevolent." My mother was miserable: my father was frequently abusive to her verbally and, at times, physically. (To this day, I don't drink red wine because one night my father threw a glass of it in my mother's face, seemingly out of nowhere. They weren't even arguing.) The physical abuse hadn't happened enough to be characterized as "a lot," but then again, it had happened too many times to be called "rare."

I spent years questioning why my father had been so cruel and my mother so helpless in the presence of that cruelty to her and to her three daughters. I pondered my parents' childhoods, and the unhappiness both expressed about those years. When I conducted research on my father's time in the army, I wondered if he'd suffered a traumatic brain injury after he was jumped by White enlisted men when he was a commissioned officer during World War II. Had this assault changed his mental health?

I never discovered the source of my parents' individual and coupled misery, but what my father did do was complain about his "Black manhood" in real life and in his published poems. By simple observation, I learned that a man's power in a relationship wasn't only about the extremes of physical and verbal abuse. Even in a contented marriage—which I had seen in my Black communities in Durham and in Eatonton—a man's power could be subtle: like a woman having to rush home from attending women's club meetings to cook dinner because her husband was "useless" in the kitchen. He could only grill hot links and ribs during the summer months. (My father couldn't even do that.) Or it being a mother's job to clean up the kitchen after she cooked every night, but a father only had to take out the garbage—which took about three to five minutes—and mow the lawn once a week or twice monthly. (Daddy didn't do that.) Or, when a father participated in child care, it was called "babysitting," as if his taking care of his own children was a special, celebratory occasion. (Nope. Daddy didn't do that, either. As a small child, if my mother left the home, I kept my own company—like so many other Generation X kids—while my father wrote his poems in his office with the door closed.)

There were some who would argue with me—who still might—that these gender roles had changed, that all men weren't the same. There were some good, non-sexist men out there. I just had to search for them, to send out the "Love me tender" bat signal in the sky. Yet the issue of power in a heterosexual relationship does not necessarily depend upon whether the individual man is nice or not. There are systemic issues at play with patriarchy, just as eradicating systemic racism and White supremacy is not simply about whether White people are personally nice to their one Black friend named Keisha or Dante.

From the time I was six or seven years old, I'd witnessed traditional roles lionized in American culture writ large, as well as in the Black communities in which I'd lived. In the latter there was a fetishizing of marriage between a man and a woman. In my majority Black elementary, junior high, and high schools, girls would talk about the time that they would get married. I'm sure White girls fetishized marriage as well, but I didn't have any White friends then.

As a young girl in the 1980s, I saw a not-so-quiet desperation about marriage that seemed to nicely match (like a wine and cheese pairing) the so-called shortage of Black men. That shortage was supposedly due to any number of issues that would come up at family reunions, college rap sessions that went off the rails in class, or after-school weed-smoking sets:

The problem was "down-low" brothers and the HIV epidemic.

No, the problem was the war on drugs waged by Ronald Reagan and George H. W. Bush, and all those brothers in prison.

That wasn't right, either: The real problem was White women stealing our men.

So many issues, and none with solutions, as we wound our way through our conversations on the Black male shortage. (We didn't use the words *cisgender* or *heterosexual* in my Black community. That would come much later.) At the end of these talks, the conclusion was that any Black woman who wanted to secure one of the diminishing numbers of straight Black (not incarcerated) men needed to let a brother lead. I didn't hear the word *patriarchy* until I enrolled in graduate school, but I understood the framework: men had the power, and any power I grabbed was what a man threw my way. That respectable basilect—"Let the brothers be *men*"— meant me (and other Black women) should accept patriarchy. Not only accept it but submit to it cheerfully.

I'd learned what feminism was when I was about nine or ten, when *female liberation* gave way as the term of choice. When either of those terms were brought up in the community meetings that my mother and father attended, they were spat out with repulsion. Female liberation (and later feminism) was supposed to be for White women, but no Black woman I encountered wanted to be—or could be—White.

Our Black female role was to protect the Black man. It was always *the* Black man, as if there were only one of him, and of course, back then, the Black man wasn't gay, and he wasn't transgender. Preferably, he resembled the titular lead of the movie *Mandingo*. And the Black woman—we were *the*, too—was compelled to stand behind her man, preferably close to his vulnerable side, where God had removed that unbarbecued rib. Our role was not to rise above our men. If there was a Christian hymn that might describe these admonitions of my African

American girl- and womanhood, it might be "Leaning on the Ever-lasting Arms of Respectability."

Yet this wasn't only a Black Christian conclusion, based on strict biblical interpretation. This conclusion was ubiquitous, taking place in discussions among nonreligious Black nationalists, highly educated, degreed Black professionals, and sometimes Black academics. There were articles taken from the pages of *Ebony* magazine, for if God had written the primary Bible, then surely the Johnson family published the secondary Good Book of the American Negro.

Later I met brothers in college who belonged to the Nation of Islam, and in graduate school who belonged to the African Hebrew Israelites. The religious teachings were different, but essentially, the message for gender relations was the same: *Let the Black man lead.* That would be my path to happiness, and if I wasn't happy with that path, I could kick rocks.

∾≈

As a young woman, I saw the politics of respectability countered by the supposed hyper-anti-respectability in hip-hop culture. For example, the early 1990s the use of the word *nigger* became publicly normalized in Black communities, seemingly because of the term's frequent use in hip-hop lyrics. Although *nigger* had been used privately in Black households, including my own, as a derisive term, I never used it in public, even around other Black people. But suddenly the word wasn't negative anymore. It was a term of endearment, or simply a descriptor for Black men.

Concurrently, anti-female terms moved into the nasty lingua franca—*bitch, ho, trick,* and *freak*—used by hip-hop MCs such as Notorious B.I.G., Dr. Dre, and Snoop Dogg—evolved as common terms, too, accompanied by hypermasculine lyrics describing sex that was either coercive or downright violent but—according to male MCs—*justified* because of the awful natures of Black women. As Riché Richardson wrote in the early twenty-first century, in "a culturally indigenous example of black masculine fashioning," even when the gangsta genre made popular on the West Coast fell out of fashion, the ideals behind the genre persisted.[10]

Wherever these masculine ideals traveled, the acceptance of Black women as degraded would follow.

Or, as a young boy once said to me, "Some bitches *is* hoes."

Just as the anti-Black desires of White men were legislated into colonial reality in this country, the (alleged) kinks, dysfunctions, and pathologies of certain African American MCs were included in hip-hop songs consumed by Black communities. Upon hearing that music, many of us Black folks were seduced into normalizing—*or even longing for*—all those (alleged) kinks, dysfunctions, and pathologies.

In the twenty-first century, Moya Bailey would invent a term specifically for Black antifemale hatred: "misogynoir."[11] Though Bailey's was a contemporary term, misogynoirist messaging maintained early negative ideas about Black women, those reaching back to early Virginia's colonial era. Indeed, the original colonial misogynoir never truly went away—it only improvised.

In younger Black communities hip-hop seemingly represented a rejection of respectability politics, but in fact it maintained a separation between "good" and "bad" Black women, in keeping with the nineteenth-century respectability politics of African American communities. Old attitudes about marriage were remixed by the hip-hop generation of the late twentieth and early twenty-first centuries. The common wisdom in communities, that marriage counteracted the (now hip-hop) messaging of the "ho" status of Black women, did not disappear. If anything, these attitudes became entrenched, for in the twenty-first century there is supposedly a "marriage crisis" among Black women. Books like Ralph Richard Banks's *Is Marriage for White People?: How the African American Marriage Decline Affects Everyone* have fed the hysteria in Black communities that heterosexual marriage is a dying institution among our people—and that that is a tragedy.

Just as hip-hop tended existing homophobic fires in Black communities, urgent discussions about marriage rates among African

American women turned rabidly vicious, landing at the door of both "down-low"—closeted—Black gay men and those gay men who rejected shame and openly lived their sexual truths. For example, in the informal discussion settings in which I participated in—beauty shops and gatherings of friends—gay men were blamed exclusively for the levels of HIV transmission in Black communities. Both closeted and openly gay men were castigated as not wanting to be "real men"—meaning they didn't engage in permanent heterosexual unions. There was little pushback against the nasty homophobia in our communities.

Only marriages between one cisgender Black man and one cisgender Black woman were counted as valid, formal unions. Few stoking the marriage crisis considered interracial marriage or marriages between African American gay men or Black lesbians as #TrueBlackLove—except to note that Black men marrying White women was the reason that sisters couldn't jump their ribbon-decorated brooms.

Every former wife can start trotting out the sins of the man she was once married to. I could do that here, but then, my ex-husband could list my own sins against him, and what good would any of that do? It won't go back and save my marriage. I still fell in love with Khalil—the man I call "the African"—and honestly, some part of me might always love him, even after it clicked that marriage hadn't ever been for me.

Though the daily events of our union were commonplace and often even boring, there was a romance to the sound of our love story. I repeated the facts as if they were extraordinary: My husband and I had met in Senegal while I was doing research on Wolof culture. We waited until we married to have sex. He called me "darling" in three languages.

I'd become an astute liar. In person, I lovingly smiled when speaking about Khalil. Online, I made witty remarks about him. Privately, though, I had started to feel salty about my social elevation as a married woman. I was a highly educated African American woman! I didn't need a man to make me! Even if I hadn't been highly educated, my deep spiritual faith told me that as a child of God and my ancestors, my singular presence in the world was astonishing.

I didn't reveal the rest, except to my closest of friends: A year or so into my marriage, I was miserable. I'd gained thirty pounds, and I spent so much time in bed. I was so tired all the damned time; it seemed I could only get up to teach my classes. I even wrote my books in bed. A few months before my husband and I separated, I developed panic attacks. On one occasion I thought I was having a heart attack, and was hospitalized for two days.

The way my marriage ended was just as mundane as I had found the marriage to be: one day, as I walked through my house—I'd purchased my home well before marrying, so it would remain mine—I noticed that my bottom lip was tucked under my top teeth, in the same petulant way my mother used to do. That was one of Mama's usual expressions throughout my childhood. She was always angry, because of my father. And here I was, decades later, always mad, after promising myself I'd never become like my mother.

I stood over the stove, cooking for the husband who had enraged me, the same as Mama had done for Daddy. My legs were aching because I'd been standing in that kitchen for about two hours: I was a southern sister raised by a southern sister, we always cook from scratch, and with West African meals, there is no such thing as "fast food." When I was done cooking, I was exhausted. I turned off the burners and headed to the living room, sitting down on the couch.

Khalil followed me into the living room. With his dazzling smile on display, he asked, "I serve myself?"

"I just cooked everything! You're telling me you can't fix your own plate?"

He kept standing there, smiling.

I sighed, then returned to the kitchen.

I wish I could tell you that I threw Khalil's food into the garbage, but that's not how it went down. I plated my husband's meal, and then I reached into the refrigerator for the jar of West African pepper sauce that I'd made, too, following a recipe online. I served my husband at the table. After the meal was over, I boiled water for the hibiscus tea he loved; they call it *bissap* in his homeland. (It doesn't look that much different from the red Kool-Aid that my grandma used to make.)

It took some time after that evening for me to file for the end of this misery. When I finally did, I was so proud of myself: I was divorcing, instead of doing what my mother had done, remaining informally separated from my father until his death. I didn't consider my decision a political one. I only thought I was tired of trying to make a hopeless relationship work.

Two years after my divorce, I detected a change in myself. Now, expelled from the sorority of wifedom, I saw what patriarchy really was. Not the dictionary version, but how I had not only negotiated with patriarchy but *welcomed* its presence—while pretending in public that my feminist politics were authentic. It wasn't that there was anything wrong with marriage to a man. I'd seen a few feminist heterosexual marriages that seemed happy, that worked. But my marriage wasn't one of those. I discarded my feminist politics so quickly, once I became someone's wife, and justified this to myself by insisting that I was just trying to live in peace.

I returned to what elder Black feminists had tried to tell me, on the page and in real life. Like the fact that, even when a Black man is solitary, he can count on the power of the African American community massed behind him, while a solitary Black woman is truly alone. She doesn't have gender power dynamics, religion, or her community on her side. Without a man to help her—first her father and then her husband—she is viewed as flawed and rudderless.

Recall the utterly handsome Billy Dee Williams in that classic Black film *Mahogany*, declaring with conviction that Diana Ross's success "is nothing" without a loving mate beside her? Then, as we all predicted, La Ross shows up to beg that superfine man to take her back.

The only surprise in that movie's conclusion is that she is unashamed to stand in a crowd of working-class Detroit residents wearing a full-length ermine coat.

But we all knew Diana would return to Billy Dee, didn't we? For where would she be without him? How would she make it by herself?

∼⤞∽

I've long suspected that, as a Black feminist woman, I'm considered weird—an example of what Cathy J. Cohen called "nonnormative heterosexuality."[12] I'm a dangerous anomaly, like my literary heroes, the protagonists of three novels I treasure: Sula, Janie, and Celie.

Nobody can figure me out: I only like to sleep with men, but I don't want a man living in my house. As soon as a brother gives me too much trouble, I block his number and keep it moving. I don't try to work things out, because I didn't survive my abusive childhood only to struggle through adult relationship drama. And though I might enjoy a bit—or a lot—of submission in bed, as soon as the lovemaking is over and my feet hit the floor, I submit to no one but God.

Then, too, I think of Great-Grandma Mandy, who never married, though she was the mother of several children. Mama passed Mandy's few stories and proverbs on to me, and always exclaimed, "I wished I had paid better attention!" I consider myself to be Mandy's child, just as much as Trellie Lee's. And if Mandy, an unmarried woman who slept with whomever she pleased, could survive scandal and gain such admiration from Mama—a woman devoted to respectability—why couldn't I live my life in freedom?

I found that it's different when you read about the politics of respectability versus when you've lived that phenomenon up close. When you've witnessed yourself surrendering to an identity that you had previously—loudly—proclaimed held no importance to you.

I have decided never to marry again. Some might say I have been forced to give up the dream of a second marriage anyway, at my advanced age. Look, I'm happy to accept whatever will make people leave me the fuck alone, but there are others like me, other Black women—of various ages—who declare that they aren't concerned with satisfying community requirements. They just want to protect their peace, and that means avoiding marriage.

Here I am, unrespectable and unashamed, waving from truthful territory. It was hard to travel here, and even more frightening to admit that once, I was a coward. I wanted acceptance so badly that I fell in love with my own defeat.

23

A Brief Note About the Election of U.S. Presidents, Annoying Progressive White Folks, and the Long-Suffering Understanding of Black Women

For me and so many other Americans (including plenty progressive White folks), Barack Obama's 2009 inauguration as the forty-fourth president of the United States was a moment we had been praying for. A needful time. I remember calling my mother and silently remaining on the phone as we watched the entire inauguration, something I'd never done. When Mr. Obama put his hand on that Bible to be sworn on, my mother burst into tears—my mother, who was not given to sentimentality. I'd only seen her cry a handful of times in my life.

"Lord have mercy, Honorée!" she exclaimed. "I never thought I'd live to see this day!"

My mother is no longer alive, but I believe I can say with certainty that, like me, she believed that the unbroken, line of White men occupying the highest political office in our nation had been ruptured. Now—*now* being those eventual eight years—this country would finally, truthfully move to "a more perfect union." That's what the preamble to Constitution declared, but we'd both forgotten that when that preamble was written, twenty-five of the fifty-five delegates to the constitutional convention owned slaves.[1]

Mama adored President Obama. I, too, loved him *personally,* along with his gorgeous, brown-skinned family: First Lady Michelle Obama, her mother, Mrs. Robinson, and those two adorable daughters, whom my mother and I called "the Little Michelles." There were no scandals, other than over that tan suit our president wore once.[2] For me, the visual rhetoric of the Obama family in the White House was like *Ebony* magazine come to life.

Yet by President Obama's second presidential term, I was disappointed at the casual violence he ordered around the globe. For example, back in 2012 I was in London and heard someone call President Obama the "Droner in Chief," a purveyor of violence. I couldn't even deny it to the man who said it to me.

"Hey, look, I'm not my president!" Despite my words, I raised my hands: *I have no defense.*

In 2016 I voted for Hillary Clinton to become the forty-fifth president of the United States, despite her enthusiastic support for Bill Clinton's Violent Crime Control and Law Enforcement Act of 1994, which saw an explosion of the prison population of Black people.[3] Today—at this writing—African Americans still are imprisoned at much higher rates than their White counterparts.[4] During Hillary Clinton's 2016 presidential campaign, she apologized to Black folks for that crime bill, and I accepted her apology, because she wasn't president.[5] I didn't hold her ultimately responsible.

I voted for Hillary Clinton because I've never not voted for a Democrat in a presidential election, from the time I first registered to vote as a young person. I voted for Hillary Clinton because I did not want her opponent Donald Trump in office. This was the man who had taken out a full-page advertisement calling for the execution of five Black and Latino teenagers known then as the Central Park Five but currently as the Exonerated Five, after DNA evidence proved them innocent.[6] Even after these now-adult men were exonerated—thus, their new moniker—Trump refused to apologize, questioning their innocence.[7]

I knew Hillary Clinton wouldn't win, though. I'd kept trying to tell folks, to prepare them for what was coming. Those folks included my own mother.

"How do you know she's going to lose?" Mama asked.

"I just have a feeling," I said.

My mother snorted. "We're supposed to poll elections based on your feelings!"

"Okay, Mama. Fine. But don't be mad at me when this thing goes south."

When the election was called for Donald Trump, my cell phone rang.

"Honorée, you tried to tell me," Mama said.

"I know, but I'm not happy I was right."

President Obama left office, and in January 2017 Donald Trump ushered in mayhem and, three years later, literal plague. Over a million people died of Covid during a pandemic that many experts assert Trump grossly mishandled.[8] More than that, during this time, I experienced a feeling of increasing hostility from White people in my town. I thought it was my imagination, but other Black folks told me that they'd picked up that same feeling. My mild social anxiety became severe; I became afraid to leave the house.

In 2020, though, there was another miraculous event: Kamala Harris, an African-Asian American woman who identified as Black, was elected as vice president when Joe Biden defeated Trump to become the forty-sixth President. As with Hillary Clinton, I had mixed emotions about Joe Biden: Not only had he too strongly supported Clinton's 1994 crime bill, but I'd witnessed his public humiliation of Anita Hill during Clarence Thomas's confirmation hearing for the US Supreme Court.[9] According to Anita Hill though Biden apologized, Hill believed that he never truly took responsibility for his treatment of her.[10]

But again—as with Hillary Clinton—I voted for Joe Biden. By this time, not only had the country changed but my approach to politics was pragmatic. I wasn't going to lie to myself. I no longer believed that a good person could be president of the United States.

⁘

There is a song that I loved, back in my senior year of college, Karyn White's "I'm Not Your Superwoman." Her angry description of the unpaid, domestic labor she performed and the unreciprocated love she gave to her man encapsulated so many Black women's complaints.

I can complain about my own people putting too much on African American women, and I do constantly. We sisters are declared to be the backbone of the Black community—but now, don't try to *travel* from the back. Those are the wages of community sexism, that a Black women should be docile and submissive while running everything behind the scenes: in our churches, homes, schools, and anyplace else where two or more Black people are gathered, whether we meet in God's name or otherwise.

What I find confusing is that every time there is a national election, there is a tacit expectation from the Democratic Party that Black women be superwomen and save the country from Republicans, while also holding up the lineage of White patriarchy. What angers me is the assumption that Black women will always be there whenever this country—or any Black community—is headed for disaster. *Give it to the sisters to fix* is the common wisdom. Even online, well-meaning White progressives praise Black women for "saving us"—*us* meaning the vision of America that these progressives, lying to themselves, believe to be true: an America of equality for everyone, regardless of race or gender or sexual orientation, and of widespread love for all fellow human beings, a country that is forward-looking, all ocular and documented evidence to the contrary.

It's true that some notable Black women voting rights activists, such as LaTosha Brown and Stacey Abrams, along with a huge number of their fellow Black women, drummed up the vote for the Democratic Party during Joe Biden's 2020 presidential run, and were arguably responsible for his victory.[11] Yet Biden kept his Black female vice president in the background, much to my frustration. I don't know why this was, but I noticed—and others did, too—that he certainly trotted Kamala Harris out in 2022, after *Roe v. Wade* was overturned.[12] Then Catholic, not-very-passionate-about-abortion-rights Biden used Harris to reassure women that his administration was very, very concerned about their legal access to choice.

❧

In 2024 Black female supernatural symbolism was exploited yet again when Joe Biden was forced to step down after challenges to his fitness to run for a second presidential term.[13] The Democratic Party plunged into anxiety until Kamala Harris stepped in, raised huge amounts of money in a very few days, and won the party's nomination.

It seemed then that Karyn White's song was a lie: Kamala *was* your superwoman. After Biden ended his presidential bid, the Democratic Party rallied, and, as with Obama's first campaign, there were all sorts of self-congratulatory comments about the historic nature of what it would mean to have a woman in office. Not only a woman: a Black woman.

Something was off, though. And somebody was lying when they said they wanted Harris for president, because Harris lost that election. As my mama liked to say, whenever something didn't pass her smell test, "There's a dead cat on the line."

In other words, many of these White folks pretending they were excited by the prospect of a Black female POTUS had lied not only to their Black friends but also to pollsters. Memories of Mama's heart-breaking tales of growing up in Jim Crow–era Georgia invaded my days as well. She'd offer those stories to explain her lifelong negotiation with racial mistrust. I nodded to myself at her memories: Yes, one never knew, for in 2024 I'd been betrayed by White neighbors again, as when Donald Trump won in 2016.

Immediately after Harris's defeat, the media pile-on began. A Black woman had failed to save us, and now she had to be punished for that failure.

The media blamed Harris's campaign strategies. They blamed her lack of outreach to Arab Americans, African American males, and Latino Americans. They blamed her for ignoring the ethnic cleansing—genocide—taking place in Gaza, although during the campaign, very few in the media had paid sustained attention to Harris's views on the Palestinian crisis. I grew so tired of that excuse about people voting for Trump because of the price of eggs, for I've been poor—truly poor—in my lifetime, and I've never been so foolish as to vote for a billionaire, thinking he'll rescue me from poverty.

The media reached for anything but racism and sexism to explain Harris's defeat. If those were the reasons, then what would that say about the engrained prejudices of Americans?[14] There had to be some other reason that, in 2024, 59 percent of White men and 53 percent of White women voted for Trump.[15] No, no, White supremacy, racism and sexism couldn't be the motivator—right? Because some *Black* voters hadn't voted for Harris, either; 9 percent of Black women and 24 percent of Black men had refused her as a candidate.[16] And since those African Americans hadn't supported her, how could White supremacy and racism enter the chat?

I'll tell you why. To paraphrase a contemporary Black proverb, it's one thing to talk about equality and equity, but it's quite another thing to *be* about it. Black women have been at the bottom of the United States' social hierarchy in general, and even within our Black communities we are oppressed. Why would everyone in the United States— even some Black folks-- suddenly be okay with an African American woman occupying the most powerful position on earth?

In their discussions of Harris's failure, the media somehow didn't remember that they had insisted Harris be perfect during her campaign. And wasn't that insistence on Black female perfection—while withstanding persecution—so familiar to me, as an African American woman in America?

⁓

Certainly I was disappointed that Kamala Harris, who had modeled toughness as a positive personality trait, and campaigned on the cognitive dissonance of "joy"—even as Israel engaged in what the United Nations deemed ethnic cleansing of Palestinian people, many of them small children, in Gaza. As a Black feminist, one of my hopes is that justice for our communities and other oppressed communities world-wide might prevail. And ethnic cleansing doesn't fit my definition of justice.

I did not anticipate change overnigh, though. Whenever I have voted—and I've always voted for Democrats—it has been for what is *possible*, not imminent. I have voted to inch things forward. My people are patient, and even more, Black women are faithful. I didn't expect global peace in my lifetime, but I expected it two or three generations down the path—if Harris won. That's why I voted for her.

I wanted Harris to criticize brutal US policies, but I reminded myself that this wasn't a realistic expectation. This was the United States; our human rights record is alarming.[17] Harris didn't start these human rights abuses, and it's unrealistic to believe that she could have ended them, all by herself, or resolved on her own a US policy in Israel that has been in place for seventy-five years. (Israel's treatment of the Palestinian people has been criticized by several of my African American literary forebears, including Toni Morrison.[18] Yet Morrison endorsed Barack Obama, whose administration did not substantially change its policy toward Israel. Remember what I said about pragmaticism?[19])

Further, anyone who'd desire this country's most powerful office—such as Kamala Harris—would already be aware of its terrible moral cost. Why would I expect more empathy from someone battling to secure that kind of power, just because she's a Black woman?

I'm not saying my spirit is untroubled by the actions of any occupant of the White House. Trouble hums me awake every morning. I'm not saying I expect universally empathetic policy changes from my president when it comes to affirming human rights, either—I don't expect empathetic faultlessness in a politician any time soon, even in someone I voted for.

When I consider Kamala Harris's campaign, I understand that this sister was expected not only to be perfect but to *transcend* perfection, taking on the role of moral Messiah—which not one of her White or African American male predecessors ever had attempted. Harris was expected to instantly lead the citizens of the United States, a nation founded upon violent, White supremacist, global capitalist exploitation, into some new promised land. Harris was expected to do this *before* holding the power of the presidential office, for she was only a candidate seeking that job.

So I understand how unfair many voters and the media were, when it came to the impossible standard that they expected Harris to meet, because I understand injustice—and in large part, I'm capable of that understanding because I'm a Black woman living in the United States.

24

Very Real (Open) Letter to Mr. Barack Obama Concerning His Speech Accusing Black Men of Sexism Because Some Hadn't Planned to Vote for Vice President Kamala Harris in the 2024 Election

Dear Mr. Obama:

You are my "Forever President" and I love you. Not only do I love you, but I love Mrs. Obama, I love your daughters, and when Mrs. Obama's mother was still living, I loved her, too. (I still love Mrs. Robinson, up in heaven.) I cannot tell you what it meant to me to see the five of you in the White House.

Although I know that any leader of this place that we call the United States is engaged in horrible events around the globe, visual rhetoric is powerful. To have a Black male president with his pretty, brown-skinned African American family residing in the White House, to have you and your family beloved and prayed for by so many—well, that meant so much. My heart is awash at the memory of those eight years.

Now, here we are, after Kamala Harris's defeat. She would have been the first Black woman leader of the free world. Before the election, more than 20 percent of African American men polled had said they weren't planning to vote for her—and they didn't.

I'm still thinking of those remarks you gave October 10, 2024— before the election—accusing Black men of sexism.[1]

Mr. Obama, you are right. They were sexist—very much so. And *they were ungrateful, too, because Black women always have the backs of Black men in this country. But it was a little late for you to have this conversation, don't you think?*

Just as I had been waiting for the first female president—I never thought I'd see a Black female in this position—I waited throughout your two terms as POTUS for a real talk with Black men about sexism and patriarchy. Instead, when you talked to them, you fetishized what bell hooks called "benevolent patriarchy." In your autobiography The Audacity of Hope, you praised the Moynihan Report, criticizing relationship choices that led to "poverty" in African American communities.[2] This praise not only blamed Black folks for their own generational marginalization, but ignored that women of all cultural backgrounds perform most child-rearing activities throughout the globe; women perform the bulk of domestic labor is how patriarchy works.[3]

Mr. Obama, I recognized your implication: that you were the role model for a Black husband and a Black father. But while it was obvious that you loved your wife, daughters, and mother-in-law, all of whom were Black females, the fact is, you were flying around the world as president of the United States while Mrs. Obama and Mrs. Robinson, your mother-in-law, stayed behind and reared your daughters.

I didn't question that patriarchal reality—even in private—because at the time, I thought, "Well, I'm just happy to have this brother in the White House." Many other Black feminists didn't question you, and I suspect this is because like me, they adored you. You seemed like a tender, good guy, even though you celebrated patriarchy. There wasn't even a question of forgiveness for us; we didn't blame you to begin with. You were our brother, so we gave you a pass.

This quandary is familiar: I loved Vice President Harris. I loved her as my African American sister, and I had dearly hoped she would become the first Black female POTUS. I was ready for the symbolism of a woman of African descent in the White House, what it might mean for sisters in Black communities, though I knew that Harris, too, would authorize horrible actions as POTUS—that is the unfortunate history of the leaders of this country.

I want to live according to my human being and feminist principles, and those principles do not include supporting the United States stomping on other people or paying other countries to do our stomping. I cannot say that having a Black woman authorize violence around the world represents some sort of feminist victory for me—simply having a brown woman be as brutal as a man is no reason to celebrate.

However, I know symbolism is important—visual rhetoric is important—and that's why I voted for Kamala Harris. Also, I voted for her because I wasn't interested in living in the dictatorship that Mr. Trump had advocated during his campaign.

Mr. Obama, again, I love you so much. (Not in a creepy way. Don't be alarmed.) I love you not only for myself—I love you because of my mother. I was on the phone with Mama during your first inauguration. The moment you became forty-fourth president, Mama and I wept in happiness together; I began shouting like I was in church. I was grateful that my seventy-five-year-old mother, who had grown up under southern Jim Crow, who had seen so much horror in this country—who remembered the assassination of Dr. Martin Luther King Jr., who remembered lynchings— could witness this moment. And that's why I pretended not to notice when you ignored your many opportunities to address the evils of patriarchy in African American communities.

On the day of your speech about Black male sexism, I was still waiting to see if our republic, this complicated country with an enduring, terrible legacy, would survive. I think of how you criticized Black men who weren't planning to vote for Harris. You accused them of sexism—and though you are very right, I must ask, Mr. Obama: Why did it take you so long?

You are an insightful man. A kind man—I truly believe this, though I know that, as president, you ordered some very bad things in service of maintaining our republic. I don't believe in those bad things you ordered, and so my love for you is as complicated as my love for my country—but let me tell you, it's still love, Mr. Obama. It's always going to be love.

Today, though, I'm exasperated with you, for you could have done so much to move Black men's gender politics forward. You could have advised them about the dangers of patriarchy. You could have led our brothers to the profound anti-patriarchal, feminist works of Kimberlé Crenshaw, Patricia Hill Collins, bell hooks, and Alice Walker.

You could have explained that, though your marriage with Mrs. Obama appeared wholly traditional on the outside, as the first African American FLOTUS, she was forced to publicly negotiate with patriarchy. And why? Because the United States of America was not ready for a gorgeous, dark-brown-skinned, brilliant, Ivy League–educated, haute couture-wearing, fly Black woman First Lady—let alone one who identified as a feminist.

And okay, maybe you couldn't have helped to take down patriarchy during your two terms as president—but you could have done that when you completed your terms and Donald Trump became POTUS. You have had so much time to teach and prepare your fellow Black men for this moment. Why didn't you?

Less than a month before the election was when you decided to give what amounted to a pop quiz on sexism and patriarchy? I am not surprised that 24 percent of my brothers failed this quiz: not only hadn't they studied for it, they didn't even know the existence of the text(s) upon which the quiz was based.

Just as your election as the first Black male president of the United States did not erase nearly five hundred years of White supremacy, your one speech calling out Black men was not going to reverse the patriarchal brainwashing inflicted on them over the centuries.

And your one speech won't ameliorate five hundred years of the theft of Black women's physical, reproductive, and emotional labor; the diminishment of our roles as activists for Black and American equality; the ridiculing of our bodies, hair, and facial features; or the questioning of our right to whatever iteration of womanhood has been called "real" in this country, either—and sometimes the very people questioning our womanhood have been Black men.

Mr. Obama, I write you this letter because it is twenty-five days after election day. I sit with my grief, fear, and anger at what my fellow citizens have done by electing Donald Trump. Yet though Kamala Harris—and truly, Black women—lost this current election, it's not too late for you to teach our brothers about the evils of patriarchy, even if those lessons might be learned amid the smoking rubble of our republic. Black men admire you. They will listen to you dismantle patriarchy, they will understand your logic, and they will follow your lead. I have seen you in action. You are a powerful teacher.

But I am praying that our country will hold, and I remain grateful to you for that moment fifteen years ago, the moment that I shared with my late mother, when you placed your hand on that Bible for the first time and became our president.

May you and your family always be blessed.

Respectfully,

Honorée Fanonne Jeffers

(who voted for you, twice)

V

BLUES FOR BOYS, BLUES FOR MEN

Little brown baby wif spa'klin' eyes,
Who's pappy's darlin' an' who's pappy's chile?
Who is it all de day nevah once tries
Fu' to be cross, er once loses dat smile?

—PAUL LAURENCE DUNBAR, "LITTLE BROWN BABY"

25

The Little Boy Who Will Be My Father[1]

For Robert Hayden and Sharon Olds

Rides on a train through the once frontier
because his mother finally has sent for him,
her remembered duty.

He has a tag around his wrist,
that's how he knows who he is.

I like to think of him this way:
Skin of pale gold,
hair brushed into obedience,

eyes narrowing with too early wit, the old-fashioned
white linen collar wider than his shoulders.

A child, not the man who would stand
in the light of the kitchen, naked,
looking me straight into my own child's eyes.

What have I done
What have I done

Why have I entered this place as a girl,
left a thing unnamed? Why didn't I stay
in my room, pray for the best that night?

I was too greedy, that's it.
The kitchen called me.

Bread, jelly, lots of milk is what I wanted,
not to see my father naked in the light.
I'm closing my eyes to that memory.

I can still see him
I can still see him

Now.
I'll open my eyes and see the little boy instead—
face like my own

what a glory of a smile!
This child will let me sleep through my life.

He won't climb into my bed,
leaving the scrim of bad dreams.
This little boy.

I love him
I love him

I like to think of my father this way
before he is changed into what I should not say.
He rides on a train headed west into the unknown,

away from his only home, away from his milk
breath clouding the prairie morning.

26

My Life with *Roots*

A few years after my sister Val taught me to read, my daddy began giving me a monthly stipend of $50 to buy books. I couldn't use this money for anything else like clothes, shoes, or candy. At the Scholastic book fair at my school, I would buy at least a dozen books, and collected the bonus poster they'd give out. (I continue to miss my poster of a baby seal. Where did it go?) And Mama would take me to the bookstore at the local mall in Durham, where I'd roam through the Young Adult section—buying Mildred Taylor, Louise Meriwether, Judy Blume, and Naomi Klein—and then I'd move on to what the grown folks read.

The year I turned nine years old—1976—Alex Haley's *Roots: The Saga of an American Family* was published. In my memory, I try to piece this together. Did I read it that next year when I was ten—or the year after that? I can't offer a definitive answer, but I entered the world of *Roots*—there's no other way to describe it—after watching the miniseries on television. Not very much later, my father and I did a buddy-read.

Then, after my father took away my television in a fit of his predictably unpredictable anger, when he ordered me to read Tolstoy's thick *Anna Karenina*—a tome that weighed even more than *Roots*—I'd understand that not only Black men wrote books that were actual as well as metaphorical weapons. But *Roots* was my first "big book," the story of an African American family's journey from freedom to slavery, and back to freedom again.

꧁

Reading *Roots* represented rare, calm moments spent with my father, a Black Arts Movement poet who, though he was very light skinned, was a Black nationalist and pined for Africa. Those times I wasn't afraid of him: I called him "Daddy," and that word wasn't bitter on my tongue. Reading was so tender, even as we talked through the horrors of slavery, the individual trauma that Kunta Kinte must have suffered. I learned that Kunta Kinte wouldn't make it out of slavery. There would be no supernatural Negro moments for him, his wife Belle, and his daughter Kizzy.

I had such affection for my enslaved ancestors: I linked them with my own suffering as well as my confounding, lasting love for my father, a man who treated me like something he owned and could harm any way he saw fit.

Kunta couldn't break free, the same way that I could never leave my father. He was part of me. My smile. My blood. My introduction to the life of the mind—and even my academic territory: A few years before I arrived at my eventual alma mater, Talladega College, my father had taught there as a visiting scholar for an academic term. These days, I run into Talladega alumni who sat in his classes; they will quote his poems to me, while I try to smile and pretend to be proud. I don't want to hurt them. I want to protect them from the truth: the man they admired was an abuser of girls and women, in the worst, most destructive ways.

I suffered under the power of Daddy. He could be so kind, and then in an instant he would turn cruel with words. In the night, there were sometimes odd and ugly touches. My mother would weakly contest his daytime verbal abuse, but that didn't stop anything. He'd turn on her, and then my sisters and I would defend her. It was a skipping song on an old record player.

I protected the memories of others so that I wouldn't have to relive my own. Up until a few months ago (at this writing), the very memory of Daddy—his emotional, physical, and sexual abuse of me—continued to affect my mental and spiritual health.

But recollection is like that, isn't it? A hybrid creation flexing and cracking bones. An ever moving, mysterious target. An unpalatable, poisonous drink—no, a piece of sweet, long-lasting candy.

As a little girl—all while reading *Roots* and then slave narratives—I had no idea how I would escape my father. He was all-powerful: brilliant, Ivy League educated, a college professor. He was the author of me: I carried his last name. Though I was much darker than he was, other Black folks we encountered constantly remarked upon how much I resembled him.

Outside of our house, my mother preened when she stood beside him, so proud to be called Mrs. Jeffers. There was no indication from her that he was the mean, spitting ogre that her children endured at home. She told us never to tell anyone how terrible he was, and I was forced to keep our secret. I was that girl that Harriet Jacobs had described in *Incidents in the Life of a Slave Girl*: "She will become prematurely knowing in evil things. Soon she will learn to tremble when she hears her master's footfall. She will be compelled to realize that she is no longer a child."[1]

In my room, I'd lie in bed with a plate of food that I stuffed into my mouth until my stomach was ready to explode. I read about books about the horrors that my ancestors had survived, the White slave masters who beat, raped, and denigrated them, and then I'd think about how I suffered in my own home, that kelly-green split-level house on a small hill at 2608 East Weaver Street in Durham, North Carolina, the dwelling my mother was so proud of.

When I was thirteen, I began telling my father to keep his monthly $50, though my mother urged me to take the cash. There was a grimy significance attached to his gifts, for his abuse had escalated into threats: he told me that Mama and he "were going to get rid of me." I didn't know what he meant. Was he going to send me away—or even kill me?

One evening, after Daddy had slapped me, I suddenly—strangely—filled with power: I ran to the kitchen, grabbed a knife, and brandished it in his face.

My mother objected, "Honorée, that's your father!"

"You shut up!" I shouted. I was shaking, for I was breaking another taboo for a Southern Black child: you do not raise your voice to your mother. You do not disrespect her.

After that night, I began sleeping with the knife under my pillow, and Daddy never hit me again—or visited my bed again. When he kept up with his litanies of verbal abuse, I reminded him of my knife.

"If I were you, Daddy, I wouldn't go to sleep," I taunted him. "I'll gut you like a hog."

For my entire young life, he'd been such a bully, but now he stood useless in front of me. I saw his fear of me, and I was thrilled beyond calculation.

I think of my knife like the talisman Frederick Douglass mentioned in his autobiography, the "root" that an enslaved elder gave him that allowed him not to be beaten by his White overseer. The knife was my own hoodoo charm, like that of my people who had once been enslaved: Douglass and Harriet Jacobs and Olaudah Equiano and Mary Prince.

But I grieved over Kunta Kinte, who hadn't been able to escape bondage. Did his own hoodoo not work against his masters? Or had it been too weak? Yet I knew Kunta had been strong: he had labored and bred and suffered psychological torture. He had withstood far more than I. It was my duty to make it to freedom, for Kunta and all the others before me, those whose names I would never know.

~❧~

When I'd moved from *Roots* to the autobiographies of Douglass and Jacobs, the message behind these narratives was clear: Slavery was not a joke. It was horrific and traumatizing. In our contemporary times, when we watch slavery movies or read slavery books, the trauma becomes more real.

Equally—and perhaps more important than needing to garner White sympathy—these formerly enslaved people wanted to testify, like the old ones in Grandma Florence's church used to do, when I spent my summers down south in Eatonton. They would stand and speak on the goodness of the Lord, how He had brought them "through many troubles and trials." They had come through a path populated by the terrible creations of Satan, who somehow made ugliness seem exquisite to the weak.

And wasn't slavery Satan's evil creation? Wasn't it against the glories of God—despite it being in the Bible beginning with Genesis, and ending in Revelations: "And cinnamon, and odours, and ointments, and frankincense, and wine, and oil, and fine flour, and wheat, and beasts, and sheep, and horses, and chariots, and slaves, and souls of men."

~⁂~

I will never forget a White man approaching me in the Oklahoma City airport to argue that Black people in the United States had it better than those in Africa, even though they had been enslaved. He had interrupted a conversation I was having with a brother I'd just met. (There's something about talking with a Black person that I know I'll probably never see again that mutes my social anxiety.)

I was headed to London to marry Khalil, the man I'd met in Senegal six months before. It was December 2012, four years before Trump took office as the forty-fifth president, but this White man at the airport didn't need (alleged) corruption in the White House to empower him, to interrupt a closed conversation between two Black folks and presumptuously lecture me about my "luck" as an American descended from the enslaved. His blue eyes widened in shock—how dare I?—when I informed him that it was not his place to tell me about my life as a Black person in America. And further, I told him, please stop talking to me. Because he really didn't know me like that.

Twelve years (at this writing) have passed since that time, and I've seen White-supremacist-attempted erasure of slavery history, one that has come under the purview of anti-critical-race-theory movements. It's true that the anthology *Critical Race Theory: The Key Writings That Formed the Movement* contains essays that document the historical, structural ways that US law frequently usually benefited White people. But critical race theory is far too complicated for most people—of whatever cultural background— to understand. (Let alone for children.) These attacks against CRT are not about complication, but rather, I believe they carry an easier motivation: It's about shame.

For many White folks, shame and its repercussions fuel the desire to erase slavery history in the United States; for example, to ignore the fact that money earned from the international and then internal US slave trade helped to build this country. And the development of the insurance industry in the West can be traced to the maritime insuring of enslaved Africans.[2] Nobody White wants to admit that their ancestors traded in an unspeakably filthy commerce: selling Black women into forced breeding, violently raping and beating men, women, and, yes, children; frequently breaking up Black families for economic purposes. Who would believe that such actions were okay?

I think of shame so much whenever I think of history. My history as a person whose African ancestors knowingly sold them into slavery. (Most likely *West* African, but I have no sure documentation.) My history as a Black American whose ancestors were dragged to this soil. My history as an abused child.

I have my own shame about those nights when my daddy came to my room and lay in my bed naked, so I can understand the shame of my distant White kin. The kind of shame might be different, but the feelings of indignity remain. Those White Americans descended from slave masters either won't accept their lineage, or pretend those crimes no longer matter—as my mother pretended that what my father did either didn't happen or wasn't that big of a deal.

I have blood kin who refuse to claim me or whom I have tried to escape from. I am the ancestor who was transgressed against. I am the taken child of Africa. I am the darker sister. I am the ruined daughter of a mother who could not protect me from the sea.

27

Blues for Boys, Blues for Men

Once my mother hinted to me that my father was abused himself as a child.

"His stepfather was cruel to him, you know," Mama said. "Forest Jeffers did things to Lance, back in the day."

I didn't ask for further information. I didn't want to feel sorry for the man whose abuse drove me to burn my bedroom light all evening into mornings, well into my late thirties.

When I thought of my father, I hid my trauma behind anger or toughness, ignoring the wisdom that vulnerability would (eventually) send my way. Even as I learned to wrestle with my abuse, I covered my pain with euphemisms, "back in the day" or "when I wasn't my best, because of certain things." I learned to play this game.

Everything that was inside my daddy, I found out secondhand, through Mama. What happened to him as a little boy. What happened to him as a young man, in England in World War II, when he was attacked by a group of White enlisted soldiers, even though he was a second lieutenant, a commissioned officer.

The soldiers beat my father bloody, then reported him—and Daddy was the one who was court-martialed. He made it out of the army with an honorable discharge—at least according to a declassified FBI surveillance file of him that I found online.[1] (When I applied to see my father's army file, I received an email saying there were no records.) But Daddy never talked about those years to me, or told me who helped him out of that trouble.

⚬⚬⚬

In so many histories about enslaved Black women and girl, intimate assault is rendered in elusive terms evoking a polite knock on the door of a charming cottage, instead of a man stalking the halls of the big house or kicking down a cabin door.

These vagaries continue when discussing the abuse of Black men and boys. The assumption is that Black males weren't raped during slavery. That the only violation they witnessed was the assault of "their" women and children.

This sort of argument ignores the stark realities of slave life, to make sure that Black males remain patriarchs—and *straight*—in our historical imaginations. And this erasure is part of the seduction of White supremacy in *Black* communities, that male might is not only preferred but the *correct* way of doing things.

To follow correctness, we must forget that Black men and boys were sexually assaulted, too--because when one is assaulted, the implication is that one becomes a receptacle. One is affirmed as a weaker vessel, if one is female—but one is transformed into weakness, if one is male.

⚬⚬⚬

"Did you try to fight?"

That is always the first question posed to a woman, after she is raped.

"Why didn't you call for help?"

That's the second.

But if you are *male*, you shouldn't need help. That's what patriarchal wisdom tells us.

Why would you admit to weakness, Black man? You should be the powerful one, Black man. That's the lie to tell yourself, Black man. Remain silent and suffering, always unsmiling in photos, with your arms around the truly fragile ones, the small ones with tender bones. You should never be caught with your heads in the laps of women.

I don't excuse what some grown Black men do to those who are physically weaker than themselves. The children they are supposed to help raise. The women who beg them for assistance or peace. I only consider the emotional and ancestral riches if we could find a place where we did not expect—demand—Black men to protect, provide, and lead—as if grown Black women were helpless and stupid—while many times, these men suffer themselves.

I'm not talking about the police and the violence they do unto Black men. That's where you're expecting me to go. I'm talking about what happens in our *homes*—the places where my people live. Where little Black boys are made.

I am praying for a time when we don't raise those boys to be stoic, to stop their crying, to learn to be what we require men to be—when manhood in this country is ugly and equals war and cruelty and violence. I want these boys to evolve into kind human beings who can admit they aren't always strong. I want them to be able to cry.

And I don't need a Black man to lead or protect me. I only need him not to be who I'm forced to run or hide from.

⁕⁖⁓

There on my ancestral altar the little boy laughs: my father who is not yet my father. A gorgeous toddler, looking at something off camera that wasn't captured in permanence. His dimple an impression of happiness.

I am aware of what the years brought my family—my mother, sisters, and me—because this child grew into a man. As my father made me with my mother. The two of them formed me, then unbaked me back into clay: I had to re-create myself and shape my own way into something better.

Yet there is some place where I sit with this child. A timeless plot—green, surrounded by flowers—where my daddy would have grown into something better than what we call "manhood," when he fought for a country that would spit in his hopeful face, upon his return from the battlefield.

I send my young father who is not yet my father blessings, as a mother might. I wave at his image, and then I pray for what was possible, in another time: Little Black boy, may you always find happiness. May your hands stay tender and not curl into bludgeons.

28

Lexicon[1]

for my mother

This is the end for you two, though he doesn't see
it or that he'll be dead in four years,
heart just stopping but not this day

when he sits in the armchair
which sags under his will, reads a book.
You speak a simple word to him—

we are leaving for good this time—
but I lose what it is,
so quick to be gone.

Something to indicate that we won't be coming back,
no last chances
like his assuming he can show up at the shelter

or drive further down south
to Grandma's house to collect us.
Or, I get the moment wrong and he goes down

to the basement first, puts on a record

—Rachmaninoff, loud—
walks upstairs, and then he sits down,

opens up his book, ignores you,
stops, cocks his head in the fine, sensitive
way that I continue to adore, ignores you some more,

tries to find blues in that European music.
A paradox,
but that is my father, kind to strangers,

slapping one of us upside our heads
at home, searching for beauty
in everything except his family

or his own reflection,
not bothering to plead with you
like he has the other times,

I'm sorry, baby.
Don't go. Please don't go.
The way a man is supposed to in the best songs.

I want you to toss something hard at him.
I'm scared we will return.
I'm scared we won't return.

I'm so angry with you and I haven't yet learned
how much weaker than a girl a woman can be.
How silly I am to assume you are stronger than he.

How arrogant I am to assume you are not.
The point is that I live, you live,
whether my father's music plays or doesn't play,

and we are driving off in the truck,
Mama,
leaving him turning the pages of his book.

What is that word? Forget about it.
We leave him there.
We left.

29

Blues for Paradise

2018

It is a Friday, and I'm in the theater in the Oklahoma town that I never will call home, waiting to see *Black Panther*. Despite myself, I've gotten caught up in the hype, the year-long publicity campaign for this movie, leading up to its release. It is silly, I think, for so many Black folks to be this excited for an action movie. Yet here I am, wearing my orange wool poncho as protection against the chill of the air conditioner.

I deserve this break. Finally I have finished *The Age of Phillis*, my book of poetry on Phillis Wheatley Peters, the eighteenth-century Black poet. A formerly enslaved woman who lived and died in the eighteenth century, she was taken as an approximately seven-year-old child from her home in the Gambia, the tongue of land running through the middle of Senegal's head.

I'm not finished typing up the notes for this book that I've been writing for fifteen years. At times I have been depressed, wondering if I ever would be done. At others, I have been stricken with grief, because Miss Phillis's era was drenched in the blood of slavery. There is no getting past that.

I am here in this theater for a night of celebration and forgetting.

⁀⁓

1783–1900

It all comes back to a young time. The dawn of childhood or an idyllic, Edenic place. That hankering that many Black folks in American have for Africa, what we call the motherland.

Our people came here enslaved on ships, and there are tales of those young ones. That after they were taken—usually teenagers or children, and no older than twenty to twenty-five—some flung themselves over the railings of those ships to try to swim back home. The open, jagged mouths of sharks awaited them, but those suicidal kids were welcomed in paradise.

There are tales that these young ones walked over that same water—skipping over the heads of those same sharks—to get back to Eden.

There are tales that these young ones lifted themselves into the sky and flew, enmeshed in clouds, to voyage back home.

And their shipmates were left behind in this place called America: not a motherland, not a paradise. The ones left behind labored, and they suffered, but they lived to tell those tales. They were in awe of their determined kindred who had escaped.

Later, when no more room for magic existed, those enslaved Africans existed in logic. They were recorded in the *Book of Negroes* by British officials who had promised freedom for those who fought on the side of King George III.[1] Some of these Africans traveled back to lands like Sierra Leone, where slave ships hugged the shore and anchored. There were many African—yes, *Black*—slave traders willing to sell other Africans—*us*—to European ship owners. The *us* comprised of the many tribes on the right side of the water: Wolof, Igbo, Ibibio, Serer, Asante, and so forth.

On the left side of the water, we became Negro or Black. One people. One nation. But we didn't want to stay in this place where we became *us*. There was too much blood here. The people who had been here already had been murdered or scattered, their land stolen.

And on that land, we had been slaves who worked. And our children did not belong to *us*. And our wives did not belong to *us*. Or our husbands, wives, fathers, sisters, brothers. Only the *idea* of *us* belonged to us, and we tried to keep our traditions. We looked to the East. We directed our eyes toward the place of our dreams. Our repatriation societies collected money, and a small group of *us* sailed back home. They waved at that mythic place on the horizon, where African slave traders still lived.

∾

2018

Black Panther begins with a prologue in Oakland, California, in 1992. Strains of Too Short play as little Black boys play basketball with a milk crate net. The city is an eyesore, pitted with urban blight, as befits a place of sorrow. This is not a motherland. This place was stolen from somebody else.

Then, an apartment. A Black American man is engaged in the selling of guns, the contemporary scourge of Black folks in this country. But no, he isn't American. The moviegoers find out that he is a citizen of Wakanda when he pulls down his lip and shows a blue tattoo. His king and two of the female royal guard appear—the Dora Milaje, bald-headed and arrayed in gold necklaces and red leather garments. They hold spears. I look around the theater, calculating how many have heard of the women warriors of the Dahomey Empire of what would be called Benin, when it was colonized by Europeans.[2]

The Dora Milaje are gorgeous, not as objects of curiosity but as courageous Black women. I, too, have been courageous (sometimes), and so has my mentor and friend, Lucille Clifton, the great Black poet. She wrote that she descended from Dahomey women.[3] The stories of these women were passed down in Miss Lucille's family. They did not forget tradition.

∾

1977

I am living in Durham, North Carolina, where my father teaches college. He is a poet, too, and well-known among the African American community of artists in that city. My mother teaches college as well, but she's not a tenure-track professor like Daddy. Mama is a hardworking woman. Raising her children. Baking bread from yeast. Keeping a garden: she is descended from tenant farmers.

Today is a Saturday, and she is baking devil's food cupcakes. She is baking for Black folks who live outside our home, but still, she is baking for *us*. It is for an African-themed festival, and thus the cupcakes must be chocolate. It would be insulting to bring angel food cupcakes to an African event sponsored by Daddy's artist friends.

Mama is mixing up chocolate frosting. And then she is mixing up plain butter cream, but she will use food coloring to make the butter cream red and green. She will frost the cupcakes and arrange them on a cookie sheet and cover with foil carefully, so that it doesn't stick to the cupcakes. The cupcakes will make up the shape and colors of the map of some unnamed country on the huge continent of Africa.

My parents, my sisters, and I will dress in the garments of African cloth, outfits that my mother sewed on her new Singer machine—so this must be 1977, because Mama didn't buy her sewing machine until that year.

I am scratching at the scalp of this recollection. The color of the cupcakes' frosting: red for the blood of Africa, green for the land of Africa, black for the people of Africa.

I wear braids that fall down my back because my hair is wavy. It will curl up, after I reach puberty. Never mind, my fair-skinned father says. All of *us* are Africans, no matter what we look like. My father is a poet who writes about being a Black man, who writes about aching for an African motherland that he will never see. (Later I will encounter Daddy's FBI file online, from the 1950s, when the federal government surveilled Black artists.[4] That is before Daddy knew Mama, when he was married to his second wife, prowled the Village in New York City, and kicked it with other writers, like James Baldwin—who also was surveilled by the FBI.[5])

At the festival there are vendors selling tiny brass replicas of the ivory Queen Mother pendant masks, the image of the Edo people of Benin. My mother has one of these brass replicas at home. Years later, when I am in my third graduate program—it will take that long for me to succeed—my mother will give me this pendant, and I will pass it on to a White female professor who is battling breast cancer. I will tell her, there is healing power in this talisman of my people.

✦

2018

I'm waiting in vain for a real discussion of slavery in this movie. That as an African who wasn't displaced, the Black Panther, T'Challa, was probably descended from slave traders.

While writing my book on Miss Phillis, I encountered so many horrors that for over a decade I've had recurring nightmares. One dream is about James DeWolf of the wealthy Rhode Island slave-trading family and captain of the slave ship *Polly*.[6] On one of his trips, his sailors reported that there was danger of smallpox among the slaves in the hold below. This was the eighteenth century, and though a century had passed since Onesimus, the enslaved Coromantee servant of Reverend Cotton Mather, had introduced his master to smallpox variolation—what would evolve to inoculation—variolation was still not common among Europeans, though it was among West Africans.[7]

Many Europeans viewed variolation with suspicion; thus most of the crew of the *Polly* probably weren't immune to smallpox, and James DeWolf couldn't have known how many of his human "cargo"—the Africans he was trafficking across the Middle Passage—were immune. Like the African woman his sailors brought to him.

As I absorbed what DeWolf did next, I tried to reassure myself: Don't judge history. I failed.

DeWolf's fear of a deadly disease spreading through that ship took hold of him; that's why he did it. Yet there was no justification for his murder of the woman he suspected of carrying smallpox. He strapped her to a chair and threw her, alive, into the Atlantic Ocean. When sailors from the *Polly* gave testimony in DeWolf's murder trial, they would say that their captain never expressed remorse over killing the African woman. He only expressed regret about losing the chair he'd strapped her in before he threw it into the sea.[8]

⚮

1990

I am back in North Carolina, after having graduated from Talladega College in Alabama. a Black college. I am so lonely here at the University of North Carolina, where I am now enrolled, and where there are only a handful of Black students. This is the first of my three graduate programs.

My friend and I are attending a gathering of the Black Graduate Student Association. She is an officer of the BGSA and well regarded, the first sister in her department. They are giving her full funding; I am taking out student loans to attend this school, and I am jealous of my friend. I wanted to be a writer, so I applied in journalism, though I have no background in the field, and no interest in writing for a newspaper. The semester before, I earned my first C, and later this spring, I will earn my second, pack up my belongings, and leave this lonely White place.

On this evening my friend is talking to another graduate student about the new name for *us*. Our nation within a nation. No longer are we *Black* people, my friend says. We are now *African American*. She doesn't say where nearly thirty million folks voted for this name change. But it is a permanent change, my friend says.

Another young sister pipes up. "The new name makes you feel proud," she says. "I was feeling low today, but then I told myself, 'Girl, lift your head up! You are an African American woman! You come from kings and queens.'"

❧

2018

There are so many beautiful costumes in this movie. Not only red, black, and green, but purple, blue, and orange. White garments decorated with golden embroidery. But I do not suck my teeth over the indiscriminate heritages depicted in these costumes: Zulu, Masai, Igbo, Ndebele, and so many others. It's all right.

And so many pretty people on the screen. So many shades of *us*. A few lighter-skinned people, though they don't get much screen time. Most of the characters are richly dark in Wakanda, the fictional country where the Black Panther is king. T'challa is his name, and he has the swagger to match the rhythms of this moniker. The strength. The broad shoulders that cannot be broken.

There are many women, too: Okoye, the general of Dora Milaje, is coffee colored. So is Nakia, the Black Panther's love interest. They offset the women of his family, who are merely brown: Romonda, his mother, and Shuri, his sister, who handles the beads that resemble real-life African trade beads. Her laboratory is where she practices science, not magic. The room is painted in abstract renderings of the Queen Mother mask. On the trays where she keeps her inventions is a script that resembles Nsibidi, an ancient iconographic script from the area that English/British slave traders—and eventual colonizers—would call Nigeria.[9]

Then, another nearly light-skinned person in the movie. This time, a major character, and the villain. Erik Killmonger, who played basketball in that tattered park in Oakland, back in 1992. The nephew of T'Challa's father. A Black American of noble African blood who wears marks all over his body, though these represent abominations. They do not name his tribe, but instead mark his taking of lives.

The adult Killmonger travels with a White man—the first hint at his betrayal—to a museum in London. A place where stolen artifacts of Africans are kept on display. Among others, there is the Queen

Mother mask of Benin.

As a Black American, it is only right that Killmonger stands in relief against these glass display cases. He is a descendant of slaves. He is an artifact of stolen blood, and since he is not truly Wakandan, he does not respect tradition. He uses fire to destroy. He does not respect his elders. He uses violence toward women. I hate him, this abomination, this monster.

~≈~

2012

It is late spring—May—and I have made the sixteen-hour journey to West Africa. (Or eighteen or twenty. Something like that.) I fly from my home in Oklahoma, where I teach at the state's flagship university, to Washington, DC. Then from there to Senegal.

All this, to do research on my book of poetry about Phillis Wheatley Peters. She wrote a grieving poem about this land in "To the Right Honorable William, Earl of Dartmouth":

Should you, my lord, while you peruse my song,
  Wonder from whence my love of Freedom sprung,
  Whence flow these wishes for the common good,
  By feeling hearts alone best understood,
  I, young in life, by seeming cruel fate
  Was snatch'd from Afric's fancy'd happy seat:
  What pangs excruciating must molest,
  What sorrows labour in my parent's breast?[10]

I fly into Léopold Sédar Senghor International Airport, named for the Négritude-era poet and the first president of Senegal. Two years later I will read an article about President Senghor's visit to New York in the 1970s, in which Senghor names my father, the poet Lance Jeffers.[11] Senghor says that he admired Black poets, but the poetry of White Americans, not so much. I will claim this connection as a sign.

I arrive in Senegal in the dark: when I look out the window of the place, hoping to spot the edge of the coast, there is nothing to see. My imagination cannot not help me. How can you imagine what is only in your blood?

My tour leader is an expatriate American, Ibrahim, who called me days before. In a few months, when I marry Khalil,[12] the beautiful man who is one of my two younger tour guides, Ibrahim will become my brother-in-law. His name was something else, before he changed it and married into Khalil's family.

"My sister, you are in for a wonderful experience," Ibrahim exclaimed. "You will connect with your people in a way you've never known."

During my trip, I will discover that Ibrahim has not only one Senegalese wife, but two.

"I'm not coming for all that," I said. "I don't even know how I feel about Africa. I'm still mad about the slave trade. I'm only here to research my book."

There was a chilling on the other end of the phone, and I speculated that I had violated one of Ibrahim's rules. I'm supposed to think about Africa as home. I'm not playing my part.

Ibrahim is not there inside the airport to collect me; he waits for me in the van. Another Senegalese guide, Sadick,[13] meets me after I have made it through customs. Outside, the air is balmy and smells of food and urine. We pass a man with no legs, who is begging for money. Sadick keeps going, but I want to stop and give the man money.

"I haven't yet changed my dollars," I say. "Can you give him something? I can pay you back."

"No, my sister," Sadick says. "I don't have any money, but you can get him next time. I can tell that you have a good heart."

In hours, he walks with me through the House of Slaves on Gorée Island. I stand in the corner and weep in the room where the women were kept in the days before they were sold to slave ships, before they passed through the Door of No Return. I stand in that room and learn that other Senegalese women—*signares*—slept with White traders and bought and sold Africans, too.

Sadick pats my shoulder. "Don't cry, my sister," he says. "You are home now. It is okay."

Bougainvillea and graffiti wound the walls of the House of Slaves. Beyond the Door of No Return, a view of the sea, generously blue. Hungry. Our guide lectures in a monotone, describing the breasts of the young kidnapped women: if high, then chosen for "favor" by slave-trading white men before demanding "a good value" on the market. Those with fallen breasts were left in peace but "reduced in price." I stand in another place—in the corner—and cover my face with my hands.

The history is that the European traders lived in this apartment above the Slave House and seasoned their food with misery. On the wall there are belts of African currency but no explanation. Who did it buy? Who was sold? Who was taken over by reconciliation? And what was the season? And the name of that ship? And the names of the White men? And the names of the Africans?

The island's Catholic church was founded by the European traders so they could bless themselves and their ships. **After leaving the Slave House,** I genuflect and dip my fingers in the huge shell font. Outside the church, I buy a rosary for my mother, who believes in prayers inked in bone. I buy nothing for myself, only for Mama who taught me that God is everywhere. In this church. In a three-foot shelf cradling a five-foot body. In the shit, piss, vomit of history.

Outside, when a woman pushes her trinkets close to my face—asking in Wolof that I purchase them—I want to strike her. I tell her in English—I understand a bit of Wolof but cannot speak it—that I want no souvenirs from this horrible place. She understands me and rolls her eyes to the other women huddled with her. Moments pass as I remember my manners—I don't want to appear as the ugly American—then I slip off my embroidered pink shoes, reaching for the pair of sneakers in my backpack. I offer the woman the pink shoes, and she takes them, suddenly friendly. I tell her I know my shoes aren't new, but I'd be so grateful if she would wear them sometimes, so I can walk this earth again in my absence. I hear her say "Teranga," a word that refers to Senegalese hospitality, which is generous to a fault. She is complimenting me; it feels like a genuine kindness.

At lunch, a curious hunger: I'm revolted by the flies lighting on my *yassa poisson*, but I keep eating. Around my table the obligatory Afrocentric noise: Black Americans speaking in their newly acquired, broken Wolof, expressing their debt to Africa. I roll my eyes: Why do I, the descendant of the stolen and sold, owe this continent anything?

Afterward, a walk along the beach of Gorée. I hear screams: a swimming boy has dipped three times, the number of death. Two other boys dive after him. They stay gone so long that I start to moan: *Oh no no no no no oh God oh please—*

All three boys rise and laugh in pleasure, their wondrous teeth bright and faithful. I give thanks and I give thanks and I give thanks. Oh, Lord, Black children have been saved today.

That evening, Khalil makes me tea outside the door of my seaside hotel. (He has not been with us at Gorée, but was visiting his mother.) When this gorgeous, coffee-colored person had invited himself to see me that night, I thought he was a young boy of nineteen or twenty, who would try to make a move. When I meet him that night, he walks outside the lobby and settles us outside the front door. We are treated to a partial view of the beach and the water. Other dark men sit a distance away; one smiles as he moves his motorcycle to provide us an unobscured view. The men exchange knowing glances as Khalil heats water on a charcoal brazier, and offer greetings with him, first in Wolof and then in French. They nod approvingly when I sit down.

I realize I'm in trouble when Khalil hands me his driver's license, after I insist that he is way too young for me. I am old enough to be his mother, but when I spot the date on the license, I see that he is twelve years younger than I am. A little over a decade, but I understand I'm dealing with a grown man now. Our age difference is the same as between Janie Crawford and Teacake in *Their Eyes Were Watching God*—and we know what happened there.

"It doesn't matter. I'm too old for you," I insist. "You need a younger woman."

I pat his hand in a "big sister" manner, and he places his own on top, then rubs his thumb over my skin. Instantly, I want him inside me. If it weren't for the men sitting a few feet away, I don't know how scandalously I might behave. I think of what my mother used to say, that the women in our family have always been hot-blooded, going back to Great-Grandma Mandy.

I slip my hand from his, telling him his charm is dangerous. He laughs, and I wonder if, despite his gentlemanly manner, he can read my naughty mind. As I sip my *ataya*, I know I won't be sleeping. This stuff is full of caffeine, and this pretty man has awoken me in places I'm embarrassed to acknowledge.

I tell myself that Khalil is just a man, and I've been celibate for far too long, but something about him makes me drop my guard. I find myself confiding how humiliated I was when the toothless man Ibrahim paid to guide us through the House of Slaves dungeon looked at me every time he spoke about the *signares*, the biracial African mistresses of the European slave traders.[14] I believe I'd seen contempt in the guide's face when he looked at me, though that might have been my imagination.

"Oh, Honorée, it is all right," Khalil says. "You will travel to Saint-Louis soon, and you will feel very comfortable. That is where the *signares* lived. It is on the Petit Côte, and there will be many mulattos like you."

I erupt into laughter. "Khalil! We don't say 'mulatto' anymore! That is a rude term. We say 'biracial' now."

"Oh, I am sorry." He flashes his entrancing smile. "Forgive me, Honorée."

"And both of my parents are African American. Look"—I offer my arm as proof—"see how dark I am?"

Khalil tilts his head, offering an amused smile. "You are not dark to me. Are you sure you are not a mulatto? You look like one."

"Yes, I'm sure!"

"Okay."

He offers more *ataya*, and I accept.

I will write a poem about this night. I will wonder, did I really fall in love with Khalil for a simple domestic act, watching him pour *ataya*—muscularly strong green tea—from one glass cup to another? Because in a week, when I travel back to the States, I will run up horrible phone bills calling Khalil. Two weeks after that, when Khalil asks me to marry him, insisting that we cannot live together the way I have offered, I will say yes. He is a Muslim, he'll remind me. Proper Muslims don't live together unless they are married. What would he say to his mother? When we have our religious and civil ceremonies, it will be in London, where Khalil will go to graduate school. We will only be married three and a half years, but the memory of our first, chaste night on the beach will remain tender to me.

2018

There are so many African Americans in this theater to see *Black Panther*, more than I've ever thought lived in Norman, Oklahoma. Probably every single one of us here is descended from the Middle Passage. When the screen goes dark, I get up to leave the theater, assuming everyone else just wants to read the credits. But at the entryway a Black woman lingers.

"It's not over yet," she says.

I stop beside her, and there is the scene of T'challa wearing a red-toned scarf draped across his body. He is flanked by three richly hued African women: his beloved, his general, and another soldier of the Dora Milaje.

The sister beside me breathes praises to God, and I want to laugh at her: This movie is based upon a cartoon superhero. But then I begin crying, thinking of Khalil, who is no longer my husband. I think of Senegal, where we met, and how sometimes, moments in my kitchen make me wish I could cook for him again.

I think of my father, who always wanted to journey to Africa but never did. Daddy missed a place that never truly existed, and I miss that place, too. And I am longing for Wakanda. I am longing for home.

30

Eighteenth-Century Illustration of a Slave Trader's Free, Mixed-Race Mistress, Standing with Her Child Under an Umbrella Held by an Enslaved African Woman

GORÉE ISLAND MUSEUM, SENEGAL

May 23, 2012

Even now, after crouching
   in the tiniest space of the Slave House,
      after translating from French
       the meaning of
       Cellule de Récalcitrants—
a place nearly the size
of a coffin, where they locked
   the ones who would not
      get in line—
       even after weeping
      over two centuries' losses,
   after tasting ancient vomit
and my survivor's guilt—
   the drawing of this languorous
      woman tricks me to comfort.
      Her dusky toddler pulls
   from her, the mother
who fans her colonized beauty.

Curls like my own peek
   from her headcloth, beckoning:
      White man, look at me.
         In this image, there is no rain.
      The umbrella that the other, unfree
woman—*son esclave*—
raises will protect
   the mistress's
      skin, securing her privilege
         from darkening fates—
      chains and the cruel feet of birds.
      I have squared sadness in a mother's land.
For the sister holding
   the umbrella and who
      cannot leave this page.
         For her owner,
         dodging the sun: a woman
   my own color,
not even fair enough to pass.
   The fingers of commerce touch her:
      Wolof, Français, Métis,
         all kinsmen of some kind.
      This is how it happened:
   Some lullabies are sins.
How she willingly showed her teeth,
   bore the weight of a White man,
      accepted his gift of a human
         being, accepted
      increasingly pale,
   forgetful children. We women
sometimes bend to accommodate
   and sometimes that is blameless—
      but some crimes
         must be sung.

VI

MISBEHAVING WOMEN

"All my life I had to fight."

—ALICE WALKER, *The Color Purple*

Honorée, if you can't be good, then be good at it.

—MAMA'S SAYINGS

31

A Brief Note Concerning Another Late Brother-Friend Who Led Me to This Discussion of the Black Woman as Soul Sister Shapeshifter in These United States

I will start with a message from an ancestor, another brother-friend who was tender to me: the poet-scholar Vincent Woodard.

When we met, Vincent was a graduate student and I had just defended my thesis at the University of Alabama; I would officially graduate two months later. It was June 1996; we were poets, and in our twenties. We had come to Cave Canem, a workshop-retreat for Black poets, located in a former monastery in the Catskills. Vincent was Queer, gender-fluid, unabashed, and vocally devoted to the ancestors. I loved him instantly, and our friendship was kept alive by many expensive long-distance phone calls, for unlimited minutes on smartphones were not available back then.

I will admit—with abundant shame—that being friends with me required too much heavy lifting on Vincent's part. I was completely ignorant about gender fluidity, and at the time I wasn't very interested in finding out what I didn't know. I continued to have romantic relations with Black men who used slurs against Queer people; when they voiced offensive words or opinions about Queer people, I'd give weak objections.

I thought that if I'd just ignore my conscience and my professed politics, sooner or later I'd find my very own straight, benevolent patriarch to order me around and make me happy.

I can only praise God that I'm no longer so stupid and treacherous.

⁓

It took me years of intensive reading—and rereading of texts I'd already encountered—and then more time to create an intellectual scaffolding for my own ideas. Finally I reached a (hopefully) greater understanding—a reconciliation—and arrived at a personal theory: The performance of many Black women/femmes constitutes improvisation, a form of shapeshifting.

As a Black woman writer who has written short fiction that could be categorized as speculative, I am a devotee of Octavia Butler, and her shapeshifting novel *Wildseed* is a favorite of mine. And as a blues poet, I know that the blues is an example of African American improvisation. Finally, as a weird, cishet Black women whose rebellious ways have brought constant challenges to my womanhood, the notion of improvisation has been on my dome for at least twenty years.

But to be randomly googling my late friend Vincent and happen upon his writing on shapeshifting? To me, that was more than a coincidence.

I found it interesting—more than that, *spooky*—that I'd been grappling with the notion of Black women/femmes' gender performance as improvisation before encountering (online) Vincent's unpublished dissertation from the University of Texas at Austin, "The Shapeshifter Figure: A New Cartography of Sex and Gender Formation Within Radical Black Antebellum Culture."[1]

It was 2023, and I'd come up with a name to describe Black women's mortal improvisation—that is, the changing of our behavior in public and private spheres, to survive—"Soul Sister Shapeshifter." I thought, was this too much? Too bold or too vintage sounding?

And then I came upon Vincent's words.

⁓

Throughout US history, a Black woman's improvisation has been a necessary survival strategy. She never knew what the courtroom or the town crier would bring.

Our shapeshifting has attracted criticism: We aren't "real women." We should be weak and wait for someone—a man—to help. Leaving aside the question of what truly is real—like colonial law, gender remains a morphing construct—I'm preoccupied with the gifts that we Black women seem to find. Even when somebody plops shit into our open hands, there is a possibility. We have known we were holding filth; we have accepted that it was wrong—but after we cried over this outrage, we have had to adapt, or we and our children would die.

But when we are called ugly, weird, unfeminine, the possibility in those cruel labels can be found in shapeshifting *away* from what this nation deems womanhood. I'm not only concerned with cisgender, heterosexual women, because I'm always thinking of my lesbian and trans sisters, the kinship and survival strategies we share. What "woman" is *supposed* to be in this country is what a Black woman has never been. Did the Atlantic change us, when we came across that water?[2] Or were we already different because of our African cultures? I'll never know, but I have searched my entire life for an identity that respects and embraces me—time and again, however, I've been labeled an odd-shaped thing.

I was born of a weird woman: Mama, who could be loud and soft-spoken, sexy and coy, angry and calm, ladylike and raucous. A woman of Christian faith who dreamed in hoodoo messages. An explorer of the formal archives who kept oral history safe through storytelling. Who read the Black vernacular of Hurston and the formal French of Colette, and fully understood both. Mama shaped and unshaped herself to meet the moment. She taught me to do the same.

Regardless of what so many of my African American kindred insist, we cannot let go of history. All roads lead back to the ancestors. They continue to lead me—and this is what they say:

To begin with, Black women weren't free.

To add injury to that initial insult, the laws and customary rules for us have relentlessly morphed, sometimes every few years, sometimes within a matter of months, and Black women have learned to improvise to keep pace.

First, unfreedom for Black folks lasted a few years. Then it lasted a lifetime.

First, baptism into Christianity made Black folks free. Then it didn't.

First, a White father could free his biracial child by a Black woman. Then he could not.

Maybe that's why Toni Morrison considered Black women the original modernists, because of our talent for meeting challenges.[3] Modernism has meant not just reacting to these challenges but *anticipating* what oppressive forces would bring.[4] Like physically vulnerable tricksters in a folktale come to life, Black women have had few material weapons—few guns, few knifes, smaller muscles, no protection from the law—but they've had their intellects and their spirituality. Somehow, their descendants remain.

⟨✤⟩

I remain.

I am still alive, because my women ancestors taught me to improvise—to shapeshift.

This is what Vincent taught me, reaching from his ancestral plane. He was my hoodoo kindred, guiding his two-headed sister. Me, the descendant of root-working Southern Black women who were not always kind, but utterly powerful. Me, the woman who has (finally) acknowledged that I am a seer. Now I understand what Vincent's spirit was saying to me.

Honor the ancestors, Vincent told me. Bless your line and tell your truth: that you have moved how you should. That you have changed out of need.

32

In Search of Our Mothers' Handles

When I tell you that I learned from my mother about the real lives that informed Southern Black history, will you believe me? I can confirm that there is existing documentation for Mama's birthplace and date: a 1940 Eatonton/Putnam County census report estimates her birth year as around 1934. (Actually, she was born in 1933.) The names of her parents, Charlie Sr. and Florence James, are on that census.

But I hesitate to keep going, in this time of fact checking. For how can I prove that my life took place?

In the last days of her life, Mama's memory was clouded by early dementia. Again, you'll have to take my word for that, although there are living relatives who can confirm her declining health—but *will* they? In many Black families, talking about inside business is viewed as forbidden.

So I will give you a hypothetical history, which I suspect is the history of many Black women. I will go back forty-five years and come forward to the present. I'll tell you what might be in my imagination—or what might be the truth sipping slowly at my blood.

~~~

It is a year in the 1970s.

There is a Black woman's voice, raised and contemptuous—no longer a harmonious drawl—at a doctor's office or a store at the new shopping mall where that Black woman lives, in Durham, North Carolina—the midsize city where she lives with her husband and three daughters.

Somebody will call that Black woman Trellie instead of her married name, Mrs. Jeffers. If that transgressing somebody is Black, she'll remind them of their manners: she is not their friend, and they do not know her. She'll put on her schoolteacher's voice, but there is love and warmth rippling under the surface of scolding. A nudging toward African American cultural lessons: "You know better," Mrs. Jeffers will say. Usually the other Black person will instantly self-correct, with an apology and perhaps a respectful dip of the head.

But if that person who doesn't use an honorific happens to be White? Mrs. Jeffers's alto voice will pitch very close to shouting. Her contempt will coalesce into speech. She'll correct that White person: "I am Mrs. Jeffers to you, and we are not social equals." If they have the nerve to try to exchange words with Mrs. Jeffers, to tell her they didn't have to put a handle on her name—there will be trouble. She'll begin to lecture the White clerk—or nurse or doctor—about the historic disrespect of Black people. She'll take that White person all the way back to Alex Haley's *Roots* and remind them how other Whites have demeaned and oppressed an entire race of people.

As Mrs. Jeffers stands there, her voice will climb, while the air in the room seems to be whispering, "What on earth is the big deal? What is wrong with this loud Black woman?"

In the car ride back home, Mrs. Jeffers will sputter even more and shout.

"These White folks don't have any manners," she'll say.

Sometimes, she'll use another word for "White folks" but I'm too polite to mention that word here. Beside her, Mrs. Jeffers's youngest daughter will cringe and agree with the air in the room they just left: Why is her mother so upset? What is the power in an honorific, or—as her relatives said down south—in a handle on a name?

༺❧༻

I was about nine or ten. My middle sister Sisi, some neighborhood kids, and I had only recently integrated the pool on the White side of Eatonton, Georgia. As with many southern towns, segregation was no longer legal in the 1970s, but still de facto custom. That summer Sisi had tired of the postage-stamp-size pool at the public park on the Black side of town. It was far more convenient, only a short walking distance from the back of Grandma Florence's house on Concord Avenue. Entry to the pool was free, but it wasn't even as large as Grandma's living room, with no space for swimming—or even to move around. Sisi decided that we should all walk to the "White" pool on the other side of town.

As a former Black nationalist—or maybe, just a currently rowdy woman—Mama encouraged our youthful activism by giving Sisi ten dollars to pay for the children whose parents wouldn't have the fifty cents entry fee. Grandma Florence was hysterical with terror, however. She invoked the threat of the Ku Klux Klan—she was close to tears— but Mama laughed at her and told us children to head on out.

Initially there was resistance from the White lifeguard who stood at the entry turnstile, until Sisi haughtily declared that if he kept us from paying and entering, he would be breaking the law. I remain shocked that he surrendered to our group of Black children so easily. There was no fuss or cursing or calling the police—but as we Black children jumped into the pool, the White children scrambled out.

After a few subsequent visits to that pool, though, our dark presence was no longer an outrage. Instead of immediately exiting the pool, the White children stayed, and a wary détente ensued.

One afternoon a blond girl of about eleven or twelve approached me, asking if I was related to a "colored lady named Florence." I was used to this question from other Black folks, as it was constantly remarked upon how I "favored" my grandmother. Grandma's elderly friends always used "colored" instead of "Black" as well. (Calling somebody Black was considered an insult in the deep country in the 1970s.)

"Yes, I am Mrs. James's granddaughter," I said.

"I knew it! You look just like Florence," the blond girl said.

As the conversation continued, the girl kept calling my elderly grandmother by her first name. Aware that I was still considered an invader—or at the very least, a guest—in this pool on the White side of town, I stayed calm. Instead of telling the girl that she should know better than to call an older Black lady by her first name, I kept calling Grandma "Mrs. James." I hoped the girl would take the hint, but she never did, even urging me, "Tell Florence that Miss Sally said 'hey'!"

Several moments passed before I understood that this blond girl was referring to herself as "Miss"—a social superior—while still refusing to respect my grandmother, a senior citizen.

That day at the pool was when I learned that Grandma had once worked as a maid. It took several years for me to discuss that incident with Mama. Until I broached the subject, she never discussed the issue of domestic work, but I didn't need to ask why. Although I'd been raised to respect my elders, I also understood that my mother was an interloper too. Her transgression had been invading the Black middle class of Durham, North Carolina, where with rare exception, all the wives were light-skinned, no matter the shades of their husbands.

Mama had shame about those class hierarchies. It was one thing for her to tell funny stories about working as "a babysitter"—she never used the term *nanny*—for a Jewish family during her summers off from Spelman College. The way she framed it, she was treated as a social equal by her employers, for they knew that she was a college girl and headed for something better. But when questioned about true domestic work—not labor done in service for a better, educated future on layaway—Mama became angry about the way that Grandma was viewed. Imagine a fully grown woman past the age of seventy calling a little girl "Miss," like she was a British servant in that show my father had loved, *Upstairs Downstairs* on Masterpiece Theatre.

It takes a while for a daughter to see in her mother the woman the daughter might become, or even acknowledge that womanhood is possible. It seems so far away when you are a little girl, a daughter who doesn't understand that one day your smooth skin will begin to wrinkle. You are not capable of miracles. You cannot change anyone's idea of womanhood. You can only imagine yourself.

Buried underneath this story is the fact that no daughter ever thinks—or wants to admit—that she, too, will become a grown, disrespected Black woman in America. Like many daughters of the past, she will relive small pieces of history.

I reside in womanhood now, clutching my mother's wisdom and my daughter's duty, but I never wanted to have anger and obsessions. Here I am, a tender of history, but this is not what I dreamed of, this constant reaching back.

I see that those moments have meaning, though, not only for protecting ancestral lore but, unfortunately, for my own life.

⁘

Anyway.

Mrs. Jeffers's daughter might have become a college teacher—*Professor* Jeffers—who moves to Norman, Oklahoma, in 2002.

Yes, let's say that.

Born in 1967, Professor Jeffers will research the history of Norman, a former sundown town—African Americans were only allowed in the town during daylight. She will imagine what her already imaginary life would have been. How, in the past, she'd have to watch the sky for darkening, to make sure she wouldn't be caught on the wrong side of time.

After living a decade in Norman, Professor Jeffers will find a favorite grocery store, filled with natural foods and friendly young White kids who smile at her. There is peace in this formerly historically troubled place. Except there is a young White woman who works at the store, who will insist on calling Professor Jeffers "girlfriend."

The older Black woman will seek all sorts of strategies to alert this young White woman that it is not appropriate to call someone old enough to be your mother "girlfriend." And they aren't friends: they only see each other at the store. Professor Jeffers will begin to refer to herself as "Miss Lady," a (hopefully) polite nickname that catches on with everyone else working at the store, everyone besides this young

White woman who tends the produce section.

Until one day—finally—Professor Jeffers informs the young woman that it isn't appropriate for her to call her girlfriend. "I'm an educated woman. I teach at the university, and I'm too old to be your girlfriend. I'm over forty."

Then the young White woman begins to justify why it is okay for her to set aside honorifics. "I'm educated, too," she said, explaining that she is a freshman in college.

The professor proceeds to give a lecture on racism in America. That, while White people are automatically given respect, nobody these days White seems to want to call a Black person "Mr." or "Mrs."

The young White woman turns pink, and abruptly she turns and leaves the produce section. But Professor Jeffers doesn't look around her, frightened at how she'll be perceived by others. She feels powerful and full of righteousness. After she pays for her groceries, walks outside, and settles behind the wheel of her car, she congratulates herself. At least she hasn't shouted at the young white woman. And besides, look: There is the sun, a sanctuary on the horizon.

33

Imaginary Letter to the White Lady Professor Who Might Have Extended an Invitation to Read Poetry at Their Prestigious University

Dear Professor _____,

Thank you so much for your email. Please forgive my directness in the words below; I sincerely beg pardon if I am not as gracious as I would hope to be. The semester is in full swing, and I'm teaching; in addition, I'm (always) on book deadline.

Let me start with your appalling lack of home training in addressing by first name an accomplished Black woman—who you don't know and have never met—who has clawed her way up the professional ladder and walked over metaphorical hot coals to become the first Black full professor in the history of her English department at her Research I institution.

I am not "the one" or "the two"—or any number you can count through infinity. You might not know what that means, but every Black woman who has reached a certain professional level in her field remembers the small and large humiliations that she has had to swallow. The way she has been underpaid and assured that this is all she deserves. The way that her colleagues assume—sometimes out loud, in her face—that she is a "diversity hire," an unqualified racial token, instead of someone who had to work like a Hurstonian mule to achieve success.

Further, we Black folks don't automatically assume familiarity in my community. You and I are not friends—again, I don't even know you— and you are seeking something from me, which is my presence on your campus. So please keep your familiarity to yourself, until I have indicated that we have moved past formality.

Now that I have made that point clear to (and perhaps past) the brink of obnoxiousness, let me continue.

I have looked up your university online, and to my shock, I discovered that the endowment of this university is several billion dollars. Thus I'm flabbergasted that the honorarium you offered me to visit your campus is 99.9 percent less than my asking fee. I'm bewildered that, after I sent you information regarding my fee, you wrote me back by telling me that I am not "within the budget."

Did you think that I'd feel guilty? I do not.

Did you think I'd change my mind and take this incredibly insulting low fee? I will not.

Did you think I would care about your budget? I do not. The same way that the carriers of my car note, and electric, water, internet, phone, gas, and mortgage services don't care about my financial situation—my budget, as it were—when they send me monthly bills. They just want their money, like I want mine.

Let's talk about what I do.

I conduct research on and write about African American history and culture. This work is emotionally taxing. It takes a toll on my spirit, and sometimes my physical health. Unless I'm on book tour, I save my energy for teaching and writing. When do make campus appearances, invariably there are students—or even faculty members—who want to know "how we heal America." They ask this question because of the nature of my work. However, most of the students and faculty in these university audiences are White, and they don't seem to grasp that the wound they're inquiring about is my own wound.

I am the Black person in America.

I am the one in ancestral and contemporary pain, and my Black kindred are in this pain, too.

The wounds that my people and I carry are not self-inflicted. They are wounds that White people—perhaps your very blood kin—inflicted upon us during slavery, in the time of Black Codes and Jim Crow, and even today. But no one in these nearly all-White audiences offers specific ways to heal my pain. They do not ask, "Professor Jeffers"—not Honorée—"what can we do to make this situation better for you and your people?"

These audiences don't give a good goddamn about me and my community. They are only paying me so that I will pretend that everyone White in that audience is just as vulnerable and injured as my Black kindred and I are.

But let me tell you that these days, I'm fresh out of chocolate breast milk.

In the past, I went along with this racial charade. But after these presentations, I'd be exhausted and grief-stricken and demoralized. The reason I would tax my spirit was that I needed that little bit of money I was being paid, to help build the Black generational wealth that your White ancestors denied mine.

These days, if I don't receive an offer for what I have deemed my worth—not what you decide is my worth—I am not about to marshal my courage and hide my social anxiety, get on a plane to fly to your town, make polite, sparkling conversation with the graduate student or faculty member you have sent to retrieve me from the airport—or pay for my own taxi to the venue—and deal with hundreds of White people who want me to act like I'm over American history, when I'm not.

And before you tell me that your European family did not emigrate to the United States until the late nineteenth century, so you have no ancestral debt for slavery, I will remind you of the Scramble for Africa beginning in 1885, when European nations carved up the African continent—and White imperialism, settler colonialism, oppression, and genocide inflicted on other African peoples ensued. I'm sure your ancestors came from at least one of those European nations.

Finally, please know that I do believe in cultural tithing. I have presented (and will continue to present) free or deeply discounted lectures to bookstores, public libraries, historical societies, and nonprofit and literary organizations that benefit underserved communities.

Unfortunately, your invitation to your incredibly rich-yet-cheap university does not fall into any of the above categories. I'm so very sorry.

Warmest regards,

Professor H. F. Jeffers

34

Blues for the Sanctuary

1.

In 1976 I announced to everyone who would listen at Fayetteville Elementary School in Durham, North Carolina—students as well as teachers—that there was no god. Not only was I self-righteous, but that probably was the moment that I claimed my enduring logic and critical thinking skills. My announcement resulted in a hoopla at my 99.999% African American school, an uproar much like the one that I patiently (and with pity, I thought) explained to my classmates that there was no Santa Claus. This was why some folks received great gifts on Christmas day, and others (including me) received the 1970s equivalent of a lump of coal in their stockings.

I was in fourth grade, smart, and the child of well-known activists in the Black community; my parents had taken on racism in the local school system and earned renown in our community. I believe this is why my teachers—also Black—tolerated my eccentricity, but only to a point.

Women teachers would take me aside and lovingly yet sternly debate me. Who created the earth and the first people? they asked. Sure, there had been a Big Bang—they were willing to give me that, when I presented my youthful research—but who had caused that Bang? I had anticipated debates, and I was ready with counterarguments: What about Cain and Abel in the Bible? What kind of sense did that scenario make? Why would God show favoritism to Abel because he offered God meat, and Cain offered fruits and vegetables? This was clearly some sort of story somebody else had made up.

The teachers presented new counters to my counterarguments, which turned personal: How did I get here, if there was no God?

"My parents." I didn't get into specifics. I wasn't that courageous. I had learned that, outside of my nuclear family, nobody wanted a little girl talking about sex.

"And how did they get here?"

"*Their* parents."

Soon they tired of me and sent me back to the lunch table, or wherever they had called me from.

There was never a time—not once—when I considered informing any of these God-fearing Black women about the agony I was experiencing at the hands of my father, the head of my family, according to the biblical designation. I knew enough that this kind of information would get Daddy in trouble for what he was doing. Even more, I was nearing contempt for anyone who believed in religious fairy tales. I was afraid I'd stub my toe on downright hatred if any one of these women told me to just pray on it, and give it to God.

My father didn't give me the idea not to believe in a higher power, only the word: *atheist*. A man like my father validated that absence. If there was a sweet, merciful God, how could He/She/They have created somebody I despised as much as my lowdown, abusive daddy? How could I be living in the personal inferno that was 2608 East Weaver Street in Durham, North Carolina?

Nights were horrible. I'd lie in my bed, afraid to go to sleep lest I hear Daddy's daunting footsteps coming up the steps. The days were nearly as bad, for he had the most changeable moods of anyone I'd known—including my grandmother Florence, and that is saying something.

In public, Daddy was charming and sweet, and everybody Black in Durham seemed to love him. Women would weep when he read his poetry at African American community gatherings to benefit the community. Men would call him "brother." At home, if Daddy was in a cranky mood, nothing could soothe him. If he came back home from the university in Raleigh where he taught after he'd been chastised by his department chairperson, surely everyone in that house on Weaver Street would be punished.

(At this writing, nearly fifty years have passed since my daddy has taught at North Carolina State University, and nearly forty years since he's died, and I still remember the name of my father's White male chairperson. I hated that man so much, and until I knew better, I blamed him for my father's behavior. But even when you thought Daddy was having a good day, he could flip on you: If you forgot to say good morning, he would launch into a rage.)

I found no comfort in God, unlike my mother, who had joined St. Joseph African Methodist Episcopal in Durham. That all-powerful being did not exist to me. I knew He didn't, because I had called out to Him on those nights when my father stalked the house, and eventually abused either me or one of my sisters. There was no sign from above.

I can't recall whether I prayed, but I was a little girl. There shouldn't have been adult rules for faithfulness for children. Little ones deserve to be saved, whether or not we give our problems to the Lord.

2.

The first time I was intimately abused by a non-family member, I was seventeen, a sophomore at Clark College, and happy to be in what I thought was an exclusive, committed relationship with a young man . My "boyfriend" (who I later found out did not consider himself my boyfriend) decided he wanted to have sex that night. We'd slept together several times, and though he was a horrible lover who could barely forestall his orgasm for all of ten seconds (if that), I'd always been willing. My orgasm never seemed important to him, but I liked the cuddling before and afterward.

That night was different, though. I'm not sure why. Even memories of rape can be fuzzy, but I do know I fought him until he slapped me very hard, and then proceeded. Afterward, I was dizzy, or maybe numb. I was surprised, too. Here I'd tolerated bad sex already, but now I realized that it could get worse. My boyfriend—no, *not* my boyfriend—ridiculed me for "pretending" to be upset. I took him back to where he lived in an apartment with his mother—he'd threatened me, saying I didn't want to know what else would happen if I forced him to take public transportation or call one of his friends to pick him up. And he was right. I didn't want to know.

Unfortunately, despite what I believe to be my immense creative talents, I don't have many lyrical terms to describe that night. Only that this dude had raped me, after hitting me so hard that I temporarily lost consciousness. After he raped me, he made me drive him way out on the interstate in the dark and drop him off at his place. When I returned to the apartment that I shared with my sister Sisi—she had been asleep while all this happened—I rocked myself into soothing.

When I saw my rapist on campus a few days later, he waved at me as if I was an acquaintance who hadn't seen him naked several times. He never thanked me for not ruining his future by calling the police on him; I'm sure he never even believed I had that power. I wondered: Is that what being a god feels like?

I continued to be an atheist, though I'd learned to keep that identity to myself. Black folks could turn nearly violent if you dared to challenge the existence of God, like that preacher who hit the male student in Ernest Gaines's story "The Sky Is Gray."[1] If you talked to the wrong African American about your belief in the absence of God, there could be shouting. Or worse, you could receive the same contemptuous dismissal—devoid of any compassion—given to the crack addicts that had begun to populate the streets of Southwest and West End Atlanta, where my mother, middle sister, and I had lived, after leaving Durham and my daddy.

Those poor addicts: their lips whitened by chemicals and prepared to spill out any lie. Their readiness to pleasure any part of someone's body to gain the five dollars to buy a vial of crack.

Four days before my eighteenth birthday, my father died. That might have been enough to convince me to change my mind about God: My tormenter was finally dead.

To my surprise, a Black priest showed up at my atheist father's funeral, a man named Father Bruce. He talked about how he'd spoken to Daddy the day before he died, that Daddy had wanted to give his life to God. I sat near the front of the Lincoln Cemetery Chapel and huffed. What kind of religious trickery was this? I was wisely stubborn.

It wasn't until I was sitting in the chapel at Clark College (now Clark Atlanta University) during mandatory chapel that I finally acknowledged the presence of God in my own life. The choir was singing something rousing that had everybody clapping their hands. Some were on their feet, swaying. Bored, I looked toward the window, where a light was doggedly shining.

I felt something shock me, and I shifted in my seat. Then an immeasurable joy—that's all I can say—entered my body. Instantly, I accepted that this was God, which confused me: Where had God been all these years?

I wasn't ecstatic, though; instead, I was cranky. Dammit, I'd been wrong, and now I'd look like a fool, changing my mind. I thought of that proverb of my country grandmother: "Don't shout 'til you get happy." That was supposed to be about catching the Holy Spirit in church, but in this case, I took it to mean that I should have kept my atheism to myself.

In my dramatic way, it wasn't enough to simply acknowledge the presence of a higher power. I had to receive the full parcel: I decided that I was going to become a nun, like Julian of Norwich, who I was studying in my English literature class. So naturally, I had to convert to Catholicism. The problem was that I was AME Methodist—we were redundant down South in our religious terms—like my mother. Even though I didn't believe in God as a child, I got dragged to church in Durham.

In Atlanta, there was one majority Black Catholic church in Atlanta, St. Anthony of Padua in the West End, two blocks from that janky mall, whose nicest store was a Sears. I'd done my research and discovered that because I was eighteen, I'd have to attend adult classes to join. When I showed up to my first class, the priest was the same man who'd spoken at my father's funeral, and who would eventually baptize me: Father Bruce. This was my sign.

The priest seemed so old to me then, so mature. Thirty-eight years later, when I contacted the parish for my baptism and confirmation of faith certificate and asked about Father Bruce, I learned he'd only been thirty at the time of my conversion.

⁓

Spoiler alert: I never became a nun.

But that time of light through the window of Clark College's auditorium was not the only time I would feel a divine presence.

There was the night after one of my religious classes at St. Anthony's when a tiny figure appeared at the side of my bed. I was nineteen. He—somehow, I knew he was a *man*, though he had no facial figures—was made of light that cast a malevolence.

Was this the devil? If so, he wasn't asking for my soul. He only giggled, which terrified me. I was sure he was about to murder me. My door was closed—how had he gotten in? I questioned my sanity, but at the time I owned a cross necklace. That night I had taken the necklace off and laid it on the bedside table. I quickly grabbed it and began to pray. A taller figure—again a man—appeared beside the smaller man. He, too, was filled with light, but somehow it symbolized safety. The taller man pointed a finger at the small man, who laughed in a taunting way; a few seconds passed, and they both disappeared.

I didn't tell anyone about this incident, lest I be called severely mentally ill; already, I'd confessed to friends my desire to kill myself, which negatively shifted our relationships. I was dating a new young man who beat me constantly. With him, there would be sexual assaults and other truly unimaginable humiliations that I'm (still) too embarrassed to detail here. I was doing poorly in college, but I did not connect the fact that I was living (off and on) with a man whose violence had rapidly escalated from slaps to choking to punching and raping with my academic failure.

My grade-point average plunged to a 1.9, and Mama insisted that I transfer to Talladega College, where she had accepted a teaching job after Daddy had died. She needed to look after me, she said, though she didn't say why. I hadn't told Mama about my abusive boyfriend, but she probably already knew what was going on—after all, she'd been married to my father.

Though our relationship remained rocky, I know my mama saved me by making me transfer schools. I don't believe I'd be alive if she hadn't intervened.

3.

As a poet and writer, I have found so much peace in my words, even while experiencing such emotional upheaval: I experienced constant racism in Oklahoma, where I had settled in 2002. My sister Sisi died in 2014. I fell in love with a man in 2012, married him that same year, and divorced him in 2016. After this latter event, I began to question who I was, as a Black woman and a human being.

The notion of Christian devotion that I had witnessed during my lifetime plucked at my guilt: Didn't I see long-standing heterosexual marriages in every Black community I encountered? If Black women gave up on these unions, what would happen to our communities? I had made serious vows under God with my ex-husband. How could I so easily discard those?

Before I married, I'd heard God-fearing Black women mention "submission." Forgive my shade here, but I assumed biblical submission was some trend that nonintellectual—*non-reading*—so-called Holy Rollers followed. After my divorce, though, it seemed that every college-educated sister I met believed that the man was the head of the household—her leader—and that this was the key to a happy union. There was the Black female friend who laughed when I insisted I would never submit to a man. She told me I just hadn't found the right man. When I did, submission would be easy for me. (A while later, I stopped being friends with her.)

In my twenties and thirties, as I interacted with writing communities, I experienced some shame over my Christianity. White feminist and Black atheist friends ridiculed my beliefs as backward and anti-progressive. Understanding that Western Christianity was not *designed* for the liberation of women—and certainly not for Black women—I felt silly trying to argue with my critics. But when I encountered the womanist theology of Katie Cannon—*Katie's Canon* is an essential read—learning that Christian faith had been instrumental in Black women's liberation struggles and achievements I felt myself on firmer ground.[2]

Cannon used the framework of Alice Walker's definition of womanism as a working philosophy that would allow gender equity in Black churches.[3] For Cannon, the tenor of female-specific biblical stories preached from the African American pulpit highlighted grim issues in Black churches. For example, in the Book of Genesis, Eve's transgression—the eating of the apple and tempting of Adam to consume this same fruit—set the tone for how women were viewed in patriarchal society at large, and in Black churches. But Cannon argues that a womanist approach to these negative messages in biblical scripture would allow for intersectional liberation—the freedom of Black women.[4]

As I considered Cannon's words, I returned to Jarena Lee, the nineteenth-century Black woman preacher whose journal I'd encountered in an African American literature class at Clark College. Lee's story resonated, for like me, she had unsuccessfully attempted suicide.[5] I had tried to kill myself at fifteen, twenty-two, twenty-three, and twenty-six. I'd stopped myself before leaving this earth, but the core of despair—and shame—of my depression always seemed to be my difference. Not only had I been abused, but my personality was weird: I didn't fit anywhere. I couldn't be at peace in my own family and community, as a girl and woman who wouldn't get in line.

Jarena Lee wasn't only like me because of her suicidal ideations, however. She was a pushy woman, too—and because she was a woman, the Reverend Richard Allen—the founder of the African Methodist Episcopal Church—had criticized her aspiration to preach: "He said that our Discipline . . . did not call for women preachers."[6] But on the day of this conversation, Lee felt "a holy energy" inside her: "If the man may preach, because the Saviour died for him, why not the woman? seeing he died for her also. Did not Mary [Magdalene] *first* preach the risen Saviour, and is not the doctrine of the resurrection the very climax of Christianity—hangs not all our hope on this, as argued by St. Paul? Then did not Mary, a woman, preach the gospel? for she preached the resurrection of the crucified Son of God."[7]

While reading Lee, there was another flash of recognition: I, too, had pondered the meaning behind Jesus's Resurrection, that He'd first shown himself to a woman who had gone and spread the Good News. When ministers and priests discussed this moment, they didn't find this evidence of Jesus's—or God's—feminism, but rather a coincidence that should not weight the bag of Christian faith. Every other moment in the Bible carried import, but this evidence of a woman's responsibility for two thousand years of Christianity was no big deal—or it only emphasized the importance of Black women's *service* to the church, as secondary figures. But like Jarena Lee, I didn't accept this secondary notion.

By the time of my return to Lee, I'd encountered the term *patriarchy*, and learned that such a male-led system of oppression was both African and European, then re-created as a whole new animal waiting to bite at the flesh of Black women, after their journey over the Middle Passage—a misogynoirist creature who *also* exhibited anti-Queer attitudes and behaviors. This patriarchal animal seemed immortal, unable to be killed.

Especially in Black churches, cisgender, heterosexual Black women encounter patriarchal strictures. They have it hard enough, but as I evolved and forcibly sloughed off the repulsive homophobia and transphobia with which I'd been reared, I saw that my Queer kindred truly were denied their very existences in most Christian settings. This denial was made acceptable and supposedly unbigoted because it was part of traditional biblical interpretation and teaching. The most virulent African American homophobe and transphobe could—and would—quote from Scripture to justify their prejudices. The softer bigot would declare, "Hate the sin, love the sinner."

What does that mean? What is the sin?

Surely not fornication—unmarried sex—for two Queer folks who are legally married? When I asked my dear friend, the poet Jericho Brown, what the phrase "Hate the sin, love the sinner" meant to him, a Southern gay Black man with an abiding faith in God, he told me he'd never seen "the love part. . . . it sounds a lot like a retrograde plea to try segregation again but this time with Black people having real access to the equal part of 'separate but equal.' It is not possible."[8]

While I would never pretend that my life as a straight Black woman is as difficult as a Queer person's, I ponder what the church taught to me, that anyone who goes against what is considered the natural order cannot be a devout Christian— "natural" being the cisgender, heterosexual male-led nuclear family. And this order is lionized in most churches as God-ordained.

Not only is patriarchy supposedly natural, it is considered the destroyer of oppression in Black communities: If we African Americans would but accept patriarchy, our community could heal; we could throw off the weight of White supremacy. Thus Black woman feminists *and* Queer Black folks are seen as threats not only to patriarchy but to the very existence, health, and survival of our African American communities.

꒰ঌ

I encountered so much confusion in the three decades following my vision in chapel services at Clark College. That's a long time. Longer than a Jesus-year interval.

I craved community, and the reminders of the good parts of my childhood, when Grandma Florence would take my sisters and me to worship at Flat Rock Primitive Baptist. The way the Spirit would rush into the sanctuary. The line singing that gave me so much joy. The fellowship picnics of fried chicken, potato salad, and butter pound cake after service, if weather was calm.

There were a few years that I tried with Catholicism, but there was too much to get past. To begin with, nobody sang like Mahalia Jackson or caught the Spirit during mass—what kind of praise was that? The fact that women couldn't be priests was the biggest issue for me, though—until the child abuse scandals painfully reminded me of my father's tormenting of me. The final barrier was my encountering information of the Catholic church's complicity in North American Indigenous genocide. I could get past different cultural performances—but the latter outrageous trinity blocked my reconciliation. Even the eating of that wafer—which I'd considered made me better than ordinary, non-Catholic Christians—couldn't sway me.

In Oklahoma I avoided a Catholic parish, but rarely I'd visit churches of other denominations. After my divorce and the emotional agony that followed, I attended a missionary Baptist church with a sister-friend of mine who taught at my university. Signs appeared at my new place of worship: I fell in love with the line singing, my beloved Black cultural holdover.

But again, as with the Catholic church, there was the unmovable patriarchy in this sanctuary. It was heavy, like that oft-referenced Rock that Jesus had moved on the third day. So high you can't get over it, so wide you can't get around it.

Nobody wanted to talk about what I believed was a scriptural justification for the equality of women: that when Jesus was crucified, only women remained during his ordeal. As Jarena Lee had told Richard Allen, when Jesus was resurrected, he'd shown himself to a woman, Mary Magdalene, who went on to spread the Good News.

Yet there was the sexism again: Mary Magdalene's presence, which had begun the Christian movement, was not viewed as a feminist act, unless women considered being under the dominion of men as empowerment. Somehow, women could occupy only secondary roles in my new house of worship: the unseen work of the temple. The cleaning, and the cooking of delicious chicken and those wondrous butter pound cakes. (Real talk: that chicken and them pound cakes *were* bomb.) And if we women weren't happy, that pointed to our lack of acceptance of our ordained roles as dominated beings. If I couldn't get with it, I'd remain what I'd always been in every middle-class Black community I'd entered: an abomination. An unnatural being unworthy of God's love.

There was one day in adult Christian education class where I challenged the gender of God.

"Why do you keep using the pronoun 'He?'" I asked.

"Because God is a man," the (cisgender) Black male teacher replied.

"How do you know that?"

"It's in the Word."

"But men wrote the Bible." When I snorted at his lack of evidence, the other sisters in the room rolled their eyes at me.

I persisted: "Let me ask you this: Have you ever seen God's genitals?" I put things in simple terms, because already I was in complex territory. I knew this man wouldn't understand, even with reproductive organs assigned as "male" or "female," gender was a social construct. And that's how it was obvious—to me—that God had been made a man by other men writing this Bible.

Brother-teacher gasped, then began laughing.

He liked my spirit, I could tell, but maybe—I'm only speculating here—as a thing to be crushed. When I would see him during services, he would head my way during altar call, smiling. Once he shook his finger at me in a joking way. I thought I knew what he was thinking: I needed a good man—and maybe some strong dick—to calm me down. There were plenty single men in the church, too, those who eyed me in my elaborate Sunday dresses, stockings, and special-occasion shoes. I'd been reared in the Deep South: A lady didn't come looking raggedy to church on the Lord's Day. I was proud to have purchased my own Bible purse, too, a clever contraption that included a large Good Book that fit inside a zippered compartment.

But there was that last day, when a guest preacher filled in for the regular pastor at my church. Suddenly—I don't remember how he logically arrived at this place in his sermon—the guest preacher began railing against transgender women being allowed to use the women's bathroom.

I sat there in my gorgeous dress, whispering to myself as I plucked at the fabric.

"What is this foolishness," I asked myself. "What is going on? I woke early, skipped breakfast, and drove from Norman to Oklahoma City for *this?*"

Only a few days before then, I had completed my LGBTQIA ally training at my university. Three of my former students were gay men who adored me, and who believed I felt the same about them. (And I did.) Could I really stay in this pew and listen to this bigoted bullshit, along with the *amen*-ing I heard around me, and be at peace with myself? Was I that much of a cruel hypocrite?

A few more seconds passed.

I picked up my Bible purse and my regular purse—it was quite the fashionable load that day—and I stood. When I walked out, tapping my medium-height heels, I didn't go through the back of the church. I walked up the aisle so that everyone could see me—and my stank attitude.

After that Sunday, my church attendance began to drop off. Eventually, I stopped going.

❧

I can't muster a rousing ending here. I'm not like James Baldwin, a former child preacher called to exhort the masses. I can say that healing is a miracle that finally happened for me, even though the world hasn't changed much, and neither has my own Black community—or my own family.

I need to say this again, lest I give the impression that my gratitude and faith are nonexistent: Healing has happened for me.

∾⤫

If this *were* a sermon, though, I'd point to that evening in January 2024, when I reread Paul's Epistle to the Ephesians. I'd been hearing that word again—*submission*—among Black women in my college alumni circles, and I decided to return to Paul's admonition to women in chapter 5, to refresh my memory: "Wives, submit yourselves to your own husbands as you do to the Lord. For the husband is the head of the wife as Christ is the head of the church, his body, of which he is the Savior. Now as the church submits to Christ, so also wives should submit to their husbands in everything."

Here, it's clear that the husband has been placed in an almost godly position: he controls his household. I'd heard Black folks try to lighten the load of this verse—a man couldn't toss his weight around; he had to lead with a gentle authority—but the gist was, all power rested in a husband's hands.

For some reason, though, despite my irritation with Paul—and yes, with Black women talking about the joys of "submission"—I continued to chapter 6, only to finally comprehend that in Paul's rules for the marital home, the submission of women in chapter 5 is tied to the obedience of children and that of enslaved people: "Slaves, obey your earthly masters with respect and fear, and with sincerity of heart, just as you would obey Christ. Obey them not only to win their favor when their eye is on you, but like slaves of Christ, doing the will of God from your heart. Serve wholeheartedly, as if you were serving the Lord, not men, because you know that the Lord will reward everyone for whatever good he does, whether he is slave or free."

As someone who had studied the institution of slavery since I was a little girl, I'd been familiar with this passage: in the nineteenth century it was read by southern slaveowners who wanted to scare enslaved people into obedience. During my adult study of slavery, I'd read about the "Slave Bible," which had elided pesky portions about resistance from the Good Book.[9]

I reread these two passages from Ephesians, sure I was missing something: Paul had been making separate points, right? But no, the authority of a husband over his subordinates—wives, children, and enslaved people—were one and the same and contained in immediately adjacent chapters. But at no time during my visits to any church had a Black or White priest or minister or even a layperson ever made this logical observation of critical analysis from the pulpit—or even during postservice fellowship. I'd heard justifications against slavery, but I'd witnessed no subsequent point that should be obvious: In a section of the Bible that speaks of household authority, you cannot logically jettison one item of oppression while embracing the others. You cannot be against the institution of slavery, which holds human beings under the complete authority of an owner, but be in support of the submission of women to the *same* complete authority.

Yet just as slaveholders had scared the Black people that they owned with the illogical logic of Ephesians 6, so had patriarchal-minded priests, ministers, laypersons, and ordinary salty, sexist Black folks used Paul's words on submission in chapter 5 to keep rebellious Black women in their place—up until and through the twenty-first century.

Rebellious Black women like me.

This small moment was a needful revelation, for I'd assumed, even with my visions, even with my study of womanist theology—even with my years of therapy—that something was terribly wrong with me, that I was dirty and atrocious: an abomination.

But this day, when I read Paul's Epistle, I knew then that, as He/She/They had done since I was eighteen years old, I had been given another sign to keep walking in the direction I'd been headed. That sign was from God: a womanist Creator.

Discussions about what is known as "the Black church" don't truly get at the pain of those of us who don't attend services anymore. Those discussions don't dive into the issues that currently face Black churches, in terms of respectability politics: sexism, homophobia and transphobia, and misogynoir.

I miss going to services, though. I miss the songs and the history and the cultural fellowship, and somebody from the pulpit assuring me that I had a friend in Jesus, that if I prayed very hard, my Savior would work it all out.

But I gave up going to church, because I needed to feel better about who I was as a Black woman—and who some of my friends were, those who were gay and lesbian and feminist. (These are not imaginary friends, as in "some of my best friends are Black." These are my actual friends.) I needed to know I was doing right by my Queer students, who depended upon not only my kindness but sometimes my protection of them from other, bullying students. And they depended upon my rejection of hypocrisy.

I didn't have the energy to fight within the sanctuary, either, a place that was supposed to deliver the message that anybody of any background was called to be there, if there were two or more of us gathered in God's name.

My experiences that led to my leaving Christian worship are not unique among many Black folks, and neither are the questions I've asked. I've fallen out with or distanced myself from so-called devout Black Christian friends over misogynoir and Queerphobia, the same ways I've cut loose White friends who revealed "benignly" White supremacist leanings. But I must be honest, I miss my former Black friends more. When you lose somebody from your own community, you lose something deeper than friendship: a shared culture, a history you both can claim.

We are supposed to be made in God's image. It is a primal wounding to be told that you are not painted divinely because you don't believe you should obey a man or that you should remain silent in the church; because you might romantically love someone the same gender as you; because someone calls you "man" but you know you were born "woman"; or because you question what you read in Scripture, the stories of gang rape, slavery, murder, and dysfunctional, abusive family dynamics.

To be dismissed or ridiculed in the name of religious fellowship can be an agony. It can hurt so much, when your own version of God has come to you at night and called you by an anointed name, has told you, "Your feelings aren't wrong. You are valid, my child. You were and are made whole. You are loved by me, and I insist that you are enough."

35

Toni Morrison Did That

It's a term I invented while watching the late, great Toni Morrison masterfully take down her critics: "The Morrisonian Moment."

My favorite of these instances took place during a 1998 interview with Charlie Rose, who verbally poked Morrison—at least, it appeared that way to me—with questions about "race."[1] Specifically, why did it annoy Morrison so much when journalists asked when she would stop writing about race—meaning, writing about Black culture and Black people?[2]

"You see," Morrison answered, "the person who asks that question doesn't understand that . . . he or she is also raced."[3]

At this point, I always giggle. (Oh, I've watched this interview at least ten times.) Not only did Rose seemingly misunderstand what the word *race* means, he didn't realize that he'd brought a knife to a gunfight. Perhaps he'd thought Morrison would be stumped, this African American woman who'd won the Nobel Prize in Literature, in a debate about Blackness and its profound creative relevance. What I loved about Morrison's response—besides her melodious, withering tone—was her historically informed argument that, although her critics might not understand how race works exactly, "White" has always been a racial category—at least since the *invention* of "race"—just like "African American." After all, White folks are the ones who invented the concept.

Morrison's unflustered logic is also what I love about "Recitatif," her only published short story.[4] "Recitatif" depicts an interracial friendship between two girls—one White, one Black—who meet in a shelter. They have different reasons for being there: Roberta's mother is sick, while Twyla's likes to party. In the story, told from Twyla's point of view, we encounter the girls over many years, but Morrison never identifies either's cultural background.

As Morrison later explained in *Playing in the Dark: Whiteness and the Literary Imagination*, she eliminated racial markers in "Recitatif" on purpose.[5] Absence is Morrison's central point: once racial markers were stripped from the girls, each reader of "Recitatif" would experience the story in a purely subjective fashion. This subjectivity appears in literary criticism as well. Some insisted they'd cracked Morrison's racial codes.[6] However, when I went back to "Recitatif" some twenty-five years after my first read, it was clear that Morrison expertly used racial codes as a shell game: You never can find the prize. After a third and fourth read, I remained confused. Frankly, I liked it that way.

When Morrison published "Recitatif" in 1983, it appeared in *Confirmation: An Anthology of African American Women*, a collection edited by the Black Arts Movement's Amiri Baraka and his writer-partner, Amina Baraka. That Morrison, a mainstream novelist, maintained a friendship with Baraka (who, like Morrison, was an attendee of Howard University) and with the radical activist-intellectual Angela Y. Davis should tell us so much about Morrison's firm grounding in Black literary communities. And that in "Recitatif," Morrison overtly refuses to include racial markers for its characters makes it undoubtedly a *Black* story written by a *Black* writer. There is an unspoken political allusion here: Morrison wants to protest the absurdity of "race" because it doesn't really exist, while evincing her understanding that "race" is a figment of an imagination—the White supremacist fancy.

Yet Morrison's twentieth-century readers probably wouldn't have searched for signifiers of *Whiteness*, the "normative" identity. Most readers would have searched for *Blackness*, its assumed imagery, music, vernacular, and performance. They would search for Blackness's static US stereotypes, especially because the story had appeared in the (married) Barakas' edited anthology, a collection compiled by self-proclaimed Black radicals.

Remember, though: Morrison tells us in *Playing in the Dark* that "race" *is* contained in "Recitatif," though we (her readers) can't identify it. Twyla and Roberta—two wounded, mostly unmothered girls, growing up with material and emotional uncertainties—are playing the cultural hands they've been dealt. Yet because we don't know who holds which hand, we become aware that these two women's social realities have become increasingly absurd—just like "race."

There are no men in "Recitatif," either. Thus the power of White supremacy in the patriarchy created in the United States isn't quite as obvious. This is a story about women, and it seems that Morrison asks us: Are we really going to play this game invented by White men? Are we that weak-minded, that susceptible to a power we don't truly—and won't ever—possess?

∿

When we talk about racial issues and racial history, the conversation will automatically descend into pain. Whether we want to admit it or not, we Black folks want an acknowledgment of what happened. When many *White* folks talk about racial issues and racial history, they receive our complaints from the vantage point of power, their ability to accept or reject the crimes of their European and American ancestors; they assume that their White point of view is the final authority of truth in history. Morrison's theory of rememory—oral stories and undocumentable experiences such as ancestral dreams or visions passed down—has no place in authority, because that authority is assumed to belong to Whiteness.

As bell hooks tells us, for those who aren't African American, non-Whiteness is a "spice," a piquancy hitting cultural taste buds.[7] Whiteness is *not* spicy: it is peacefully bland and normal—and innocent. In *Playing in the Dark*, Morrison talked about the "thematics of innocence," a concept that James Baldwin previously explored before her.[8] But what Morrison insisted upon is that, even when a White

American never mentions "race" in their writing—and I continually place the word in quotes to indicate the unnuanced political, cultural, social, and legal shorthand that this one small word connotes—"race" *is* present in any creative text generated by that White writer. There is knowing of what "race" means, despite racial innocence—because that innocence is patently false.

I've tried to unpack what Morrison meant in that 1998 interview with Charlie Rose, when he asked her about writing White main characters. After thinking about her words, here is what occurred to me:

The *absence* of racial markers—in monochromatic neighborhood demographics, majority White universities attended, socioeconomic privilege (for some) and attitudes shaped by cultural upbringing—signifies *White* racial identity. And this absence points to the power of Whiteness, because as a White writer or poet, when you don't have to consider your history in society or in a country; when the blank page of a book does not constrain or conflict who you and your ancestors are, have been, or have done; when you can automatically assume that you only have to depict an individual, deracinated story and not your own cultural background, proverbs, vernacular, or folklore; when you don't have to keep in mind that *deracinated* shares an etymology with the French word *deracinée*, "pulled up from the roots"; when every literary allusion you make to other texts is taken at its unspoken face value instead of having to be painstakingly explained and justified in detail ad nauseam; when you don't even have to identify the racial categories of your characters, because until those categories are noted, their Whiteness is assumed, and more than that, apparent by its referential absence—all that indicates the power of Whiteness in literary spaces.

This absence, taken with a refusal by White readers, critics, academics—and yes, even editors—to acknowledge that what has happened in this country continues to impact literary production and publication, creating a false sense of White blamelessness, an off-tune, childishly pitched *Who, me?*

It is only when someone like me, someone who is *not* the default—which, if I have not made myself clear, the default is White—enters the room that there is suddenly a sea change from a "normal" conversation to a "race" discourse. That is because it's assumed that the primary, most essential conversation is always about White people: about White men and then about White women, in that order—and of course, both are cisgender and heterosexual.

It might seem a contradiction that Black people, historically depicted as ignorant, stupid, and intellectually incapable, could concurrently possess a "racial" wisdom that Whites can't understand, while Whites are represented as all-knowing and intellectually extraordinary—until it comes to their White innocence over slavery, settler colonialism, imperialism, Jim Crow, and a US legal system designed to replicate slavery in a metamorphized form. Yet that is the nonsense of White supremacy. The rules are ever-changing. There is no logic, just something made up and pushed through.

～※～

Toni Morrison's first novel, *The Bluest Eye*, appeared in 1970. In the fifty-plus intervening years, many critics have merely moved the marginalizing emphasis from one question (which I have configured here), "Do Black writers have the right to depict themselves?" to an (implied) declarative statement: "Yes, Black writers *can* depict themselves, but that depiction lies in the specific category of 'writing about race.' " These supposed generosities and inclusions—thank you so very much, progressive White critics—maintain Black writing as an oddity in opposition to the more important, default norm of writing produced by Whites. Or maybe it presents African Americans as a defiance, because if all God's Black children got rhythm, we got that real sassy backtalk, too.

Like that of most writers, my life is filled with curiosity. Something will strike me in a dream or in waking life, and I move to questioning: What would happen if I thought about this—or that—longer? If I chased my curiosity and waded into the ensuing confusion until I learned to swim instead of drowning?

So here's what I want to know: When did "race" become shorthand for so much? For slavery, colonialism, lynching, disenfranchisement of Indigenous folks and people of color—and, especially, for talking about the everyday lives of Black folks?

And when did "race" become shorthand for so *little*? Such as, whatever isn't White?

When did we Black writers, so desperate for publication and fame within our tiny, insular artistic communities—or even, outside of that, on a national scale—become so terrified of White professors in our master of fine arts programs, White editors at publishing houses, White critics at newspapers and magazines, that we completely accepted that our depictions of our own culture(s) need be crammed into the category of "writing about race"?

And by "we," understand that I, too, have been included in this petrified number.

I will accept that there is such a real thing as "writing about race." I've done that: I've written about how the social category of "race" came to be; for example, with Enlightenment philosophers like Immanuel Kant, who created a cultural hierarchy with Europeans at the top and Africans at the bottom: "The Negroes of Africa have by nature no feeling, which rises above the trifling. . . . Not a single one of them has ever been found that has performed any thing great, either in the arts or sciences, or shown any other commendable property."[9] This from Kant, one of the Europeans who gave us our ugly pseudoscientific notions of "race"—Kant, who in his lifetime never even left his Prussian hometown, let alone traveled to the African continent to observe those darker folks that he held in such contempt, and *lied* that he knew so much about.[10]

However, writing a novel where a narrator discusses, say, the crack epidemic in Black communities in the United States, or the way that *one* Black family deals with multigenerational sexual trauma? That is *history*. Not simply Black history but the history of the United States. After all, when most scholars talk about the White guys who framed the Constitution, the men collectively known as the founding fathers, we never say, "Oh, wait, these dudes are all White, so this discussion is about 'race.' "

Or when we discuss the current opioid addiction epidemic in Middle America, we never make it about "race" explicitly, as we did with the crack epidemic. There isn't a national conversation saying, "Look at all these White kids who became dope fiends! White communities sure are dysfunctional! Now let's start another national war on drugs and put a bunch of White men in prison—and then let's talk about the shortage of White cishet male marriage mates in White communities, and the absence of White fathers in White homes. Let's talk about fentanyl babies and how White women can't ever be good moms, even after they've shaken their addiction, so we constantly send social workers to their houses and make them afraid of losing their legal rights to their White children."

When it comes to those who write about Black life, certainly there is an ease in promotion when we finish our books. I know what it means to hustle, to earn out an advance on a book. If my publishing company uses "race" as a shorthand in publicity materials sent out to magazines, newspapers, and (now) podcast hosts, then the critical and thematic points of departure will be obvious: Is this a serious book? Is this a book about issues—and is that issue "race"? If so, reviews of the book and interviews with the author can be directed toward a specific subset of readers: Black readers, or White readers who want to learn about African Americans. (Because, you know, we Black folks are so *complex* and *unknown* and *exotic*—even though we've been in this country since the sixteenth century.)

Marketing is about business. It's about selling books, and as the Black kids might say, "Secure your bag, sis." But I'm again curious: when did so many of us Black writers give up carrying forward the critical legacy of Morrison (who only died a few years ago), whose mind, analyses, and intellectual evisceration of others remained sharp and peerless until the end? When did we surrender to shorthand, instead of reminding others that we're writing about our own people—Black people—and that those people are worthy?

~⁂~

The original version of this essay was a (much shorter) review of "Recitatif" for *The New York Times*. In preparation for that, I reread Morrison's nonfiction. It felt like coming home, though not to a geographical place: It was a home within my outrage. I felt as if I'd inherited Morrison's outrage over the question that I was asked about my novel: "Why did you feel the need to write about Black people in *The Love Songs of W. E. B. Du Bois?*"

As if an African American writer deciding to creatively depict Black people—*their own people*—represents a striding through brackish, nonpotable waters. This question is never asked of White writers: "Hey, fill-in-the-blank White dude, I notice that your entire novel is about some White family living in rural Ohio. Why did you feel the need to present only White characters in your book?"

Even expanding this essay from my original review of the reprint of "Recitatif," I felt scared. When you're a Black writer—or when you are *this* Black writer—you think about gratitude so much. You think about your blessings, about how you've been allowed to occupy a privileged space, and how your Black ass might be ejected from that space at a moment's notice. No matter how educated you might be, to be Black in the United States is to live with daily precarity—in your body *and* your mind. There are so few writers who look like you who have made it here to this mountaintop of publication, where sometimes, some real nice money awaits in a pot. The mountaintop where *Greek* gods reside—nobody is ever going to point to the highest place where the Yoruba orishas live, because that Yoruba hill is a *Negro* place, and a Negro place is not where well-behaved Black girls should go when they become successful writers.

Yet I consider Morrison, whose unflappable calm (no matter the ridiculous questions asked of her) probably hid some of the same concerns as mine. It seems almost blasphemous to say, "Morrison might have been afraid, too," but, knowing what I do about the lives of Black women, I'm almost positive that she was afraid a few times in her life. And when I return to "Recitatif," it is with a renewed understanding of the courage that story took to write. Not simply Morrison's artistic curiosity, but her sustained insistence that she had a *right* to write such a story.

Knowing Black literary history, I know that, along with other African Americans like W.E.B. Du Bois, Ann Petry, Amiri Baraka, James Baldwin, Sonia Sanchez, Alice Walker, Angela Davis, and Lucille Clifton—the latter two edited by Morrison during her years at Random House—Morrison depicted Black culture while *also* considering politics, while *also* considering United States history, while *also* considering White supremacy, while *also* considering economic class, while *also* considering gender, while *also* considering intergenerational trauma.

As the Black kids might say, Toni Morrison *did* that.

She did that decades ago, so it's not her fault that we haven't learned simultaneity, that we need a blunt hammer to break the American experience into tiny, sharp-edged pieces that we can touch—and maybe hold—only one at a time. The fault is ours. The lack of understanding is ours—but within any lack, there exists possibility. And that is ours as well.

36

In Search of Our Mothers' Tar Baby

1.

In Eatonton, there is a museum honoring Joel Chandler Harris, the White man who wrote a new framework for "The Wonderful Tar Baby Story," a folktale that my mother used to recite to me, like her father before her.[1] The museum is named after Uncle Remus, the elderly Black man that Harris invented as the placid storyteller who narrates Tar Baby's tale, as well as the other stories of Bruh Rabbit.

The character of Uncle Remus is an old man who seems to experience no greater pleasure than to sit around all day and tell stories to a bothersome little White boy. Uncle Remus's name is one of those monikers from classical literature: White folks liked to make fun of us during slavery, so they named us for Roman and Greek divinities, then tormented us and took away our dignity.

Her whole life, my mother refused to visit the Uncle Remus Museum. "I'll never step foot in that place," she declared. "Not while my head is hot!" She didn't like Uncle Remus the character, and didn't think much of Joel Chandler Harris, the real person: "Look at that White man, making his money off poor Black folks."

Her voice would turn angry when she talked about the outrages that she'd withstood growing up in the country South. If Uncle Remus had been a real person, Mama was sure Harris would never have given the old man a nickel with a hole in it. And we can assume no dark woman ever got her share, either.

In my thirties, I visited the Uncle Remus Museum once when I drove to Eatonton by myself. It was inside a cute little log cabin and furnished with rustic bibelots. The guide explained to me that Harris was the author of the folktales in his books.

I corrected the guide. "No, he *transcribed* them. These are traditional African American folktales. But he did invent the little boy and Uncle Remus. We can give him that."

The guide blinked, turned pink, then quickly told me the total of the items that I was buying from the gift corner.

It took me another decade to understand why the Uncle Remus Museum infuriated Mama so much. I hadn't been born in central Georgia in poverty. Both my parents had attended and finished graduate school, while my maternal grandmother used her finger to point to words when she haltingly read the newspaper, and my maternal grandfather—well, he never even learned to read.

Unlike Mama, my matriculation hadn't included Flat Rock School, her one-room schoolhouse that doubled as a Primitive Baptist church on Sundays. I'd never had White children spit at me from the windows of their nice, segregated school bus while I was walking three miles to secure my education, no matter the pitiless season.

Lord, sometimes thinking about my mother's pain is too much to bear.

2.

My mother's former student at Eatonton's Butler Baker High School, the novelist Alice Walker, took her issues with Joel Chandler Harris to the page in "Uncle Remus: No Friend of Mine," responding to both the appropriation of the African American versions of the folktales as well as the creation of Uncle Remus, a seemingly harmless Black man.[2]

Walker's well-earned resentment counters what I call "Remusfication," the sanitizing of White southern terrorism against African Americans, during and after slavery. An example of Remusfication is when Harris describes his titular character as having nothing "but pleasant memories of the discipline of slavery"; this during the time that Jim Crow was in full feather in the US South, which makes Uncle Remus seem either ridiculous or contemptible.[3] According to Harris's logic, not only was White supremacist violence exaggerated—or even nonexistent—but African American enslaved persons, freed domestic servants, and sharecroppers had been happy and content.

3.

I remember Mama telling me—*telling*, not reading, for she knew several by heart—the Bruh Rabbit tales. "Bruh" is the pronunciation she used, one I explained in a poem of mine:

Consider my brother as the Rabbit—
Bruh, not *Br'er*, as Mister Harris mangled
on the page. *Bruh*, like the sound of the hoe's
swing hitting the earth's face: *Take these blues—huh—
plant them in the garden—huh*[4]

Just to clarify, nobody Black in the Deep South uses a word resembling *burr* to indicate kinship. Neither do we rhyme a sibling phrase with *hair*. When we shorten "brother," it sounds like a grunt in the back of the throat: *Bruh*. My mother told me that her father had told these folktales to her. She reassured me that, like Joel Chandler Harris, Grandpa Charlie was born in Eatonton, but he couldn't have learned the Bruh Rabbit tales by reading them, because Grandpa never did learn to read.

4.

The Bruh Rabbit folktales do not belong to Harris or even solely to what we call the United States. Some trickster folktales that made it over the ocean were Africa-specific, such as the Anansi the Spider tales or the Bouki and Lapin tales of the Senegambia region—the latter include a trickster hare figure.[5] Like the Bruh Rabbit tales, both Bouki and Anansi tales feature a smaller, physically weaker protagonist who outsmarts their larger, vicious opponent.

On the left side of the water, in what is now known as the southeastern United States, the Cherokee (Tsalagi), Creek (Muscogee), and other southeastern Indigenous peoples had their own versions of Rabbit trickster tales. In the Cherokee version of the tales, the rabbit is called Jistu or Tsisdu.[6] In the Creek/Muscogee versions, the rabbit is Chufee.[7] What does it mean that cultures—the African forcibly pushed across the ocean, and the Indigenous forcibly settler-colonized—collided and, thus, those different tales became Afro-Indigenous?[8] And though the "Indigenous" portion was unacknowledged or outright erased by Harris, what does it mean that his version of the Rabbit tales is the loudest, most lasting sound we hear?

As for this specific folktale, according to Bryan Wagner's *The Tar Baby: A Global History*, many cultures around the globe carry some version of it.[9] Even Toni Morrison was fascinated by Tar Baby: she wrote an entire novel as an allegory based upon the tale.

5.

Whenever I return to "The Wonderful Tar Baby," I think about who the doll is supposed to be.

Initially, Tar Baby serves a traditional role. She is gendered as "she" or "her," and she is silent, dark, and unmoving. This is the acceptable behavior for real-life Black women. But there's so much complication in this tale, for it quickly violates gender expectations: Bruh Rabbit, gendered as a male, exhibits many traditional *female* characteristics. He is small and physically helpless and cannot beat Bruh Fox at his own game, which is centered on physical strength. By taking on these female qualities, Bruh Rabbit shares a kinship with Tar Baby. When he sees the Tar Baby in the road, however, and she refuses to speak—

because she *cannot*—he gives in to misogynoirist behavior: he becomes enraged and attacks someone weaker than himself. This stupidity is what leads him to fall into Bruh Fox's life-threatening trap.

Yet it's Bruh Rabbit's same encounter with Tar Baby that allows him to exhibit intellectual strength. After becoming stuck in the substance of the doll, Bruh Rabbit turns to improvisation. He changes instantly, a behavior that enslaved Black people—and especially Black women—turned to for survival: he begs Bruh Fox not to toss him in the briar patch. Thinking this would be the worst kind of death—instead of being boiled, as Bruh Fox first planned—Bruh Fox throws his smaller, weaker enemy in the patch. In this way, Bruh Rabbit ends up happy and free and alive.

6.

I never think of Uncle Remus as a man—I don't think of him as a woman, either. I think of him as nonbinary. I know that Harris means for Uncle Remus to hold nothing but desire to please his White benefactors, but this Black elder is a shapeshifter: always doing what he must to live. Even if Harris depicts him as worry-free and in no danger from Whites; even if, on the surface, Harris's Uncle Remus happily accepts his status as an inferior person speaking to his White superior; even if the latter is a child.

The trick is that Uncle Remus seems submissive. Though slavery has ended, he moves according to the whims of his former enslavers. Supposedly, he has no anger, no ambition, no late-age plots to get ahead in life.

When we examine Harris's versions of the folktales, though, we might find it interesting that he chose a Black *man* as the narrator, for the tales with which Uncle Remus entertains first one White male child, and then another, constitute a form of caretaking. Essentially, Uncle Remus is a nanny for this White child, which goes against late nineteenth-century traditional ideas of heteronormativity. Given the nineteenth/early twentieth-century emphasis on lionizing the Black Mammy, Harris's choice of placing Uncle Remus in this role is interesting, if not downright odd—why not choose a cisgender Black *woman* for his narrator?[10]

Besides Uncle Remus's role as nanny, Queer-leaning language appears in another volume of Harris's stories, *Told by Uncle Remus: New Stories of the Old Plantation*.[11] The narrator describes Uncle Remus's subsequent young charge, the son of the first—now grown—White male landowner that the elderly Black man had tended:

> This little boy was not like the other little boy [his father]. He was more like a girl in his refinement; all the boyishness had been taken out of him by that mysterious course of discipline that some mothers know how to apply. He seemed to belong to a different age—to a different time; just how or why it would be impossible to say. . . .
>
> "Miss Sally," said Uncle Remus, a few days after the arrival of the little boy and his mother, "what dey gwineter do wit dat chile? What dey gwineter make out'n'him?"[12]

The "difference" in the little White boy mirrors Uncle Remus's, because neither are performing traditional gender expectations. Both are "off" in some way—according to their era's requirements for males—which makes them a tiny community of two, despite their different races. When considering what Uncle Remus's real-life improvisations—his survival tactics—might have been during the early Jim Crow era, I can't help but think about Bruh Rabbit's tendencies to say whatever is needed at a particular time, to survive.

7.

As an African American woman, I am descended from blood, but also from the *ideas* of this country. As an imagined figure, Tar Baby is my ancestor, too.

In reading this folktale, I know I'm supposed to be on Bruh Rabbit's side. After all, clearly, he's a stand-in for the oppressed southern African American man. And Bruh Fox is the tool of White supremacy, though he, too, speaks in what Joel Chandler Harris imagined as a Black vernacular, however much he butchered it.

But as a Black woman, I think about the "sister" in this scenario: Tar Baby. I imagine her as a luscious, dark-skinned woman-creature, one who is free with her love. My imaginary Tar Baby is totally different from the wordless figure tugged between two trash-talking brothers.

What would Tar Baby say, if she could really speak? She could tell all the places she had traveled throughout the world. How she'd perched on the mouths of chained African peoples who survived the Middle Passage, and crawled out to accompany Lapin, the ultimately victorious trickster hare. How Tar Baby crouched around the fires of the clans of the Indigenous folks in this country, listening to the antics of Tsisdu or Chufee, a rabbit who always triumphed, too.

I wonder how Tar Baby came to be on a red dirt road in Georgia and where she was going, before them two Negroes—Bruh Fox and Bruh Rabbit—decided to hem her up and make her a boxing prize. The place on which she sits might be one I've encountered too many times: a crossroads, two of those narrow throughways traversing in a town so dear and familiar to me. You turn off the highway, and the tiny rocks fly toward the windshield.

I want to believe that Tar Baby's silence isn't stupidity. She is only careful about keeping her own counsel. She's vigilant with her words, but sure enough, if you treat her right, an abundance might be told.

In my mind, Tar Baby is every woman I've ever considered beautiful: Black and comely, like Sheba in the Bible. *Black* meaning *dark like molasses*. So delicious, she is forbidden. Tugged back and forth by sometimes violent hands, but one day, she'll raise her voice to whoever touches her: "If you know what's good, you better turn me loose."

37

Imaginary Letter to the White Lady Colleague Who Might Have Sat Next to Me at One of the Now Eliminated University Workshops for Diversity, Equity, and Inclusion Training

Dear _____:

I want to use one of my mother's cherished phrases: "You meant well."

Because when I met you at the workshop, you seemed so kind, and that had made me want to trust you. Your outwardly gentle countenance streaked with hints of pink, your whispery, baby voice, a peculiar trademark in the feminist stronghold of academia, almost made me unafraid.

The night before, when I was thinking about my terror of White people, I'd thought about when Barack Obama was elected. Those delicious eight years had given me a reprieve from fear. White people had voted for Obama, so not all of them could be so bad.

But the next morning, as I scanned the gathering at the workshop, my fear returned. I carefully searched for other African Americans in the mass of Whites. *Please let some other colored folks show up*, I prayed. *Please, Lord. Don't let me go through this alone.*

There were twenty-three faculty members. We sat at a cluster of round tables, a shape that indicated that there would be no hierarchy. No beginning and no end. No alpha and omega. I glanced at the front of the room. No, not the *front*, because there was not supposed to be a front. The empty space farthest from the door.

There was only one Black person besides me. She didn't count, however, because this woman—this *sister*—was the moderator of the workshop. And she was doggedly avoiding my significant glances, looking past me to the others. They were the ones who counted. They were White people and truly needed this workshop. Sister Moderator and I, we already possessed a commitment to diversity, equity, and inclusion. Our history was our commitment. Our skin.

Sister Moderator nodded vaguely at the entire group, her nod indicating that everyone in the room was great, and we'd be great together. Perhaps just for these three hours—minus a twenty-minute break—but as occurs at university gatherings, some of us might exchange business cards after this event was over. We might continue to discover each other.

She reminded us that each attendee of this workshop would receive a medium-size sticker that we could—if we chose, but no *pressure*—place on the outside of our office door to indicate that we had attended this workshop and were indeed committed to its stated principles. I silently assumed that even that White dude over there from the Classics Department, where the faculty only teaches European texts—even that dude would get his sticker.

I wanted my sticker, too, even though it would be cheating, considering I'm Black and already in the know.

The gathering assumed a lack of knowledge, and so there'd be a presumption of respect. But then again, if we didn't know each other, then we were strangers, and my mama had warned me against talking to strangers, especially White men: "Don't sit down next to a strange White man in any room or even the bus stop. Don't show your teeth to a strange White man. If you have the nerve to laugh or get friendly, he might think you're flirting with him, which will make him remember what he's learned about the loose nature of Black women."

You arrived about ten minutes after the workshop officially began, though Sister Moderator had only given innocuous remarks. You settled next to me: there was only one space left in the room. If you'd been

Black, I might have whispered something to you about "CP Time." I couldn't take that chance with a White woman. But you *were* a woman, and that meant I was almost unafraid of you. So close to being at ease.

There was opportunity here: We might become friends, if we chatted nicely, sipped the free dark roast coffee, and ate the free pastries provided. There were nice pens in the center of the table, too: rollerballs. I was already scheming on taking three of them back home with me.

You placed your messenger bag on the table, right in my space. Or the space I'd claimed for myself. I scooted away a few inches to reestablish my territory. You smiled at me, hesitantly, nervously, and I moved into White-people-pleasing mode as I saw the other seats filled with people who didn't look like me either. I tried to calm my panic.

"Hey there," I said to you. "It sure is early! Those pastries better be yummy, if they want us here at the butt-crack of dawn."

I laughed, making sure there was warmth in my voice. I was so good at being warm. It's a trait that I inherited from my Georgia mama. Your smile lengthened, and I was relieved I hadn't lost my maternal superpowers. We introduced ourselves: our names, our fields, our departments. The subjects of our books. You were in the Modern Languages Department, one of only two women.

I told you I was a poet, but I was working on my first novel.

"Oh, gosh! That sounds so wonderful," you baby-whispered.

"Sometimes," I whispered back, though like a grown person. "Other times, not so much."

"But it sounds so much fun!"

"Well, it's work, just like any other field."

"But don't you just love it? Isn't it fun?"

When you repeated the word *fun*, I tried to self-soothe. I reminded myself that usually only other artists respect the labor of writing. I was trying not to feel defensive.

"Not like what I'm working on," you said. "These footnotes in Chicago. This index. I'm exhausted."

You gave a brief shudder, then began explaining that "Chicago" stood for *Chicago Manual of Style*—but in a normal voice, I cut you off, telling you that my latest book of poetry included a bibliography and an afterword with endnotes in *Chicago.*

I continued that I was an elected member of a well-known historical society to which fourteen US presidents have been elected. If somebody woke me in the middle of the night, I probably could recite that line about the presidents. It's straight from the website of the society. Every time somebody made me feel intellectually inferior, I informed them of my membership.

"Oh, wow," you said. "How did that happen? You know, for a poet?"

"I guess because I'm brilliant. You know, like the *rest* of the elected members."

I'd failed: I was definitely defensive. I remained silent for long seconds, unsure of how I should tread conversational waters.

I spoke again, but my warmth was faked. I was disappointed in you, when I'd been somewhat hopeful: You had a ring in your nose, and one side of your head was shaved. Cosmetic attributes that might have indicated progressive sensibilities. Tolerance on your part, though one never knows in this state. And one never knows about White academics.

I hopped up, dashing to the bathroom to wash my hands. I prayed that the cinnamon rolls wouldn't be gone when I returned to the workshop room. And God was good: I took the last three and avoided thinking about whether someone with unwashed hands had already touched them. At our table, your eyes lighted up at my generosity, but I pushed the cinnamon rolls to my side. I needed you to understand I wasn't sharing. These suckers were for me. I deserved them. I wrapped two of the rolls in a napkin, placing them in my purse. I tried not to shove the other one in my mouth, but I needed the sugar to calm me.

I looked at my watch. How much longer? Two hours and forty-one minutes. (Minus the break.) If I ate another cinnamon roll, I might move from calm to drowsiness.

As a last resort, I began rocking slowly in my chair.

There was historical and visual rhetoric in that room. I'm a dark woman with tight curls usually caught up in a rubber band. Looking at my skin, features, and hair, you might assume that I'm African American, and that assumption would be correct, because although my family always has insisted on Cherokee ancestors, I can't prove that. I'm not enrolled in any tribe, I wasn't reared among people who identify as Native American, and none of my Indigenous ancestors' names appear on the Dawes Roll. Those family stories don't mean much as documentation. And I didn't really *want* to claim my White ancestors, though I didn't lie about having them.

You were pale-skinned with a European-sounding last name. I thought I could guess some of your background. Even if your ancestors came over to this country in the post–Civil War time, you identified as White. That means you could claim privilege—otherwise, you'd be calling yourself something else.

I wondered if you told yourself lies about your ancestors' exceptionalism, about their racial tolerance, all evidence to the contrary. I, too, thought about Black falsehoods propagated as iron truths, like how we tell ourselves that West Africans who sold other West Africans into slavery didn't know what they were doing. That because African slavery was different—benign, kind, even—that they couldn't have known the horror that awaited dark people on this side of the water. That, even after several centuries of West African slave-trading, participation in selling war captives, those newer slave traders had been naive, unaware that the enslaved would never return to the motherland. Those lies always make me furious, though I'm aware that everyone avoids some bits of reality.

Sister Moderator began distributing the questionnaire, though she'd prepared a PowerPoint with colorful, eye-catching graphics as well. We'd need all this stimulation early in the morning on a Saturday: already, there were yawns no one bothered to conceal.

I picked up a rollerball and wondered who'd put these handouts together, because anybody with sense would know not to pick "(D) Honestly, I don't want to be here" as one of the four answers to why we decided to take this workshop. I chose the safe and obvious alternative:

"(A) I'm sincerely interested in learning how to be sensitive to those who are different than myself."

The other questions seemed simple enough, and I finished quickly, choosing my answers in under a minute, but when I looked around the room, everyone else seemed to be in deep, painful contemplation. I lowered my head and pretended to read back over my answers. A few minutes passed, and Sister Moderator lightly clapped her hands.

"All right, let's see those questionnaires," she exclaimed, and the others reluctantly pass her theirs.

You nudged my arm. "That was so hard!" The room was lively, so you'd raised your voice. I didn't have to lean in to hear you.

"It sure was!" I made sure to match your earnest energy. The wheels of my emotional labor machine remained oily. I had to sit at this table with you for the next two hours and twenty-nine minutes—minus the break. Besides, I've always been too harsh with people of all backgrounds, even my own. I needed to be more patient.

Sister Moderator continued that we'd go around the room and introduce ourselves. She suggested that we offer one piece of information that was unique. Something about ourselves that might make us different than anyone else. You and I were closest to where Sister Moderator was standing, but I prayed that our table would go last.

It was supposed to be a secret, but word on the university streets was that this workshop was a punishment for badly behaved faculty. I was curious: How many of us in the room weren't here voluntarily?

How many of us had been strong-armed by our chairperson to attend this workshop because we had wide gaps on our curriculum vitae under the "professional development" heading? Or because we might be coming up for tenure and/or promotion and wanted to seem sensitive to the university committee? Or because anonymous students had commented on the end-of-semester evaluations that it seemed impossible to believe that a cisgender White male professor who hadn't changed his syllabus in fifteen years could truly believe that Black lives mattered, according to that heartfelt statement the professor had placed in sixteen-point bold font at the top of said syllabus?

During introductions, about half the attendees mentioned their pets by name.

One person was very proud of their vintage T-shirt collection.

Someone else knew how to fly a plane and ski—"Though not at the same time!" Obligatory, strained laughter followed.

The classics professor from across the room informed us that he really believed in the First Amendment, as if we might not know that: The man *was* wearing a bright-red T-shirt with a matching cap, and both announced THE FIRST AMENDMENT (DAMNIT).

"It's gotten to the point where you can't even read particular words from a published book! People are so sensitive these days," Classics Dude said. "I mean, what's next? Proctors in our classrooms? I'm supposed to be a full professor. I've taught at this university for thirty years."

I fixed my face, keeping my eyebrows raised in a neutral expression. My lips stretched in straight line. I looked around to see who was nodding in agreement with Classics Dude—only about five others—and who maintained noncommittal blandness. I was pleased to see that you were one of the latter. I shifted so that I could catch your eye, and you quickly winked at me.

When it was your turn to introduce yourself, you mentioned that you spoke six languages fluently, and before I could stop myself, I burst into applause.

"That's so amazing!" I exclaimed.

Sister Moderator reminded me to respect everyone's time, but you said, no, it's completely fine. Wonderful, in fact, since I seemed way more excited than your parents were about your being a polyglot. Again, laughter from the others in the room, but this time, it seemed sincere.

When I introduced myself and said I was a full professor and a poet, you clapped, too.

Then the Power Point started, filled with boilerplate. I pretended to be taking notes—looking up from time to time and nodding and making attentive noises—when actually I'd started writing a poem in my notebook.

After the twenty-minute break, Sister Moderator encouraged us to feel free to return to the refreshments table without asking. She said there were three more boxes of coffee, and plenty of pastries, too—though no more cinnamon rolls—and gave me a lingering side eye. Then she announced it was time for the discussion sessions, to talk through the original handout in more detail.

When you and I remained in our places, Sister Moderator chided, no, let's meet new people.

"Professor J," she said to me. "Why don't you try sitting a while at that other table? But only if you're comfortable."

She gestured toward the table where Classics Dude sat.

The troublemaker in me debated saying, I'm deeply uncomfortable talking to any White man in a red shirt and matching hat. But it had been a surprisingly good morning: I picked up my purse and my belongings, though you'd told me you'd watch those for me.

"No, I got it," I said. "But thanks!"

I hoped you understood, it was no longer you that I didn't trust: You had proven yourself. It was the others who had been sitting with us, those who reminded me what Ntozake Shange had written about somebody and her stuff. I didn't want to be a victim of academic settler colonialism.

At my new table, Classic Dude decided he was in charge. He began reading out the questions. The others at this table—three White women—didn't object.

"Get a load of this one," he said. "'Has there ever been a time when you made someone who was a different culture, gender, or sexual orientation uncomfortable?'"

He sighed loudly, but I jumped in.

"I'll go first!" I said. "Let me see . . ." I tapped my top lip, but I didn't need to think. I already remembered the moment. "Okay . . . well, before I went through LGBTQIA ally training, I didn't really understand how problematic it was to call my trans students by their dead names. I hadn't been keeping up. I'm pretty absentminded, too, and one day I called out a name on the roll that was a student's dead name. I didn't know whether to say something or not, so I just froze, but then I just apologized to them, and it was fine—"

Classics Dude cut me off. "You did what? I'm sorry, I'm not getting this."

The other women at table turned in my direction: *Tell him*, their expressions urged. *Do this for us.*

Because I'd had an extra cup of coffee with cream—so much cream, though I felt proud that I'd brought my own stevia packets—I began to explain what I knew about the gender spectrum. My tone signaled virtue, claiming good intentions, as I told Classics Dude that a dead name is the name of a trans person before they affirmed their true gender.

While I gave him the official spiel, I held back the full, shameful details of the day when I called out the dead name of that student. I hadn't wanted to draw attention to myself. I hadn't wanted to feel foolish or admit weakness, so when the student looked at me, their eyes widening, I'd only said "Oops," in a breezy way, as if it wasn't a big deal. I quickly followed up by calling out the student's living name, but all through class that student was withdrawn, looking down at their desk, and I felt their pain pulling at me. Their embarrassment. Their disappointment, because I was supposed to be the cool professor. My students had told me that I was one of a few on campus that even asked for preferred pronouns. After class, I'd called to the student I'd offended, waited for everyone to leave, and then apologized, sucking up tears because I couldn't stand when somebody hurt my feelings and then cried to try to make me feel guilty. I kept asking the student to forgive me, and I knew that I'd finally made things right between us when they had smiled and joked, It's okay, Professor J: I was old, and sometimes old folks forgot, and we had laughed together—but even after that, I'd been ashamed for weeks. Sometimes I would cry, and then, I'd think, I was making this about me, and it wasn't. It was about that student. And I'd feel ashamed again.

"But if that's the name on the registrar's class roll, that's the student's name." Classics Dude folded his arms and nodded several times, agreeing with himself.

"No, that's *not* their name," I said. "That's the name that someone else gave them for a gender that's not theirs. That's why it's called 'dead.' "

Classics Dude raised his voice. "You know what? This is why so many people voted for Trump the first time around! I mean, I didn't, of course. I'd never vote for a Republican. I'm a registered Libertarian, but I totally get it."

"Get what?" I laughed. "Get ignorance? Get transphobia? Get homophobia? Get racism? Get misogyny? Just what kind of lowdown shit are you getting?"

The three women at the table gasped.

"Hey now," one said, in a whisper. The other two women whispered, too: something about keeping things civil.

"Hey nothing!" My own voice raised. "Y'all really just gone let this man be a bully?" My southern drawl was in full effect, but I was hot. I was ready to fight somebody, to feel righteous, to erase the shame of that past day, long ago, when I'd hurt the feelings of my student, somebody only two years out of high school. "These are kids we're talking about! We might as well be teaching thirteenth grade!"

I felt others around the room staring at our table, staring at me. I looked over to where you were, seeking your support. Your eyes met mine for a second, and then you looked away.

Sister Moderator appeared. "How we doing over here?"

"Oh, we are doing just fine," I said. "I was just explaining transphobia and humanity to him." There was only one man at the table, so I didn't feel the need to gesture.

"And I was just explaining the First Amendment to this—" He stopped. "I was explaining to her."

He pointed his finger in my direction, and I was grateful he was sitting across from me and not beside me. Because if this Latin-reading-and-speaking motherfucker had put his finger in my face, I would have thrown my cup of rich, dark French roast at him and then flipped this goddamned table. And then, I wouldn't have a job no more.

The three women at my table began speaking in soothing tones. They recounted the exchange between Classics Dude and me, taking his side, saying he hadn't meant any harm. He wasn't a bad person. We needed more dialogue and less accusation. I had become so angry, and that's why the country was so divided right now.

"Actually, I'd have to agree with Professor J," Sister Moderator said. "Her reaction to dead-naming her student was very appropriate. Now, it *is* best for us not to shout or curse"—she chuckled—"so maybe you two should lower your voices? But as Professor J was saying, sensitivity to others is key. That's why we're all here, isn't it?"

Classics Dude refolded his arms.

I looked up at Sister Moderator. Nothing too obvious, but enough to register gratitude. Before she moved to the next table, she patted my shoulder.

Finally, it was noon. The workshop was over.

Sister-Moderator told us she'd now exit the room, so we could fill out the evaluation forms without feeling uncomfortable in her presence.

I returned to my original table, where you waited. After a couple silent minutes, you turned to me. You were friendly again—you looked in my eyes this time, instead of glancing away—and I surrendered to chatting about our shared ordeal. That wasn't so bad, you said. This was kind of fabulous, and I agreed.

You leaned toward me.

"But oh, my fucking god," you baby-whispered. "That guy in red. White guys are the absolute worst. Aren't they the worst?" You discreetly pointed at Classics Dude, who was sitting alone at his table, intensely filling out the workshop evaluation.

"Take care of yourself," I said. "It was so good meeting you."

You reached for my hand and squeezed it. "Oh, thank you! That means so much, coming from you."

You rose and offered your business card, saying you were grateful you had met me. I was so funny. So stylish: look at my shoes. And wise, because you'd learned so much from me, even in three short hours. I made this university a better place—this world even! And you wanted to have lunch or dinner with me, sometime very soon. You couldn't wait.

I placed your card on the table. When you playfully demanded my own card—give it over, you said, giggling—my rage began to rise, like the thickest cream.

I thought about what had happened at the end of Mr. Obama's peaceful eight years as president, when 53 percent of White ladies had betrayed my people and voted for a racist crotch-grabber. Before then, if somebody had told me what would happen, after that interval of a well-behaved, handsome Black man leading this nation, I would have questioned their sanity.

"You know, I don't carry cards," I said. "They seem so wasteful, when I can just give somebody my number to put in their phone. I'm not going to give you my number, though, because I don't ever want to talk to you again." My mama's drawl was back, but I made certain that my voice stayed low: there aren't too many places where a shouting Black woman can prolong safety. "I'm tired of you already. I'm tired of even thinking about sharing a meal with you, much less picking up a fork in your presence. And if I do spot you on campus, I'm going to walk in the other direction, because after fifty-plus years on this planet, I'm just exhausted by progressive White folks. But God bless you."

You stood over me, repeatedly apologizing. "Oh, no, what did I do? I'm sorry! I thought we had something here. I thought we could be friends. I'm so sorry."

The rosy color in your face had deepened and overtaken your cheeks, your chin, your forehead. Your eyes welled with tears, and I knew I should be very afraid. There's nothing more dangerous than a crying White woman standing in front of a Black person unwilling to make the amends that will keep history at bay. You were wrong about me: I wasn't wise, because I didn't care about your tears, even when Classics Dude stared over at us, smirking.

I gestured to the post-workshop sheet, telling you I should complete the evaluation. Please leave me in peace. I looked down at the table instead of attending to your monologue: You didn't understand why I was angry. Why was I so angry? You were sorry. Did I think you were a racist? Because you weren't. I had to believe you. You were so sorry. What was it that you'd said?

Finally, you were gone, and I praised the creator that my Georgia mother had worshipped, though He wasn't entirely merciful: Classics Dude remained across the room.

I used one of the free rollerballs and began filling out my evaluation:

"On a scale of one to five—five being the highest, most positive score, and one being the lowest, least positive score—how was this workshop?"

Five.

"How well did the moderator facilitate this workshop?"

Five.

"Please rate the following, again on a scale of one to five: 'I have learned many useful things today that will positively impact my future interactions with others who are different from me.' "

Five.

In the "Further comments" section, I wrote long, positive passages, making sure to eliminate any cultural cues that would reveal my solidarity with Sister-Moderator. The evaluation remarks would be anonymous, but I suspected that, in addition to Classics Dude, several other seemingly gracious White attendees had given Sister-Moderator the lowest scores possible. They probably had written hostile details in "Further comments" too, after smiling and thanking her for such a fantastic Saturday-morning experience. So I wanted to help my sister. I really needed to help this Black woman out, because only she and I were in this thing together.

Sincerely,

Professor J

38

On Being Fannie Lou Hamer Tired

1.

We Black women can call upon some empowering mantras, can't we? There's "Ain't I A Woman?" This is a quote attributed to Sojourner Truth, but which was written by a White woman.[1] (That's a long story that Nell Irvin Painter can tell you; unlike me, she's an actual historian.)[2]

There's "And Still I Rise," the poem by Maya Angelou. When I was growing up, that poem was a staple at high school talent shows. This is the "strong Black woman mantra," a resistant utterance.

Let's not forget the various snippets of lyrics from Beyoncé albums, preferably from the *Lemonade* project, which, depending on who you ask, is about empowering Black women or it's about putting her husband's cheating on blast. (I can't quote from any of these lyrics, though, because I don't have Beyoncé money to pay for permissions.)

There's a time when a Black woman is exhausted, but that fatigue comes from demands placed upon her from *within* her own community. When she feels she can't go on, but she's expected to do so much. Specifically, she's compelled—through guilt or tradition—to perform labor, in her community, church, in her family. This labor is uncompensated, either financially or in reciprocal—and meaningful—acknowledgment. (Beyond, of course, "Women's Day" at Black churches, where the women do all the work to prepare for that day and receive a couple hymns, pertinent Bible verses, slices of that ever-present lemon pound cake, and red carnations for their trouble.)

Black women's exhaustion can look like a frightening mental health crisis, when there's no scheduled therapy with a counselor that day—or when a sister can't even afford therapy. She is one step from cussing somebody out, before or after bursting into tears. She might be two glasses into a bottle of wine of nefarious/suspect vintage. Maybe she's chewed an edible, for good measure. That's the day she declares that, like the renowned civil rights activist Fannie Lou Hamer, "I'm sick and tired of being sick and tired."[3]

I'm not saying that other women of other communities don't get to be exhausted. But a Fannie Lou Hamer moment targets the historical nexuses of racial and gender marginalization(s), combined with Black cultural expectations—with some White supremacy thrown in. It is a moment familiar to many African American women, when we are just not having it anymore. When a sister approaches a Fannie Lou Hamer moment, perhaps she's spent some time in this world noticing that no one cares about those tears she's crying.

Usually, only White women's tears are noticed and honored. There is no danger to anybody in the vicinity of a crying Black woman, whereas if a White woman cries, that's a cue to assume that somebody committed a terrible wrong against her. A White man. A Black woman. A Black man who makes a White woman cry?—okay, now, that's going to be a *very* serious problem.

When a Black woman cries, she might not even be offered a tissue. But other African Americans might toss her a look informing her that she's violated the strong Black woman covenant.

Come on now, girl, that look will say. *Get yourself together.*

2.

Keisha N. Blain has written a compelling treatment of Fannie Lou Hamer, *Until I Am Free: Fannie Lou Hamer's Enduring Message to America,* which combines academic writing, personal reminisces, and political analyses of Hamer's life. We learn about Fannie Lou Hamer's early life in Mississippi, how she left school to financially contribute to her family's finances, because they had growing money troubles.[4] Hamer worked as a domestic, and Blain recounts Hamer's story where she challenges the veracity of her White woman employer insisting that she, too, had labored physically alongside Hamer, her Black woman domestic.[5] That Hamer strongly asserted herself is already courageous, but to know that this Black female assertion took place in Mississippi, known for its violence toward African Americans, is extraordinary.

Hamer's denial of a White woman's appropriation of Black female domestic labor brands the complicated relationship between African American and White women in this country. What Hamer implies about her employer is that it's possible to be a victim *and* an oppressor, but this is the largely ignored history of White women in America. It's a challenge for Black women to seek allyship with White women, for how can we hold sympathy toward those guilty of hurting us while claiming a shared sisterhood?

Hamer's denunciation of her employer's lies also represents an "anti-Mammy" epiphany, going against every condescending, racist expectation for a Black woman: that the hands that prepared the food, cleaned the kitchen and bathroom(s), and wiped the behinds of small (White) children are guided by the hands of a White employer. That thhese hands do not move independently, and their subsequent labor belongs to someone else—again, a White employer. When we shift from the hands up to the dark face of a submissive Black female domestic, there should be a broad smile, indicating that the performed labor was pleasurable. This is the smile of the idealized, (assumed) selfless Black woman.

After reading Blain's book about Fannie Lou Hamer and listening to the brief autobiography that Hamer recorded in 1963, *Songs My Mother Taught Me*, I'm even angrier at the expectations foisted onto Black women. While Hamer turned personal suffering into a Black community good, I don't consider her the quintessential, long-suffering Black woman. Fannie Lou Hamer's agency came from within herself.

It was an evening in 1964 when she spoke to an audience who'd come to see Malcolm X speak as well. When I look at these words and listen to them, I recognize a turning point of self-realization. One Black woman has moved from a collective/plural first person pronoun—*we*—to a singular pronoun—*I*—back to the collective *we*. From a rhetorical standpoint, this is an example of what I've called "the Black communal lyric," when one righteous speaker "of moral authority stands as a frontal representative of African/American community(ies) in the background."[6] As with so many utterances by Black women, Hamer's words have become sacred to me, the spoken thoughts of a messianic figure who charged forth. Despite her fear and the genuine danger that she knew she might encounter, for she already had met danger: the year before, she was beaten while in White police custody.[7]

But Hamer pressed on that evening, speaking truth to the crimes of powerful White people: "For three hundred years we've given them time. And I've been tired so long. Now, I'm sick and tired of being sick and tired, and we want a change."[8]

This moment of rejecting the status quo imposed upon African American women is one of logic and personal subjectivity. Hamer asserts that, though her work has benefited the Black community of her town, state, and country, it is not selfless: it feeds Hamer's sense of self. This is a time of naming: A Black woman has finally had enough and is ready for change. She has become. She has emerged.

3.

I remember telephoning Uncle Charles, my mother's (now late) baby brother, to ask why I hadn't been informed of Mama's hospitalization after her first stroke. This was in 2009.

I'd been on my first hiatus from Mama; these would continue throughout the years, as I hoped that long stretches of silence between us would somehow change her behavior and mute my anger about my childhood. I didn't find out about her stroke until I spoke to her, after I hadn't called her for several months; the issue *that* time was that Mama had started demanding money to pay her mortgage. I was making plans to carve out the $900 a month—knowing I didn't have it—when Mama casually mentioned that she was planning on leaving her home to one of my sisters, after her death. I was confused: I was supposed to pay her mortgage, but someone else would receive the house? I kept pushing the issue until Mama erupted into a tantrum, shouting that I was selfish with my money. Other people had it harder than I did. Why did I need a second house anyway, when I already owned one in Oklahoma? I couldn't take my money with me.

After a while of this, I hung up on her.

Later that same year, when I was on the phone with Uncle Charles, instead of apologizing or explaining why no one in our large family had thought to contact me about Mama's life-threatening health issue, he began shouting at me for neglecting the family. He told me that if I hadn't moved so far away, I'd know what was happening with my mother. As was usually the case when speaking to my family, I was bewildered. Did anybody really think I'd *wanted* to move to Oklahoma, of all places? I'd only gone there for the job at a university. It wasn't like tenure-track academic teaching positions were easy to secure, especially for a Black woman.

I didn't mention to Uncle Charles what he already knew, that for years a known male sexual abuser had been invited to our family reunion in Eatonton, Georgia. According to Mama—whom I believed—a male relative had sexually assaulted her at four years old; she'd blurted this to me during one of our many arguments. (It had been *another* maternal uncle who handed my four-year-old Mama the butcher knife with which she'd accidentally put out her right eye. Both relatives are long dead.)

Knowing that my mother's sexual abuser was given a hot rib plate, greetings, and smiles while he walked around Grandma's yard—or sat next to Mama on the pew at her oldest brother Alvester's funeral and had the nerve to speak to her—caused me panic attacks. During the family reunion, I'd try to watch over the small children while also trying to watch the abuser, to make sure he didn't go after the kids. I'd spoken to other kin about disinviting this abuser, and they had spoken to me about "accusations" and said that "forgiveness is in the Bible."

On the phone, Uncle Charles continued: he said that he couldn't stand me. There were some other choice words. Taken aback, I began crying, which made me angry at myself. I didn't want to be weak. I haltingly explained that, as a sexual abuse survivor myself, my mental health had suffered throughout the years; that's why I'd kept my distance. I needed to take care of myself, and it was hard doing that.

My uncle responded that he was "tired of hearing that story" about my abusive father, who had been dead since the mid-1980s. He revealed that my sister Sisi had confided in him before she died that our father had sexually abused her as well. This was the first time I learned that Sisi was a survivor, too—I knew about my sister Val's experiences already—and my heart felt like it was being sliced open.

This conversation and the subsequent lack of sympathy when I repeated Uncle Charles's remarks to other family members let me know that very few in my family were concerned about my mental or physical health, or the generational trauma that had been passed down from my mother, who had been sexually abused by a relative, a person who *also* abused one of my childhood friends (and yes, I believed my friend)—to my sisters and me, who were abused by our father. Though I continued to be honest about Daddy's abuse, Mama and other relatives would mention him with affection and respect, as if my mouth had been moving when recounting my childhood terrors, but no sound had emerged.

There were other women in the family whose mental health had suffered because their emotional labor had been misused and unacknowledged. The prime example of this was Grandma Florence. She had "gone down slow" for years before her death, but when family members talked about her strange behavior, they would laughingly reconfigure this behavior into mere eccentricity.

∿

That conversation I had with Uncle Charles still hurts, though he's been dead for several years. When I am trying to capture some compassion, I suppose he was angry because, since I am a highly educated Black woman with reasonably good credit, I was expected to become the next matriarch of our family, to hold up the family with one hand while clutching a Bible—a huge one with the gilt-edged pages—in the other. To "loan" money (which certainly would never be repaid) to less fortunate family members, kin who would turn around and talk badly about me, sometimes even to my face, after taking my cash.

Throughout Black communities, African American women had held it down for their families for centuries. My grandmother Florence and my mother had been two of those women. Before she became disabled, my sister Sisi was another of these women, too—one of those family helpmeets.

Black folks—this is a "Dear Reader" moment—you know what I'm talking about, don't you? You know about those older women rustling grandchildren with greased faces, knees, and elbows to church every Sunday. You've eaten the meals of these women and asked for seconds and thirds. When the progeny of these older women are either unable or unwilling to take care of their own children, they've left those kids with Black grandmothers or other female relatives to rear.

The only rest for an African American woman is death, after a grand homegoing that many times requires a "passed hat" to pay for because these women can't afford burial insurance. (We had to pass the hat to bury Sisi. I put in my last thousand dollars at the time, leaving my savings at zero.)

There will be inconsolable weeping, however. A heartfelt eulogy, and fried chicken at the repast—and then a search for a new Black woman to carry out the unpaid labor of her family and community. There might be some issues for this new woman, over the years. Maybe some large, painful uterine fibroids, with diagnoses of type 2 diabetes and/or high blood pressure thrown in for good measure. But she will endure until it's time for her to pass away, too, and another Black woman takes her place.

4.

Listening to Fannie Lou Hamer's recorded autobiography, so much of what she talked about was familiar from my conversations with my mother.

The twenty children that Hamer's mother bore reminded me of my maternal great- grandmother's brood of fifteen living children.[9] The poverty that Hamer withstood was nearly identical to Mama's as a little girl. As I heard Hamer tell the story of her parents finally getting out of the financial hole, only to have a White man poison the drinking trough where this Black family's mule drank, I had to cut off the recording.

I put my hand over my eyes and wailed, "Oh, Miss Fannie! Oh, Lord have mercy."

I thought of my mother's stories about her upbringing, how mean Grandma Florence and Ma Sweet had been to her, only for Mama to marry a man—my daddy—who would verbally, physically, and sexually abuse her girl children, and abuse Mama as well. And yet she stayed married to Daddy until he died, even after they had separated. Over my pleading and objections, when he was diagnosed with terminal heart disease, Mama brought him down to Atlanta. She moved out of the apartment that she and I shared, moved Sisi in with me (after Sisi left her roommate's apartment), and relocated to an apartment with my father.

Once I'd asked Mama to go into therapy with me so we could work out our problems, and she'd scoffed, "Nobody has problems but you."

Before my parents separated, I would beg Mama to leave Daddy, and she would respond that I didn't know what it was like to be black—*black* with a lowercase *b*, meaning dark-skinned—and poor. To have other African Americans scowl at me because I was so dark, like they thought I had no right to be born. She insisted many of her classmates at Spelman College had done this, along with my father's former colleagues at Howard University. She'd even published an essay about this colorism, "The Black Black Woman and the Black Middle-Class."

Mama broadly hinted that she'd married my father so that her children wouldn't carry her own color. Other times, she'd insist that men her own darker shade of brown wouldn't have her; only fair men seemed to find her suitable for a public, *respectable* commitment. Mama told me that dark-skinned brothers only wanted to sleep with her in secret.

I read E. Franklin Frazier's condescending history *The Black Bourgeoisie*, which included his rules for belonging to that socioeconomic class. Frazier wasn't complimenting anybody in that number, but I could tell from Mama's suddenly nasal tone when she said the word *bourgeoisie* that it meant something positive and superior to her.

Did we want to slide into poverty, Mama asked, when she could testify how horrible that life was? There was no nobility in being poor. It was dirty, it was humiliating, it was dangerous. There was only escape, if that was possible.

~≈~

At my mother's funeral in the fall of 2023, her brother Thedwron would tell a story about his big sister Trellie saving the life of a relative, my great-aunt Flossie, who died some years back. She was my mother's aunt; because Ma Sweet bore children from her adolescence through her forties, some of her grandchildren were older than Flossie, Ma Sweet's youngest child.

Uncle Ted was up on the stage talking. Down on the floor of De-Forest Chapel at Talladega College—where Mama had taught for over two decades—was the fancy casket. I'd pulled money out of my novel royalty savings to "put her away right." But the casket was closed and there had been no viewing. Knowing how Southern Black folks viciously gossip about funerals, I didn't want anybody judging my mother's appearance. When she died, she had been almost a hundred pounds lighter than her regular weight, and nearly bald, her mouth sunken because all but seven or eight of her teeth had fallen out.

The gold satin dress I'd bought Mama and the silver turban a friend had provided were beautiful, though, as were the underwear and stockings she wore. I didn't care about all that money going into the ground. My mama used to say she might not be pretty, but she sure knew how to dress. I wanted her looking extra fine when she finally met her Jesus.

Behind the podium, Uncle Ted recounted in dramatic fashion that as a toddler, his aunt Flossie—Grandma Florence's baby sister—had fallen into a creek and dipped two times already; she didn't have much time before she drowned. Mama, a little girl not much older than eight or nine, had acted quickly: she quickly found a branch, thrust it into the water, and somehow pulled Aunt Flossie to safety.

I knew that Uncle Ted like to take his time when explaining his critical analysis, and his speech this Thursday afternoon in late October was no exception. He mentioned that when the children had returned from the creek that day and told everyone how his sister Trellie had saved Aunt Flossie, none of the adults made a big deal about it. But to Uncle Ted, my mother's actions proved that she would become a great person, and she showed that quality as a woman of the family, for she returned, after her graduation from Spelman College, to teach in Eatonton at segregated schools. When she left Eatonton, she would earn a doctorate and become a college professor. Uncle Ted pointed out that Mama had students who revered her; five of her college students would speak at her service, including my cousin Todd and me, who had been taught by Mama. (And during the funeral one of my friends would read a statement emailed to me by Alice Walker, testifying to her love for and admiration of Mama, her former teacher in Eatonton.)

To me, Uncle Ted's logic revealed that though Mama had talked years before about needing to be selfish to survive poverty, she'd been just the opposite with many people: giving her strength, money—he didn't say so, but Mama died penniless—and emotional support to others. I remember what she would say during our increasingly rare phone conversations, when I fussed at her for giving her last dime to grown people who wouldn't work: "Honorée, if I don't do it, who will?" And she told me I didn't need her sympathy or her money: I was strong, like she was. I could take care of myself; she'd reared me that way.

During Mama's funeral service, I sat on the chapel pew, listening to my uncle's story about my mother saving Aunt Flossie. Though I concealed it, I was so overtaken with rage I thought I'd spew curses. I'd never heard this tale of my mother's heroism, not once. Certainly, I'd heard Uncle Ted brag on how smart his sister was; he and Mama had been best friends their entire lives. I thought I knew every bit of Mama's history, but I was thrown. No one had mentioned this story to me: not my mother, not Ma Sweet, not Grandma Florence, and not Aunt Flossie.

What I *had* heard consistently from Aunt Flossie and other members of my grandmother's (now-deceased) family was how ugly dark-skinned people were. The direct implication was that, as a very dark-skinned person, Mama was damaged goods. Further, one of my earliest memories was of Aunt Flossie cursing in the yard of our home in California. I was almost four years old—this was in the very early 1970s—and Aunt Flossie was screaming horrible words at Mama, the woman who had once saved her life.

What kind of sense did Aunt Flossie's behavior make? I asked myself.

I recalled something my mother liked to say: "I'll tell you what kind of sense, Honorée: *nonsense.*" Then she'd laugh in that musical way of hers.

As I sat on the pew, I believed Mama was trying to tell me something. She was sorry for everything. Didn't I know she was sorry? About Daddy, about calling me a liar. She knew I'd told the truth. She had been ashamed that this had happened in her house. That's why she'd turned on me—and to forget her own shame about her addiction to Valium during a time when I needed her most.

In the weeks since I'd taken over Mama's care financially and visited her in the nursing home, I had begun to heal. I had begun to find peace, something I never thought possible. But it had occurred to me that, her whole life, my mother never had space to heal.

Healing would have taken time and rest and financial resources—

and somebody telling Mama that she wasn't a bad Christian for knowing something was wrong, and instead of taking her trauma to Jesus, taking it to a licensed therapist. Healing would have taken somebody consistently telling Mama—despite what people in her own family, her Black community, and this White supremacist nation said—that she wasn't ugly because she was dark-skinned. In fact, Mama possessed a beauty that she had passed on. One day close to her dying. Mama had said to me, "Your hair is so pretty. And your face. You are such a pretty woman." And I told her, "Well, you made me, Mama, with your body. You are the beauty that I am." She'd laughed in surprise—and then delight.

But none of that healing support had been available to my mother. None is available to most Black women, either, for no matter how folks talk on social media about "self-care," caring for Black women—or allowing us to care for ourselves—doesn't mean trips to the spa or microblading our eyebrows.

What self-care means is that Black women won't be used for our money and/or overworked in our homes and communities, until our health gives out or we commit suicide. That we won't be pushed to the back to let men take the lead, because this is what the Bible tells us—and what most men of all cultural backgrounds have insisted how women should act.

On that pew on the day of Mama's homegoing, I whispered my own apology to her spirit: I was sorry, too. I'd doubted her when she spoke about the life pain she'd experienced. I'd believed that she was exaggerating. But now I understood that when Mama had said she was tired, so tired, and only doing the best she could, she hadn't been lying either.

Nobody seemed to have wanted Mama to name her truth, but now that she had died, naming it was my job. I was a Black woman born with the courage to go it alone, whenever I was called an abomination. I was—and still am—Trellie Lee James Jeffers's misbehaving Black feminist child.

39

Driving Interstate West through Georgia[1]

Already I am an outsider, a visitor
seldom and hasty to my community
of pecan, cedar, pine, oak. A forgetful witness
to the smell of peaches liquoring the air.

I see this land the way I remember
and do the same for childhood love—
the rough hand that touched me
but didn't scrape down to bone.

Like those Africans choking down
mouthfuls of home before they were loaded
onto the boats, the place
might be gone from me soon.

The clucking of grown folks'
voices as they prayed over daily meat,
the branch cradling the blood's neck,
patch of green fed by offhand screams.

If this earth is denied me, then what do I know?
That before you travel to the prairie's fields,
you must follow the southern tangle?

That if you try to pull up something

unfinished from the ground, the clotted
sounds of lament will cling to the roots?

VII

IN SEARCH OF OUR MOTHERS' FORGIVENESS[1]

Water does not forget its path.

—TRADITIONAL WOLOF PROVERB

40

August 2023

Monday, August 14

I thought I could handle flying back and forth from Alabama to Oklahoma every few days, but I can't: I finished traveling at two a.m. this morning, arriving at Will Rogers Airport in the dark. At nine thirty, Mama's nursing home calls me to say she's back in the hospital. I decide to pack, get my car serviced, and drive back to Alabama tomorrow (in two days) to set up camp for a while in an Airbnb.

On Facebook, I ask for strong prayers of safety for my travel and for my mama, that I can be with her constantly at this time in her life, to love on her. Two weeks before, when I arrived in Alabama to take over her care, Mama's doctors informed me that she had early dementia. She couldn't remember a lot, but my heart was gladdened that talk of her love of gardening led to a memory from forty-eight years ago, when I used to garden with her "over the river" in Chapel Hill, North Carolina—Mama reminded me of the river.

Later

Finished pulling junk out of my car and will load up in the morning an hour before I take off for Alabama.

I was not aware how much unnecessary stuff I kept in my car.

I don't think I'm ever going to have a pristine car. I'm good with that, but it's a sobering realization.

Tuesday, August 15

I'm on the journey back to Alabama and taking a break a few miles outside Little Rock (which I always pronounce as "Lil"). I check my email, and somebody has written from England, asking about the cost to bring me in for a Phillis Wheatley Peters anniversary event in late September. A four-week lead time never bodes well unless somebody is putting you on the short or long list for a prize.

One would think that a monumental anniversary like this year would mean years' worth of planning and fundraising—enough to respect a possible guest's time and fee requirements. Apparently not.

I just hit the delete button. I'm getting ruder with each passing day, considering my current emotional circumstances.

Later

Let me tell you when you know you're in the Deep South: when somebody tells you sincerely and with absolutely no irony to "have a blessed day."

Later

I'm so tired I feel loopy.

I just finished another professional deadline with twenty-six minutes to spare in some Hampton Inn in Memphis.

Right now, I'm Fannie Lou Hamer tired. I just want to lay my head in the same place for fourteen straight days and be weak and vulnerable.

Thursday, August 17

I arrive at the hospital, and Mama is thrilled—she says several times

"I'm so glad to see you! I didn't think you were coming back." I sit with her for the next two hours, telling her repeatedly how much I love her. I open my laptop, and we watch a bit of the Alvin Ailey dancers perform *Revelations*, and I remind her that she was in a modern dance class while a student at Spelman College—she always remembers Spelman.

Then I read a sonnet by Shakespeare, and I kiss her several times on top of her head, which tickles her. I tell her that I will be back tomorrow. She doesn't believe me, but I remind her that when I was a teenager, she would say I wasn't well-behaved, but whenever I gave my word, I kept it.

This is such a bittersweet time. I know what's coming, but I lie to myself that we will always be this way, just the two of us, like when I was a very little girl. So quiet and peaceful, in complete understanding.

Friday, August 18

It's not a good day. Mama is on morphine and completely zoned out. I'm depressed and starting to be afraid.

Later

I'm feeling so much better! The doctor came and told me it was the morphine (for a bit of her pain) making her seem so much worse. He's taking her off it.

I know what's coming—I'm not a child—but I just want to be with my mama as much as possible. She couldn't even talk to me today, and it hurt so very badly. Now at least we can have our conversations again.

Saturday, August 19

Yesterday was brutal, so I take a slow run this morning: two miles with a half-mile warm-up and cooldown. I was planning for longer, but these Alabama hills do not play, even at the park.

I cannot lie: the pretty light-skinned brother who kept smiling at me at the park did brighten my mood: A win is a win this week.

Later

With Mama right now—they took her off that morphine and her great personality is back. She just ate a whole ice cream sandwich. She loves her ice cream.

Sunday, August 20

I was thinking about Toni Morrison's *Beloved* as I drove home from seeing Mama today at the nursing home. It was a good day. My cousin came with his son, and then, after they left, my mother's favorite brother, Uncle Ted, came with his wife, Aunt Marie.

Mama was so very happy. She was dressed in the new pajamas I bought her, green with a tiny white pattern. She loves pretty colors. The nurses at the facility are so wonderful and kind to her. My heart opens every time I see the tenderness in their treatment of her.

At times when I am moved by the human condition—as I have been these few days—I long to read *Beloved* again, so that I can experience anew what I learned from this novel. I'm trying to read it in French, but it is too complicated in another language. I hope one day I will have the skills.

I've read *Beloved* seven times, so far. Five years ago, I decided that I could never love a man who has never read this book, because to read *Beloved* is to know something essential about me.

Every time I enter Morrison's world, I have such anticipation to arrive at the first of two monumental passages. A lot of my friends know how I feel about the quote at the end of the novel, what I think of as a sermon on Black love. It is a layered remembrance: Paul D thinks of his friend Sixo, who is telling a story about the Thirty-Mile Woman, and Sixo says of his cherished lady, "She is a friend of my mind. She gather me, man. The pieces I am, she gather them and give them back to me in all the right order. It's good, you know, when you got a woman who is a friend of your mind."[1]

But the other words that confused me for many years, but which I clutched, were spoken by the ghost Beloved to Paul D: "I want you to touch me on the inside part and call me my name."[2]

When I read this line twenty years ago—it took me ten false starts to finally finish *Beloved*, in my thirties—I thought, "Oh, this is about sex." And yes, the ghost was talking about the sexual act, but the third time I read this line, I suddenly realized that it rang beyond the physical. That line—to me—was about knowing. I was aching for somebody to affect the deepest part of me, yearning for somebody to truly know that deepest part—and not damage it. But very few people have this ability.

I've never met anyone who could touch me like that, though I've always been looking. Perhaps the searching is the point? I don't know. I'm not sad, just aware. It's so amazing to me what Morrison understood about the human condition. How I miss her! But how grateful I am to still have her words. How I love her, though I never met her in real life.

I think so much these days. It's like the tendons of my spirit are cracking and popping with change and I can hear them. I thought I was done with growing. I wonder what I am becoming.

Tuesday, August 22

And of course, I've now come down with the flu or something.

Later

I'm headed to urgent care to see if I've got the flu or Covid.

Later

Negative for Covid, flu, and strep swabs! No real diagnosis except I'm exhausted, and I may be having food and/or environmental allergies.

Saturday, August 26

The game show host Bob Barker died today. I remember sitting in Grandma Florence's living room watching *The Price Is Right* on one of the two channels we could get. It was so hot, the box fan in the window throwing out a useless breeze. I never failed to get excited when a contestant rolled the wheel.

I feel like I lost a family member.

Sunday, August 27

Somebody called me from the nursing home and told me a relative came and told the nurses to change my mama's diet without even consulting me. The amount of ordering around I'm getting about how I'm supposed to take care of my own mama from people who are not contributing money alongside mine for her care is absolutely astounding.

And I picked this time to be off sugar. I'm glad I still have coffee, otherwise somebody would see my mugshot on TV alongside our forty-fifth president.

It's Sunday. I'm truly trying to continue to be the classy, gracious individual I have worked so hard to be these fifty-six years, the person my therapist keeps praising. It's only prayer keeping me from cussing folks out on the Lord's Day.

Later

I've driven an hour to see Mama, only to walk into the nursing home and see a sign that says they have had an outbreak of Covid in the facility.

I considered walking in, but I've had Covid three times and just got past eighteen months of long covid two months ago. I just can't take the chance.

This is so upsetting.

Monday, August 28

When you're writing checks on top of checks to take care of your mama and your new raise at your university doesn't show up in your monthly paycheck.

Mercury is retrograding for real this cycle.

Wednesday, August 30

Sitting here with Mama, and I'm double-masked. I decided I just couldn't go any longer without being with her. I'm so glad she can't remember that my sister Sisi passed away nine years ago on this date, though at some point during our visit, she pointed out an invisible "little girl" in the corner. I wonder if she was seeing Sisi's spirit.

Thursday, August 31

I know good days for my mama are dwindling, but so grateful she has a good day today. When I put on Aretha Franklin, she tells me, "I like the tough songs!" And she even remembers the words to some of them, like "Don't Play That Song"! I was astounded.

And then Mama talks about selling eggs (from chickens that she raised) to Old Man Willie Waller, a White man with a store in her neighborhood. She was a teenager and needed money for her lingerie and feminine hygiene products.

Mama informs me that she was "a tough old dame" and that she never asked anybody to take care of her from the time she was little.

"I know, Mama," I say. "I'm tough just like you. You taught me how to be that way."

41

September 2023

Friday, September 1

I just left Mama. I played Aretha Franklin for her, which has become our bonding time.

When "Chain of Fools" came on and Miss Aretha sang about her doomed half-decade-long relationship with her man, Mama said, "Five years is a long time to stay. Why'd it take her so long?"

And we burst out laughing together!

Then, one of her favorite health care workers came in, a White lady around my age. She likes to talk to me, which is very flattering. She told Mama and me that she had a master of history education degree and had taught middle school before going into health care.

Mama said, "I knew you were something special," and I saw the lady's heart melt right there.

When she left, I told Mama, "Look at you. You always knew how to charm folks!"

"Well, it just comes natural," she said.

That's my mama: modest as always.

Saturday, September 2

There's nothing worse than calling an alcoholic relative to try to talk about serious family matters—in this case, my mama—and they are in the middle of drinking with other drunks. I feel triggered, thinking about how substance abuse has impacted my family. Food for my father and me, drugs and alcohol for my late sister Val, and drugs for Mama.

I know I should reach for compassion for this relative, but I'm just angry and tired.

Sunday, September 3

There's a sister-author on Instagram who just gave birth to her third (and final) baby. She's so happy and glow-y— and I was thinking, as I always do, how close a woman is to God when she is creating a human being inside her body. I think I would be terrified of that holy proximity—like Moses standing before a burning bush.

Later

Visited Mama today, and we had a fabulous time laughing and talking. The only issue is that the same nosy relative, who's not paying one dollar for her care, charmed the nursing staff into changing Mama's diet to puréed foods. Now Mama won't eat any of her meals, and the health care staff are trying to cajole her to eat pudding and Ensure shakes.

Of course I'm furious.

On Tuesday, when the office staff is back from the holiday, I must change something back that shouldn't have been changed in the first place. This will allow Mama to eat solid foods again. There will be paperwork to certify that if Mama chokes to death, I can't sue the nursing home.

After the paperwork is filed, I'll be allowed to bring in her food, just cutting it up in very tiny pieces. I haven't cooked big meals for anyone since I was married. But I'm going to do that for Mama. She's almost ninety years old. She should be able to eat whatever she wants.

Monday, September 4 (Labor Day)

It's a quiet, peaceful day—though indeed, I am laboring around the charming Airbnb where I am staying.

I am washing laundry—the Sisyphean task—and sitting in front of my computer. I checked my email and saw that I was sent a rebroadcast of a BBC radio program on Phillis Wheatley Peters, the brainchild of a brilliant Afro-British sister, Olateju Adeleye.[1]

Miss Phillis always finds a way to remind me of her presence, and I always think, "Mother, I haven't forgotten you."

Tuesday, September 5

Trying to tempt Mama's appetite, so I cooked her breakfast this morning to take to the nursing home: pancakes with maple syrup, biscuits made with Irish butter (inside and melted on top) and apricot jam on the side, seasoned soft scrambled organic eggs with extra sharp and hoop cheese and seasoned creamy grits.

Most of these dishes are from Mama's recipes. It's all a bit rich, but I hope she eats something solid today, even if it's only a few bites.

Later

Just left Mama. She didn't want any of the food. She could tell I was crestfallen, so she picked at a pancake, something she used to do to save my feelings when I was a little girl and cooked something she didn't care for.

"I don't want any of this," she said. "I want cornbread. You know I want cornbread."

"Mama, you can't eat that. It's a choking hazard for you. Please eat something else. I'm just doing the best I can."

"Your best isn't good enough," she says, and starts laughing. I can't help but join in: Her laugh is so infectious.

She asks about my ex-husband. What happened? Why aren't we

married anymore? I tell her a few of the details in simplified language, that he'd hurt me, when I thought we'd be together forever.

"You always had such a soft heart, since you were a little girl. You tried to hide it, but you couldn't."

I don't want to, but I start crying anyway. "I never wanted my heart to be that way, Mama. I never did."

"It's all right," she says. "I like you this way."

Friday, September 8

I know that as a radical, pro-LGBTQIA feminist, it might seem at odds with logic that I receive a daily snippet of biblical scripture each morning on my cell phone.

I get the confusion, because I'm confused, too. For nearly forty years—ever since my first spiritual vision at eighteen, which led me to the acceptance of a higher power—I've been trying to reconcile my Christianity with my political and personal beliefs. Most times, I feel like a fool.

This morning, the snippet I received was from 2 Corinthians 4:18: "So we fix our eyes not on what is seen, but on what is unseen, since what is seen is temporary, but what is unseen is eternal."

I'm thinking of the great James Baldwin this morning, and his book about the Atlanta child murders, *Evidence of Things Unseen*. I'm thinking of his outrage and his grief, and I wonder how it is possible to live a life of contentment and yet maintain anger over what should not have happened.

I'm thinking of my childhood and the transgressions that occurred, and how that unhappy little girl became a deep thinker who some-times—I hope—gives others joy with her words.

I'm thinking about this country that I love but which gives me eternal, deep disappointment.

I'm thinking about the southern landscape that daily pierces me with its beauty, even while I wonder what horrors this landscape remembers: lynchings, slavery, rapes.

So much complication this morning.

It seems that sadness is traveling through my bloodstream—my whole body hurts. But yesterday a man I care about reminded me that my mother named me for Honoré de Balzac, a great writer. My mama said that she looked at my newborn face and saw all that would come to pass and named me a word that means that I am honored.

This morning, despite my sadness, I rose at four thirty and made coffee and I wrote. I don't know what I see, and I can't seem to find the proof, either. I am only reaching.

Sunday, September 10

Mama and I have a good visit this afternoon. I cooked for her again, some breakfast food but this time also a sweet potato pudding, which is essentially the pie filling without the crust. It's her recipe, and she absolutely loves it.

I remind her that she loves sweet potatoes because when she was a little girl, she asked Ma Sweet—whom she always called mean—for some sweet potatoes out of a huge bin. Her grandmother only gave her three small potatoes.

Mama pauses, eating her sweet potato pudding. "And now my daughter brought me this good sweet potato pudding," she says. "So there."

Then I read Psalm 2 aloud: "Why do the heathen rage, and the people imagine a vain thing? The kings of the earth set themselves, and the rulers take counsel together, against the LORD, and against his anointed, saying, Let us break their bands asunder, and cast away their cords from us."

I read this passage in English and then in French. My French accent is very bad, but Mama keeps praising me.

"I can tell you are very intelligent, and you read beautifully." She grabs my hand and squeezes it.

Monday, September 11

I love this charming, beautiful Airbnb cottage where I've been staying in rural Alabama. It's on the "Black side" of town, and it just makes me so happy to wave at the sweet African Americans as I drive by.

I love being in the country. This is home, where my mother taught at the college here, made pancakes for students who stopped by her house, and kept a small patch of greens and tomatoes in the back of that old campus house. When I sneaked my townie lover into the living room in my senior year, Mama let me know the next morning that I hadn't fooled her one bit!

As she liked to say, "If you can't be good, be good at it."

Alabama has its horrors in its past—and current transgressions as well, if I am real—but this little town occupies every corner of my heart.

Later

I promised Mama cornbread, collard greens, and sliced tomatoes on Friday. Problem is, my shame as a Southern Black woman is that I can't cook collard greens. I found a recipe online, and I plan to buy a smoked turkey leg and try my hand at making some greens that do not taste like corn shucks, and have the same texture.

I'm going to pray real, real hard that these greens turn out all right, because I want to make my mama happy.

Tuesday, September 12

I now have a migraine halo, along with a writing deadline at midnight.

Thursday, September 14

Tuesday is my break from visiting Mama.

Yesterday and today, I have been suffering still from that migraine halo. The actual headache isn't that painful, but late in the afternoon—like right about now—here comes the halo, which makes it difficult to see.

I will pray that all will be well in the morning and that I can visit Mama and come back before the afternoon brings the halo again. I really miss her.

I spoke to her today on the phone, and it was a good day for her. I told her I loved her so many times.

Friday, September 15

My fourth cup of full-strength coffee yesterday coincided with my migraine halo, so I am cutting my coffee today with decaf and replacing one coffee with tea.

Later

I have bought pork ham hocks—I couldn't find a smoked turkey leg—onions, garlic, chicken stock, olive oil, salt, pepper, and smoked paprika to make Mama's greens. I don't yet have the courage to begin cooking them.

Later

I go back to see Mama this evening, but then there is drama: I finally had to snap on the relative who keeps interfering with Mama's diet. The last straw was them giving Mama a full-sugar Coke—she has diabetes and gout, among other ailments.

It is so hard to stand up to my elders, but after my rant, Mama's health care workers gave me the actual thumbs-up. When the relative finally leaves, the health care workers and I make fun of that relative, laughing so loud.

Saturday, September 16

I don't know if it's the powering down on full-throttle coffee or if it's that I finally got off my chest my annoyance with my interfering maternal relative, but the halo is gone.

Sunday, September 17

A good morning so far: I found smoked turkey wings and tails (for Mama's collards) at the grocery store on the Black side of town.

I've put the ham hocks in the freezer. I don't want to waste food.

Later

I prayed to God, and then I called on the spirits of my ancestors and decided to cook these collard greens the old-fashioned way: in a big old pot. I'd bought a pressure cooker, but it seemed so complicated, the thought of figuring out how to operate it gave me anxiety.

Now the kitchen smells just like Mama's used to, heavy with the smell of onions and smoked meat. I'm hopeful.

The maple-butter cornbread is causing me less anxiety. I used to make cornbread and biscuits for my ex-husband—the African—nearly every day when we lived together. When he knew we were breaking up, he even tried to trick me out of my recipes, but I told him, "Ain't no other woman gone be cooking my cornbread and biscuits for you. Let that heifer get her own recipes."

My literary companions for today's soul food venture are Rita Dove's poem "Sunday Greens" and Lucille Clifton's "cutting greens." And I've just started reading Blair L. M. Kelley's book *Black Folk: The Roots of the Black Working Class*, which makes me feel like a loving cousin is sitting down at my kitchen table.

For some reason, I feel some kind of mighty spirit rolling through me today. Maybe cooking these collard greens wasn't the burden I thought it would be. Who knows?

I hope today I will finally become the southern Black woman of my intentional dreams, who can feed and give and spread tenderness and sustenance and wild-seasoned wisdom.

Later

I try not to eat meat anymore, but I had to make an exception to make sure these greens are good, and they are delicious, so tender and seasoned. I even have a small container of pot liquor for Mama.

Now, what will she think? We shall see.

The greens are cut so fine because Mama must have her food prepared that way. When she used to make collards, she liked them in larger bits.

Later

Mama says my cornbread and collard greens were good! And she tells me, "This pot liquor is excellent."

This is a historical day! I am officially an African American southern woman.

Later

It seems I am crying all the time, but now I am joyful: I just wanted to make my mama happy.

Monday, September 18

As if my successful collard greens were not enough of a wonderful moment, I find out this morning that *Les chants d'amour de Wood Place*—the French translation of my novel *The Love Songs of W.E.B. Du Bois*—is on the long list for Le Grand Prix de Littérature Américaine.

If Mama didn't have dementia—if she still had her French fluency—I would tell her about it. The Mama from ten years ago would be so proud of me.

Tuesday, September 19

My French tutor is an older White lady from France. I call her "Madame," and we have the best conversations (over Zoom) about books and culture and history, even with my half-English, half-French conversations. I am understanding her nearly perfectly, even if I can't articulate the depth of my own thoughts as well. There's always a moment where I must lightly tap my head and say in English, "Ah! It's too complicated to say!"

I think about when I was a little girl, and my mama would speak in French around me. I was in such awe of her. Somehow, when I am talking to my tutor, I feel so close to Mama. It's funny how only now, after two years with Madame, I realize that I started taking French lessons to understand my mother better.

I tell Madame today, "Ma mère est le soleil—et je suis ses planètes." Mama is the sun, and I am her planets.

Sunday, September 24

Just arrived to visit Mama, but she is sleeping so soundly.

When she's awake, it's a lot of work to keep her engaged, and sometimes it emotionally exhausts/grieves me, but when I come and she won't wake up, I miss her so much.

Later

Mama wakes up for dinner! I'm so glad.

Monday, September 25

Preparing to drive to see Mama.

I'm listening to Johnny Hodges's exquisite saxophone breakdown on Duke Ellington's "Arabesque Cookie." If there's anything better than a Black man playing the saxophone, I cannot name it.

Mama loved her some Johnny Hodges, in the "before" time—before her dementia.

Later

Mama eats a lot of the seasoned cheese grits I made her, along with the buttered Hawaiian roll and the already-cooked field peas I bought from the grocery store.

She is talkative, and though she doesn't sing the words, she smiles while listening to the Staple Singers' "I'll Take You There," and especially Luther Vandross's "Dance with My Father"—her top five favorite song in the "before" time.

When the next song comes on —Luther's "Superstar"—I sing to her. It's one of my own favorites. After I finish, she tells me, "You sound so good."

"Mama, you are such a charmer," I say.

"I'm telling the truth."

I've decided to try—really try—to be grateful for these good days, instead of wishing for days that will never come again.

42

October 2023

Sunday, October 1

I'm here with Mama. She woke up when I tapped her hand.

I put on Aretha's version of "Wholly Holy," and we talk briefly before she becomes drowsy again.

I'm grateful that when I tell her, "I love you, Mama. I love you so much," she still says, "I love you back."

Today, she asks, "Is there anything you need? I can give you something."

I said, "Only you, Mama. I only need to be with you."

Monday, October 2

This evening, I arrive at dinnertime, but I'm empty-handed. I didn't cook today.

When the nurse sees me, she tells the other (new) nurse, "Her daughter's here now. She gets her to eat."

It's a little thing, but I am proud. I feel like a good daughter for once, after it took me so long to take over Mama's care. Since I arrived in Alabama, I've worked every day—hustled—to make money to pay back into my savings and replace the money I've spent for the nursing home. I thought that pulling thousands of dollars from my savings would make me resentful, but strangely, it doesn't. I'm just grateful I have the money.

While feeding Mama vanilla ice cream—she spat out the hot dog they gave her at dinner, and truly I can't blame her; it looked so nasty—Mama asks, "Where's your husband?"

"I divorced him." I don't say she's asked about my ex-husband a couple times before. I'd avoided criticizing him, but this time I decided to tell her the truth. "Being married to that man was like a blues song, like something by Bobby 'Blue' Bland. He was cheap with his money and his feelings. I'm so glad to be divorced."

While speaking, I'd expected sadness to follow, but somehow I just end up laughing.

"Oh, Lord, I know what you mean!" She joins in my laughter. "These men are something else."

"Trellie Lee, they are a mess."

Wednesday, October 4

Headed to see Mama and bringing her cheese grits. I haven't been on my job with her food for the last couple weeks.

Later

For the most part, Mama has stopped eating.

She takes a few bites of the grits and the cheese eggs I made, but I can tell she is only trying to please me. I use the jocular tone that irritates me when the nurses do the same. Begging her to eat, "Come on now, Trellie Lee. Just one more bite."

Mama smiles when I call her by her government name.

In a now-rare moment of lucidity, she tells me she doesn't want me to worry about her. That she wants me to be all right.

I tell her that I didn't want her to worry about me, either. That I'm going to be okay. That I have people who love me and who are there for me. I try not to cry—it seems I'm constantly weeping these days—

but I can't help it.

I tell her she is the love of my life. That no man—no boyfriend, no husband—has ever taken her place. She has been everything to me, even when I was angry at her. Even when I was silent. I know she doesn't understand everything I am saying, but she tells me that she loves me, and she's so happy because I am here with her.

Then I gave her vanilla ice cream, which is the only thing she willingly eats. She asks me to be there until she falls asleep.

Mama is declining rapidly. She can barely lift her head now.

Later

I log onto Facebook and ask my friends to surround me with prayer. I never knew my faith could be this strong, though I'm angry about what death is stealing from me.

Thursday, October 5

Mama still won't take meals from anyone but me. Even when she eats, it's not that much.

One of her favorite health care workers is back today, and when she sees me, she runs to me and says, "Thank the Lord you're here! Dr. Jeffers won't eat anything. At lunch, she told me I better get that food out of her face." She laughs.

I apologize for Mama's manners, but the lady tells me no apology is necessary. She says she loves herself some Dr. Jeffers. We stand there for a few seconds, our arms touching. Some days, we hug. I've become accustomed to the affection on the hall, and my social anxiety isn't so bad here.

Mama is very frail—I touch her very gently— but this evening she is lucid again.

After I feed her vanilla ice cream (of a brand infused with secret protein) and a small carton of nutritional drink, I ask, "Bonjour Madame, ça va?"

I've been doing this for weeks now—asking, "How are you, ma'am?" in French—with no response, except Mama's confusion.

Tonight, to my shock, Mama replies, "Ça va bien!" She is doing well, she tells me.

I give a little squeal and clap my hands, repeating, "Ça va bien! Ça va bien!"

Mama smiles and says, "Why are you so happy?" It seems like she's teasing me, but I can't be sure.

We listen to selections from Aretha Franklin's *Amazing Grace*, as we've been doing for a few days, but this evening, she remembers all the songs. She even sings along to two of them. I don't know why, but I am so emotional. I weep—yet again; I'm so annoyed at myself—while I listen. Then I notice that Mama is getting misty as well.

She moves her head slowly with the music.

"That lady's voice is so beautiful," she says. "She really has a power."

Mama doesn't use the familiar name—Aretha—as she did when I was a girl. For years I thought Aretha Franklin and my mother were close friends, the way Mama spoke so knowledgeably about her. I call the singer "Miss Aretha," using a handle like I did my grandmother's neighbors down in Eatonton.

It is an odd but lovely thing, this lyrical statement of Mama, because other times her syntax is scrambled, and she says words in no particular order. What she says mostly doesn't make sense, but I'll pretend that I know what she's saying. I always reply, "Yes, ma'am," and nod vigorously.

On the last song I play—"Mary don't you weep"—when Miss Aretha arrives at the place where she calls Lazarus's name three times, Mama still knows that on the last call, Miss Aretha will quickly climb the note, octave by octave.

We both exclaim, "Here it comes!"—and when Miss Aretha hits that note, we look at each other in astonishment, like we always did.

"You really feel the presence of God when you listen to her," I say.

"Yes," Mama says.

Then, she says something that sounds like "well." She keeps saying, "Well." Then, "Well water," repeatedly. Then, finally, "Clear. So clear."

"Ma'am?" I think a few seconds. "Are you saying Miss Aretha's voice is clear like well water?"

"Yes!" Mama said. "Yes. And sweet like that, too."

We look at each other for a long time. I put a hand on each side of my mother's face and stroke her cheeks.

Saturday, October 7

I just saw Mama yesterday, but today her frailty startled me.

Though she is even weaker, Mama eats better tonight. I leave the chicken in the cooler bag, because I noticed that chewing meat is difficult for her now. I only set out the greens, cornbread, and sweet potatoes. I decided that she deserves cornbread and that I will pray that she doesn't choke.

I negotiate with her about tomorrow's meal: how about more greens and sweet potatoes, but something new? A salmon patty and seasoned rice?

"That sounds good," she said. "You cook so well."

After having her "milk" for dessert—a vanilla shake infused with vitamins and protein that the nursing home provides—she suddenly announces, "I don't ever want to marry again!"

I've learned to go with these moments and pretend that all is possible, such as romance, even at this time in her life, what I've been warned is her rapidly approaching end. She doesn't have the time the doctors had promised me, two months ago. There won't be another year.

"Really?" I ask. "Why, Mama? Why don't you want to get married again?"

I brace, expecting a memory about my father to erupt, something from one of his cruelest moments. But Mama seems to have forgotten about Daddy. I can't say that doesn't make me happy, because in her early days in the nursing home, she'd mention him with fondness, and it took every bit of my self-control not to get angry. How I despise his memory—but I try to remember Mama's situation. She has dementia, and I can't blame her anymore for what she says.

"I don't want to get married, because I want to be there for my family. I want to do good things for them."

"Mama, you already have done so much for us," I say. "And you are so appreciated. I know I appreciate you very, very much."

"But I want to do more for them," she insists.

"You've sacrificed for our family, haven't you, Mama?"

"I have," she says. "But I don't mind."

I want her to stop talking like this, to cease bargaining with people for love. It reminds me of how I've run behind the wrong people for so many years, begging for affection, only to get kicked in the teeth. It took the pandemic to shake me out of that, along with three years of therapy.

I think about all Mama has done for people. It makes me more than sad; it makes me angry. I can't avoid this rush of feelings, looking at Mama in her hospital bed, so greatly diminished. All her money gone, because of people she loved taking advantage of her. Here she is barely alive but thinking of service to others.

This is the training that we Black women get in our communities—consider yourself last. It makes me wonder, when can a Black woman ever rest? When can we consider our own well-being without guilt? Will there ever be a time before death?

Sunday, October 8

Over the past couple of weeks, I've obsessively recounted a story about the day that Mama taught me compassion, when she transformed my heart into softness, like some sort of root worker.

While driving to see Mama, I repeat the story to myself, wondering, Why do I remember this?

I was six years old, in first grade, and Valentine's Day was approaching. Mama and I were downtown in Durham, North Carolina. We were either at the Rose's or the Woolworth's—let's just say Rose's. And Mama was doing that sort of everyday, mild fussing that mothers do. She was complaining because there were only twenty-one kids in my class besides me, but because the Valentine's Day cards for children came in a pack of twenty, she had to buy a whole second pack of those little Valentine's Day cards.

"No, Mama," I said. "You don't have to buy that second pack. I only need twenty."

I'm pretty sure I was proud of myself for my grasp of math.

"No, baby," she said. "There are twenty children in your class."

This was fifty years ago, so I can't remember how I got to this next part, but I do know that I told Mama that I wasn't going to give this little girl named Tee*[1] a card.

"Why not?" Mama said.

"I'm not giving Tee a Valentine's Day card because she eats glue. And she lives in the projects."

I don't know where I learned to speak unashamedly about class hierarchies. Looking back, though, I see that already I was becoming obnoxious, thinking myself above others, because of where they lived and how much money their parents made or didn't make.

What I hadn't yet learned at the age of six is that where my mother had grown up in Eatonton, the projects would have been a huge step up for her. In my adolescence, Mama would describe to me the pain of that upbringing. She would talk about how others had ridiculed her for her dark skin and her clothes made from feed sacks and her scuffed shoes—her missing eye, the result of a childhood accident. How, before a lady named Miss Janet Virginia Talley had encouraged—indeed pushed her, as Mama would later push her own students at Talladega College—to apply to Spelman, my mother hadn't even known such a future was possible.

But that knowledge of Mama's upbringing was years off for me, and when Mama told me that I had to give Tee a Valentine's Day card,

I started breaking fool in the Rose's.

"Tee eats glue!" I shrieked. "Tee eats glue!"

Mama looked at me calmly while I flailed my hands, then she leaned down and took my chin in her fingers.

"Let me tell you something," she said. "If Tee doesn't get a Valentine's Day card, *nobody* in your class will get a card. Do you understand me? I'm not raising you to be cruel to other people."

That day of the Valentine's Day party, I contemptuously tossed my card on Tee's desk, but though I was only six and still caught up in my petite, self-centered world, I noticed that I was the only person that had given her a card. Surprisingly—I don't know where this feeling came from—seeing that others had rejected Tee the way I'd planned to reject her made me feel so sad for her. When I got home and told Mama that I felt sad about nobody else giving Tee a card, she told me that she was proud of me.

Seven years later, in eighth grade, things had changed. I was no longer popular among my classmates. I wore very thick glasses—I'd started wearing them in third grade. I'd become fat. I'd shot up to nearly the height I'd be in adulthood, and I'd gotten the bright idea to cut all my hair off—my hair had been the one thing about me that African Americans treated as special, especially in school. There were only three girls who would be my friends. All three lived in the projects: One of those girls was Tee.

By that time, I was beginning to learn insight and self-interrogation. I asked Tee why she was friends with me when nobody else wanted to be. She reminded me of that Valentine's Day card.

I guess I learned from that experience that sometimes, the person that you least expect to save you will come right on time. Tee was kind to me, out of her compassion, though I'd been forced by Mama into my own.

Monday, October 9

I am late this evening, arriving at about six p.m. Though the health care workers told me that Mama had eaten some of her dinner, Mama eagerly says yes when I ask her if she wants to eat some of the food that I've brought.

She loves the squash and onions, the salmon patty, and especially the seasoned rice—even though I was afraid it was sticky—but she doesn't like the cabbage. She doesn't say anything bad about it but won't take a second bite.

"I'm sorry it's not good," I say. "I didn't remember how you made it," and Mama begins telling me that I needed an onion and a ham hock or—at my prompting—smoked turkey. I am so mad at myself, because I'd gone back and forth about putting an onion and smoked meat in the cabbage but had decided against it.

Then—out of the blue—Mama begins talking about how she'd never let anybody push her around. Her memories appear from some place I wish I could see, and always in an abrupt fashion. I don't say anything about Daddy's emotional and physical abuse, how he pushed all of us around plenty. I don't want her to remember him. I am afraid that even talking about him would steal her from me. I'm jealous of his memory.

This evening Mama focuses on Grandma Florence, and how mean she was. After all these years—and through dementia—Mama remembers her mother's cruelty, that Grandma hadn't even attended her graduation from Spelman College. I already know one version of the story: Mama has told it to me several times throughout the years, but with amusement: One of her country relatives who *did* attend sat on a pew in Sisters Chapel, pulled out a banana from her purse, and peeled and ate it! Mama wasn't upset; she was just glad somebody in her family had showed up to graduation.

This evening, Mama doesn't remember the banana story, and there is pain in her voice about Grandma missing her daughter's triumph.

"You would have thought my mother was proud of me," Mama said. "I was graduating from college! Nobody else in the family ever had done that."

"Grandma wasn't a very happy person, Mama. That wasn't your

fault. And maybe she just couldn't even understand where you had come from. You aren't like anybody else in your family."

I think how I'd never fit in, either. I've always felt like a freak among my blood kin. And I think of Grandma, whom I am positive suffered from serious mental illness.

Mama keeps talking about Grandma and her meanness, and though I can't deny that cruelty—I've been a victim of Grandma's sudden bouts of temper, and even physical abuse—I've learned to have some compassion. I remind Mama about how mean Grandma's father, Jenkins Paschal, was.

The story went that Jenkins had run off almost all of Grandma's suitors, and at the age of twenty-three, Grandma's only remaining romantic possibility was Grandpa Charlie, a good-looking man but very dark-skinned, so not considered suitable within Grandma's color-struck family. Grandpa had been a poor man, too. When he arrived at the Paschal house for courting, Jenkins wouldn't let Grandma sit on the porch with her boyfriend until all her chores were finished. According to Mama, Grandpa said he'd sometimes wait for hours.

"Grandma had a mean daddy," I say.

"I still don't understand why she couldn't love me," Mama says.

My heart aches for so many reasons, and I'm not going to scold her. Hadn't I stopped speaking to Mama for five years, tired of the mind games she'd played with me, how she had told relatives that I'd lied about Daddy abusing me, how she insisted that she'd gone bankrupt because she'd paid for my graduate school education—when I retained the receipts for those six figures of student loans I had owed?

Surely I can keep a grudge myself, but what does any of that matter now? I'm a woman fully grown, sitting by the deathbed of my mother, who I love more than anyone, dead or living. No matter what has happened between us—and plenty has happened—I couldn't stop loving her, after years of trying. This mother whose words shaped mine—whose earth called me back to the red dirt place I'd sworn I'd never return to. And I already miss her, though she isn't even gone yet.

As I have so many times when Mama spoke about the pain of her childhood and young adulthood, I feel as if we are joined. Her hurt is my hurt, and I want to make her—the both of us—feel better.

"Well, I love you, Mama." I'm holding her hand, as I do through our visits. Her hands are so elegant, with long fingers. Piano-playing hands, though she despaired that she'd never had the talent. "I love you very much."

"Of course you do!" she exclaims. "And nobody is ever going to love you more than me! I love you with everything I have inside."

My sudden weeping is violent and shocks us both, ripped out of some rusted-over place. Like a child, I can't control myself. I can't stop, and Mama squeezes my hand.

"Don't cry," she says. "Don't be sad."

"I'm not sad, Mama. I'm just so happy that you would say something like that to me." I must repeat myself, I'm crying so hard. It's true: Though the tears keep coming, I'm so happy.

I'd only expected pain from this time with Mama, what I know are her last days. If somebody had told me I'd feel anything but resentment in her presence, I would have felt sorry for them, in their foolishness.

We sit there for a while, and she asks for another bite of squash and onions. Before I gather my things to go, I give her kisses on her forehead, making loud smacks, which make her giggle.

Then, my usual farewell. "I'll see you soon, Trellie Lee, God willing—" I always wait for her to finish, and I'm thrilled that she remembers, that the dementia hasn't stolen this from me.

"—and the creek don't rise," she says.

I stand at the threshold to her room and tell her, repeatedly, I love her.

"I love you more," Mama says.

Acknowledgments

I'm no longer embarrassed by the length of my acknowledgments, for I know that when I have so many to thank, that means I was given so much.

First, as always, I give unashamed glory and praise to my mighty good, gender-full God and the ancestors who have brought healing and forgiveness to my life. My parents, Professor Lance Flippin Jeffers and Dr. Trellie Lee James Jeffers, did the best they could, and I love them: that knowledge is miraculous to me. Mama, your language and front porch-brilliance are mine. You made this creative life possible for me, and that life is now filled with so much peace and contentment. My late sisters Sidonie Colette Jeffers and Valjeanne Jeffers-Thompson, your baby sister loves y'all. I'm trying to do right so I'll see y'all again.

Gratitude to other ancestors who continue to guide me: my late friend James William Richardson Jr., who taught me how a Black feminist man should love, even in a platonic way. Big Poppa, I think of your rare tenderness and your extraordinary mind and heart every day. If I never experience true romance, still, I know I had an *agape* love from one of the best brothers to ever walk this earth: my soul is satisfied. My friend, mentor, and second mother, Lucille Clifton, I will never stop praising your name. Thank you for guiding me, even from the afterlife. You taught me that though this root bag gets heavy, the weight is worth it. My friend, Vincent Woodard, I wish we could have reconnected during your lifetime. You taught me so much that I am only now realizing—you blessed me so much! I pray we see each other in the after time.

And there is so much gratitude to the living.

To Angela Brooks, Joanna Brooks, Jericho Brown, Gillian Clifton, Alexia Clifton, Graham Clifton, John Freeman, Stephanie Powell-Watts, Jaqueline Woodson, Farah Jasmine Griffin, Jennifer L. Morgan, Donna Akiba Sullivan Harper, Fred Viebhan, Rita Dove, Ceron Bryant, Remica Bingham-Risher, Nicole Terez Dutton, Cherise Pollard, Robert L. Jones, Jr., Deesha Philyaw, Angie Thomas, Dolen Perkins-Valdez, Jodie Turner-Smith, Ava DuVernay, Jina DuVernay, Nesha Williams, Cedric Tolliver, Tracy K. Smith, Sophie Pugh-Sellers, Aru Menon, Carmen Davis, Mosiah Williams, Mungu Sanchez, Thedwron and Marie James, Queta Vessie, Phadra Carson Foster, Katherine Johnsen, Veronica Miller, Dr. Carol Anderson, Eddie Glaude, Jane Ciabattari, Kathleen Driskill, Victor Lavalle, Emily Raboteau, Rebecca Walker, Rachel Harper, Karen Chilton, Adenrele Ojo, Prentice Onayemi, Channing Godfrey Peoples, Wilhemina Jenkins, Veronica Chambers, Joshunda Sanders, Liz Velez, Caroline Strout, Christian Anton Gerard, Liz Ahl, Carole Bandy Carson, Monique Navelet, Elizabeth Watts Pope, Ashley Cataldo, Chelsea Hicks, Ghaunté Lewis, Lily Painter, S. J. Thompson, and Grant Mullican.

To the bookstores that support quirky, nerdy writers like me. To my readers and the "Bookstagram" community, especially Crystal Forte, Raymond Williams, Nia Allen, A. J. Hill, Jamise Harper, Akili Nzuri, Reggie Bailey, and Nikesha Elise Williams.

To my American Antiquarian Society "Too-Live Crew." Even if life gets in the way, we'll always have Worcester: Jonathan Senchyne, Emily Pawley, Tanya Mears, Meredith Neuman, and Paul Erickson.

To my former publicist, Jane "The Great" Beirn, thank you so much. I hope I've made you proud. Maya Rutherford Baran, thank you for your advocacy as my current publicist. Karintha Parker, you were/are a sister to me, continually giving me encouragement. Rebecca Gardner and Will Roberts, you brought to reality my dream for becoming an internationally known writer. Anna Rolen, you stepped in as my assistant in a stressful time. To Sarah Reid and Emily Griffin, thank you for looking out for me as editors.

To Liz Van Hoose (aka "the book whisperer"), you are a genius. My appreciation is boundless for your guidance for *Love Songs*, and now, this book. (I'm positive that Great-Grandma Mandy thanks you.)

To Brooke Ehrlich, Sekou Campbell, Carl Fallin, Valerie Janke, and Azura Tyabji, you don't just look after my business interests, you make my independence possible. Thank you for your nurturing, care-taking, and patience.

To my Black woman therapist—I will keep you anonymous—I thank you for not only advising me to cease cussing folks out but urging me to see/know my worth. I do miss the cussing-out, but I waited so long for this good self-esteem—now that it's here, I'm gone let it howl at the moon.

To Ms. Alice Walker, you literally made this book possible. Thank you for your words and your kindness. Dr. Henry Louis Gates Jr, thank you for being my go-to, generous genius. Ms. Oprah Winfrey, as I'm fond of saying, "First we thank God, and then we thank Miss Oprah!" I'm incredibly proud to be "Number 92" for your book club. You blessed me.

To Dr. Sonia Sanchez: Miss Sonia, your love, mentoring, and courage keep me going. I can't believe you take my phone calls. (Smile.) My life is so much more with you in it.

To my "shoulders": Remica Bingham-Risher, Sidney Clifton, Oscar Enriquez, Andrew Jeon, Bailey Hoffner, Laura Pegram, Riché Richardson, Jacqueline Allen Trimble, Ms. Tena Turner, I love y'all so much. I will never take your affection, loyalty, and friendship for granted.

Erin Wicks, I'm so grateful that you are still in my life as my dear-dear friend. I love you so very much: To the moon and back and "MAS Forever!"

To Sarah Burnes: Woman, I love you. (Excuse the mush.) Since 2005, you've been more than my literary agent: Your faith in my creative gifts, your encouragement, your big heart, your decency, your calming spirit, and your wise counsel have helped me grow not only as a writer and intellectual but—I hope—a better human being.

Adenike Olanrewaju, my sister, this is a kin-filled journey you helped me travel. I'm grateful you stepped in as editor for this book and walked me across the finish line. I appreciate you so much.

Finally, this book is for Black women: You have supported me in ways I didn't even know existed. Sistren, we are in this thing together until the wheels fall off, and then we gone get out that car and walk the rest of the way. I love y'all—I love *us*—real, real strong.

Notes

ESSAY 1: THAT DAY IN JANUARY

1. Czachor, "Boebert's Tweet History."

ESSAY 2: OUR FATHERS WHO REWROTE OUR MOTHERS

1. Landers, "Slavery in the Lower South," 23. See also Ballvé, "King of Spain's Slaves," 11.

2. John Rolfe to Sir Edwin Sandys, January 1620, in Kingsbury and Woerishoffer, *Records of the Virginia Company*, 243. For further information about the English kidnapping and refusal to return the person known as Pocahontas to her father, the Indigenous leader, Powhatan, and her likely-forced marriage to John Rolfe, see Custalow and Daniel, *True Story of Pocahontas*, 135–37. For information about the Algonquin name—Metoaka—of the woman represented by the English as "Pocahontas," see Goetz, *Baptism of Early America*, 49.

3. Thorndale, "Virginia Census of 1619," 155, 168.

4. Hotten, *Original Lists*, 244.

5. Morgan, "Partus Sequitur Ventrem,' 8.

6. Strackey, *Historie of Travaile*, 20.

7. Thorndale, "Virginia Census of 1619," 168.

8. Welch, "Law and the Making of Slavery," 2.

9. Sheeler, "Servitude and Slavery," 161.

10. Hening, *Statutes at Large*, 1:144.

11. Hening, 1:146.

12. Hening, 1:226.

13. Hening, 1:242.

14. Bernier, "Nouvelle division de la terre," 135. Translated from the original French by Honorée Fanonne Jeffers.

15. Godwyn, *Negro's and Indians Advocate*, 14.

16. Godwyn, 36.

17. Godwyn, 36.

18. Brown, *Good Wives*, 86–88.
19. Brown, 86–88.
20. Hammond, *Leah and Rachel*, 290–91.
21. Morgan, *Laboring Women*, 12.
22. Ligon, *True and Exact History*, 12.
23. Bell, *Running from Bondage*, 22–34.
24. "Wench," *American Dictionary of the English Language: Webster's Dictionary 1828*, accessed October 22, 2024, https://webstersdictionary1828.com/Dictionary/wench. For a fictionalized exploration of enslaved Black women designated as sexual partners, see Perkins-Valdez, *Wench*.
25. Banks, "Elizabeth Key," 84.
26. Billings, *Old Dominion*, 165.
27. Billings, 165.
28. Billings, 166.
29. Billings, 166.
30. Billings, 165.
31. Baldwin, "My Dungeon Shook," 5.
32. "Indentured Servants in Colonial Virginia," *Encyclopedia Virginia*, accessed October 22, 2024, https://encyclopediavirginia.org/entries/indentured-servants-in-colonial-virginia.
33. Billings, *Old Dominion*, 168.
34. Billings, 165.
35. Billings, 167.
36. Billings, 168.
37. Billings, 168.
38. Hening, *Statutes at Large*, 2:26. <AU: Again, please check page references vs. url given in bibliography>
39. Hening, 2:116–17.
40. Hening, 2:170.
41. Morgan, "Partus Sequitur Ventrem," 12.
42. Spillers, "Mama's Baby," 66.
43. Morgan, "Partus Sequitur Ventrem," 4.
44. Billings, *Old Dominion*, 168.
45. Billings.
46. Banks, "Dangerous Woman," 836.

ESSAY 3: BLUES FOR THE AFRICAN WOMAN WHOSE NAME HAS BEEN ERASED

1. Morrison, "Rememory."
2. 4

ESSAY 4: PAPER TRAIL

1. National Archives, "1850 Census Records."

2. Hartman, "Venus in Two Acts," 11.

3. Morrison, *Source of Self-Regard*, 323–24.

4. National Archives, "1850 Census Records."

5. "Georgia Census Records, 1870," database with images, Ancestry (https://www.ancestry.com/discoveryui-content/view/3931557:7163?), census report Tompkins, Putnam, Georgia; Roll: M593_171; Page: 70B; citing "*1870 United States Federal Census* [database on-line]".

6. "Acts of the General Assembly of the state of Georgia, passed in Milledgeville, at an annual session in December 1865, and January, February, and March, 1866," vol. 1, 1866, https://hdl.handle.net/2027/nyp.33433001216187.

7. "Reconstruction Registration Oath Book," https://vault.georgiaarchives.org/digital/collection/adhoc/id/70/.

8. Knight, *Standard History of Georgia*, 2452.

9. "1860 Slave Schedules: Putnam County," Mary Turner Project, SlaveCensus.com (website defunct).

10. Newton and Cowper, "Chronicles."

11. Turner, *Amazing Grace*, 50, 64.

12. "Amanda Napier in the 1880 United States Federal Census," https://www.ancestry.com/discoveryui-content/view/40996393:6742.

13. "Federal and State Georgia Census Records, Federal Census History," https://www.georgiaarchives.org/research/census_records#:~:text=1890.

14. "Georgia Census Records, 1900," database with images, Ancestry (https://www.ancestry.com/discoveryui-content/view/3931557:7163?), census report Johnson, Putnam, Georgia; Roll: 217; Page: 1; citing "*1900 United States Federal Census* [database on-line],"

15. "Georgia Census Records, 1910," database with images, Ancestry (https://www.ancestry.com/discoveryui-content/view/3712547%3A7884), census report Garrard, Putnam, Georgia; Roll: T624_208; Page: 9b; citing "*1870 United States Federal Census* [database on-line]."

16. Georgia Archives; Morrow, Georgia; *County Marriage Records, 1828–1978.* https://www.ancestry.com/discoveryui-content/view/205680%3A4766.

17. Goldenberg, *Curse of Ham*, 178–82.

18. "Georgia Census Records, 1920," database with images, Ancestry (https://www.ancestry.com/discoveryui-content/view/3931557:7163?), census report Garrard, Putnam, Georgia; T625_267; Page: 3B; citing "*1920 United States Federal Census* [database on-line]."

19. "Georgia Census Records, 1930," database with images, Ancestry (https://www.ancestry.com/discoveryui-content/view/101494751%3A6061), census report Garrard, Putnam, Georgia; Page: 1B; citing "*1930 United States Federal Census* [database on-line]."

20. Ancestry.com. *Georgia, U.S., Death Records, 1914-1940* [database on-line].

Provo, UT, USA: Ancestry.com Operations, Inc., 2011. https://www.ancestry.com/discoveryui-content/view/75910817%3A2562

21. "Georgia Census Records, 1940," database with images, Ancestry (https://www.ancestry.com/discoveryui-content/view/48957712%3A2442), Year: *1940*; Census Place: *Garrard, Putnam, Georgia*; Roll: *m-t0627-00703*; Page: *5A*; citing *"1940 United States Federal Census* [database on-line]."

22. "Georgia Census Records, 1930," database with images, Ancestry (https://www.ancestry.com/discoveryui-content/view/17970208:6224?), Census Place: *Garrard, Putnam, Georgia*; Page: *1A*; citing *"1930 United States Federal Census* [database on-line]."

23. "Georgia Census Records, 1940," database with images, Ancestry (https://www.ancestry.com/discoveryui-content/view/48957751%3A2442), Census Place: *Garrard, Putnam, Georgia*; Roll: *m-t0627-00703*; Page: *5B*; citing *"1940 United States Federal Census* [database on-line]."

24. "Ambrose Hutchinson Paschal Sr.," accessed October 7, 2024, https://www.findagrave.com/memorial/16067723/ambrose_hutchinson-paschal#source.

25. "Ambrose Paschal."

26. Wilson, *Black Codes of the South*, 63.

27. Du Bois, *Black Reconstruction*, 167–68.

28. Du Bois, 167–68.

29. Turner et al., *Captive Labor*.

30. "The Criminalization of the Homeless," National Coalition for the Homeless, accessed October 7, 2024, https://nationalhomeless.org/civil-rights-criminalization-of-homelessness.

31. "Unjust Fees and Fines," Equal Justice Initiative, accessed October 7, 2024, https://eji.org/projects/fees-and-fines.

ESSAY 5: A BRIEF NOTE CONCERNING WOMANIST IDENTITY

1. Walker, *Our Mothers' Gardens*, xi.

2. Jessica Hill, "Fact Check: Post Detailing 9 Things Women Couldn't Do Before 1971 Is Mostly Right," *USA Today*, October 28, 2020, https://www.usatoday.com/story/news/factcheck/2020/10/28/fact-check-9-things-women-couldnt-do-1971-mostly-right/3677101001.

3. Jocelyn Frye, "Rejecting Business as Usual: Improving Employment Outcomes and Economic Security for Black Women," National Partnership for Women and Families, July 2023, https://nationalpartnership.org/report/improving-employment-outcomes-economic-security-for-black-women/.

4. Hill, "Fact Check."

5. London, "History of Birth Control."

6. Bardaglio, "Rape and the Law," 759; and Feinstein, *When Rape Was Legal*, 4.

7. Jones, *Vanguard*, discusses the complicated and oftentimes racist history of the suffragist movement. Though the Nineteenth Amendment gave some Black women the right to vote, voter suppression continued, giving rise to a

movement of African American woman voting rights activists.

8. Crenshaw, "Curious Resurrection," 227.

9. Long, *Martin Luther King Jr.*, 73–98.

10. Griffin, " 'Ironies of the Saint,' " 217–18.

11. "The Combahee River Collective Statement," http://circuitous.org/scraps/combahee.html.

ESSAY 6: IN SEARCH OF OUR MOTHERS' CROSSROADS

1. Gates, *Signifying Monkey*, 4–6.

2. Gates, 29.

3. Schroeder, *Robert Johnson*, 34–37.

4. Crenshaw, "Demarginalizing the Intersection."

5. Davis, *Understanding Alice Walker*, 4–5.

ESSAY 9: THINGS AIN'T ALWAYS GONE BE THIS WAY

1. For this Walton County massacre of four African Americans, see Wexler, *Fire in a Canebrake*.

2. "Georgia Constitution of 1877 as amended through 1943," 1877, 13–16, https://digitalcommons.law.uga.edu/cgi/viewcontent.cgi?article=1010&context=ga_constitutions.

3. McDonald, *Voting Rights Odyssey*, 40–41; and Grantham, "Georgia Politics."

4. Franklin, " 'Legal' Disfranchisement."

5. "Disfranchisement Completes Program," *Atlanta Journal*, October 11, 1908, 28, https://www.newspapers.com/image/969953297.

6. "Summary of Georgia's New Registration Law (1958)," accessed October 27, 2024, https://www.crmvet.org/info/gavrlaw.pdf.

7. McDonald, *Voting Rights Odyssey*, 9.

8. "Citizenship Test, 1958," accessed October 25, 2024, https://dp.la/primary-source-sets/voting-rights-act-of-1965/sources/1387.

9. McDonald, *Voting Rights Odyssey*, 74.

10. McDonald, 46.

11. "Civil Rights Movement Voting Rights: Are *You* 'Qualified' to Vote? Take a 'Literacy Test' to Find Out," accessed October 27, 2024, https://www.crmvet.org/info/lithome.htm.

12. Gershenhorn, "*Hocutt v. Wilson* ."

13. "Durham City School Board Lists Six Black Candidates," *Carolina Times*, September 15, 1979, https://newspapers.digitalnc.org/lccn/sn83045120/1979-09-15/ed-1/seq-1.

ESSAY 10: BLUES FOR ROE

1. Thomas Codo, "Nebraska Football Recognizes Journey of George Flippin," *Daily Nebraskan*, November 10, 2020, https://www.dailynebraskan.com/sports/nebraska-football-recognizes-journey-of-george-flippin/article_a784fa2e-22fa-11eb-865a-5be14c7c7345.html/.

2. The National Archives at Washington, D.C., Compiled Military Service Records of Volunteer Union Soldiers Who Served with the United States Colored Troops, Infantry Organizations, Database with Images, Ancestry.com, (https://www.ancestry.com/discoveryui-content/view/27146:1107?) U.S., Colored Troops Military Service Records, 1863-1865 [database online].

3. "Dr. C. A. Flippen of Hillsboro and Miss Belle Reid of Morris County Were Married [. . .]," *Peabody Weekly Republican*, January 30, 1885, accessed October 23, 2024, https://www.ancestry.com/family-tree/person/tree/12054027/person/-344477829/hints.

4. "Judge Peterson Issued a License Monday to Dr. Chas A. Flippen of Stromburg and Miss Nettie M. Lohman [. . .]," *Central City Nonpareil*, June 17, 1909, accessed October 25, 2024, https://www.ancestry.com/mediaui-viewer/tree/174822575/person/252276325426/media/5fe1dd96-21cb-497a-a27c-6ef39a926e81?.

5. "Dr. C. A. Flippin Faces Grave Charge in Grand Island Court," *York Daily News-Times*, April 4, 1924, accessed October 25, 2024, https://www.newspapers.com/image/770499597. For an extensive discussion on the abortion charges against Charles A. Flippin, see Tallman, *Notorious Dr. Flippin.*

ESSAY 11: IN SEARCH OF OUR MOTHERS' JUSTIFICATIONS

1. Paul Lawrence Dunbar, "Little Brown Baby," in The Book of American Negro Poetry, ed. James Weldon Johnson (Harcourt, Brace, 1922), 5–6.

2. Year: 1930; Census Place: San Francisco, San Francisco, California; Page: 8B; Enumeration District: 0287; FHL microfilm: 2339940/. https://www.ancestry.com/discoveryui-content/view/92474478:6224/.

3. "Mertina Elizabeth Larson Flippin," Find a Grave, accessed October 25, 2024, https://www.findagrave.com/memorial/29942901/mertina_elizabeth_flippin.

4. Year: 1910; Census Place: Stromsburg, Polk, Nebraska; Roll: T624_853; Page: 7a; Enumeration District: 0114; FHL microfilm: 1374866. / https://www.ancestry.com/discoveryui-content/view/150490853:7884/.]

5. Year: 1920; Census Place: Sioux City Precinct 5, Woodbury, Iowa; Roll: T625_520; Page: 22A; Enumeration District: 209. /https://www.ancestry.com/discoveryui-content/view/44623749:6061/.]

6. Tallman, *Notorious Dr. Flippin*, 9.

7. Marriage certificate of Mahala K. Anderson and Charles Flippin, July 2, 1865,

Ancestry.com. Ohio, U.S., County Marriage Records, 1774-1993 [database on-line]. Lehi, UT, USA: Ancestry.com Operations, Inc., 2016, /https:// www.ancestry.com/discoveryui-content/view/901437465:61378?tid=&pid= &queryid=52f0a890-2622-40fb-8f4d-10c35ad8e725&_phsrc=jGP269&_ phstart=successSource/.]

ESSAY 12: GOING TO MEET MR. BALDWIN

1. "Atlanta Child Murders," accessed October 25, 2024, https://vault.fbi.gov/ Atlanta%20Child%20Murders.

2. Audra D. S. Burch, "Who Killed Atlanta's Children?" *New York Times*, April 20, 2019, https://www.nytimes.com/2019/04/30/us/atlanta-child-murders. html.

3. Toni Morrison, "James Baldwin: His Voice Remembered; Life in His Language," *New York Times*, December 20, 1987, https://archive.nytimes. com/www.nytimes.com/books/98/03/29/specials/baldwin-morrison.html?.

ESSAY 14: TRELLIE LEE'S BABY

1. Portions of this essay appeared in Honorée Fanonne Jeffers, "I Step into History," in *Southern Fiction: Photographs by Tema Stauffer* (Daylight Community Arts Foundation, 2022), 91–94.

2. <COMP: Delete this note, which has been moved above as an unnumbered headnote.>

3. Joel Chandler Harris, "The Wonderful Tar Baby Story," in *Uncle Remus*, 23–35.

4. Harvard Library, "Confronting Anti-Black Racism," https://library.harvard. edu/confronting-anti-black-racism/education#:~:text=Between%201740%20 and%201867%2C%20anti,learning%20to%20read%20or%20write.

5. "The Freedom in the Fine Arts Committee of the Durham Chapter of Links [. . .]," *Carolina Times*, June 5, 1976, 13, https://newspapers.digitalnc. org/lccn/sn83045120/1976-06-05/ed-1/seq-13.pdf/.

6. "Welcome to the Memorial Page for Barbara (Logan) Cooke," Fisher Memorial Funeral Parlor, https://www.fishermemorialfuneralparlor.com/ obituary/Barbara-Cooke.

ESSAY 15: FROM THE OLD SLAVE SHACK: MEMOIRS OF A TEACHER

1. <COMP: Delete this note, and insert above as unnumbered note for Essay 14.>

ESSAY 17: HISTORY IS A TRIGGER WARNING

1. "History Is a Trigger Warning"

2. "The Life of Sally Hemings: Drawn from the Words of Her Son Madison

Hemings," Monticello, accessed October 25, 2024, https://www.monticello.org/sallyhemings.

3.   "Life of Sally Hemings."

4.   "Life of Sally Hemings."

5.   Gordon-Reed, *Thomas Jefferson and Sally Hemings*.

6.   Gordon-Reed, *Hemingses of Monticello*.

7.   Madison Hemings, "Life Among the Lowly, No. 1," *Pike County Republican*, March 13, 1873, reproduced in "The Recollections of Madison Hemings," Monticello, https://www.monticello.org/slavery/people-enslaved-at-monticello/slave-memoirs-oral-histories/recollections-of-madison-hemings.

8.   Gordon-Reed, *Hemingses of Monticello*, 271.

9.   Gordon-Reed, 294.

10. Gordon-Reed, 188.

11. Epstein, Blake, and González, "Girlhood Interrupted," 2.

12. King, *Stolen Childhood*, 71–106.

13. King, 1–30.

14. Herskovitz, *Myth of the Negro Past*, 293.

15. Pennington, *Fugitive Blacksmith*, ix.

16. Pennington, x (italics Pennington's).

17. "Sally Hemings," Monticello, accessed October 25, 2024, https://www.monticello.org/sallyhemings.

18. "Summary: *Louisa Piquet, the Octoroon, or Inside Views of Southern Domestic Life*," accessed October 25, 2024, https://docsouth.unc.edu/neh/picquet/summary.html#.

19. Gomez, *African Dominion*.

20. Andrew Huebner, "Writing History with Emotion," Organization of American Historians, August 2014, https://www.oah.org/tah/august/writing-history-with-emotion.

21. Farmer, "Archiving While Black."

22. Jefferson, *Notes on the State of Virginia*, 147.

23. Jefferson, 148.

24. Jefferson, 148.

25. Jefferson, 150.

26. Although some attribute "thingification" to Martin Luther King Jr., Aimé Césaire coined this term (in the original French) in *Discours sur le colonialisme*, 14.

27. "Slavery FAQS: Property," Monticello, accessed October 25, 2024, https://www.monticello.org/slavery/slavery-faqs/property/#.

28. Laslett, "Age at Menarche."

29. Hamlin, "Raising the Age of Sexual Consent."

30. "We Need to Take Away Children," Human Rights Watch, last modified December 16, 2024, https://www.hrw.org/report/2024/12/16/we-need-

take-away-children/zero-accountability-six-years-after-zero-tolerance/.
31. Wiencek, *Master of the Mountain*, 113.
32. Wiencek, 3–4.

ESSAY 19: A BRIEF NOTE CONCERNING MY LATE BROTHER-FRIEND'S USAGE OF THE N-WORD AS A VERB

1. For a discussion of the theory of "John Henryism" and the diseases that prevail in African American communities as a result of racism and White supremacy, see Sherman A. James, "John Henryism and the Health of African Americans." Culture, Medicine and Psychiatry 18 (1994): 163–182. https://deepblue.lib.umich.edu/bitstream/handle/2027.42/45356/11013_2005_Article_BF01379448.pdf?sequence=1.

ESSAY 20: A BLACK BODY IS SOMEBODY

1. Honorée Fanonne Jeffers, "a Black body is somebody," *Hammer & Hope* no. 3 (Summer 2023): /https://hammerandhope.org/article/black-body-is-somebody-jeffers/.

ESSAY 21: BLUES FOR MOYNIHAN

1. Daniel Patrick Moynihan, "The Negro Family: The Case for National Action," US Department of Labor, 1965, https://www.dol.gov/general/aboutdol/history/webid-moynihan.
2. Spillers, "Mama's Baby," 66.
3. Geary, *Beyond Civil Rights*, 12–41.
4. Spillers, "Mama's Baby," 66.
5. Geary, *Beyond Civil Rights*, 139, 141.
6. Spillers, "Mama's Baby," 66.
7. Spillers, 67.
8. Toni Morrison, *Beloved*, 103.
9. After I had finished writing this book, I googled my topic(s), as I am wont to do, and surprisingly encountered Margo Natalie Crawford's essay "When Hortense Spillers and Toni Morrison Meet in the Clearing." Like me, Crawford explores the synchronicity of Toni Morrison's and Hortense Spillers's use of "flesh" in their work—without these two intellectuals consulting each other. Though Crawford's essay discusses Moynihan's rupturing of African American "kin" not through his report—as my piece does—but rather, as a "marking," for me, it's necessary to cite Crawford because of the similar, exciting simultaneity of two *other* Black women intellectuals—Crawford and myself—writing about the same issue at the same time, *also* without consultation, which represents such a wonderful, *kinful* confluence.
10. hooks, *Feminism Is for Everybody*, 64.
11. Geary, *Beyond Civil Rights*, 139.

ESSAY 22: LEANING ON THE EVERLASTING ARMS OF RESPECTABILITY

1. Name changed for privacy.
2. Martin, "Genesis of Godey's Lady's Book."
3. Peterson, "Mrs. Stowe and Slavery," 32–33; and Marshall, *Splintered Sisterhood*, 21.
4. Welter, "Cult of True Womanhood."
5. Welter, 152.
6. Higginbotham, *Righteous Discontent*, 165–202.
7. Higginbotham, 166.
8. Welter, "Cult of True Womanhood," 151.
9. hooks, *We Real Cool*, 3.
10. Richardson, *Black Masculinity*, 221.
11. Bailey, *Misogynoir Transformed*, 1–2.
12. For a discussion of cisgender heterosexuals who fall outside of conventional cishet behavior, see Richardson, "Punks, Bulldaggers, and Welfare Queens," 452.

ESSAY 23: A BRIEF NOTE ABOUT THE ELECTION OF U.S. PRESIDENTS, ANNOYING PROGRESSIVE WHITE FOLKS, AND THE LONG-SUFFERING UNDERSTANDING OF BLACK WOMEN

1. Steven Mintz, "Historical Context: The Constitution and Slavery," Gilder Lehrman Institute of American History, accessed December 1, 2024, https://www.gilderlehrman.org/history-resources/teaching-resource/historical-context-constitution-and-slavery.
2. Savannah Kuchar, "Barack Obama's Tan Suit Gate: What to Know on the Tenth Anniversary," *USA Today*, August 28, 2024, https://www.usatoday.com/story/news/politics/2024/08/28/barack-obama-tan-suit-anniversary/74979509007.
3. Ranya Shannon, "3 Ways the 1994 Crime Bill Continues to Hurt Communities of Color," Center for American Progress, May 10, 2019, https://www.americanprogress.org/article/3-ways-1994-crime-bill-continues-hurt-communities-color.
4. Shannon.
5. "Hillary Clinton Apologizes for Husband's Crime Bill," CNN, April 14, 2016, https://www.cnn.com/videos/politics/2016/04/14/brooklyn-democratic-debate-hillary-clinton-sorry-1994-crime-bill-6.cnn.
6. Lisa Herndon, "The Exonerated Five: An In-Depth Look at Their Journey to Justice," *New York Public Library Blog*, February 1, 2023, https://www.nypl.org/blog/2023/02/01/exonerated-five-depth-look-their-journey-justice.
7. Jan Ransom, "Trump Will Not Apologize for Calling for Death Penalty Over Central Park Five," *New York Times*, June 18, 2019, https://www.nytimes.com/2019/06/18/nyregion/central-park-five-trump.html.

8. Yasmeen Abutaleb, Ashley Parker, Josh Dawsey and Philip Rucker, "The Inside Story of How Trump's Denial, Mismanagement and Magical Thinking Led to the Pandemic's Dark Winter," *Washington Post*, December 19, 2020, https://www.washingtonpost.com/graphics/2020/politics/trump-covid-pandemic-dark-winter.

9. Li Zhou, "The Joe Biden and Anita Hill Controversy Explained," *Vox*, April 29, 2019, https://www.vox.com/policy-and-politics/2019/3/27/18262482/joe-biden-anita-hill-2020-christine-blasey-ford-brett-kavanaugh.

10. Sheryl Gay Stolberg and Carl Hulse, "Joe Biden Expresses Regret to Anita Hill, but She Says 'I'm Sorry' Is Not Enough," *New York Times*, April 25, 2019, https://www.nytimes.com/2019/04/25/us/politics/joe-biden-anita-hill.html.

11. Courtney Conley, "How Stacey Abrams, LaTosha Brown and other Black Women Changed the Course of the 2020 election," CNBC, November 6, 2020, https://www.cnbc.com/2020/11/06/black-women-continue-to-be-the-democratic-partys-most-powerful-weapon.html.

12. Michael D. Shear and Alisha Haridasani Gupta, "Harris Emerges as the Voice of Abortion Rights in the Biden Administration," *New York Times*, May 12, 2022, https://www.nytimes.com/2022/05/12/us/politics/harris-abortion-rights-biden.html.

13. Zeke Miller, Colleen Long, and Darlene Superville, "Biden Drops Out of 2024 Race after Disastrous Debate Inflamed Age Concerns. VP Harris Gets His Nod," Associated Press, July 21, 2024, https://apnews.com/article/biden-drops-out-2024-election-ddffde72838370032bdcff946cfc2ce6.

14. I'm not the only one who felt this way about Harris's loss. Eddie Glaude spoke at length publicly about it as well. See Marc Rivers, John Ketchum, Nadia Lancy, and Juana Summers, "Identity Politics Lie at the Heart of Harris' Loss, Academic Eddie Glaude Jr. Argues," National Public Radio, November 20, 2024, https://www.npr.org/2024/11/20/nx-s1-5188372/identity-politics-lie-at-the-heart-of-harris-loss-academic-eddie-glaude-jr-argues.

15. Steve Ross Johnson and Elliott David Jr., "How Key Demographic Groups Voted in the 2024 Election," *U.S. News and World Report*, November 6, 2024, https://www.usnews.com/news/national-news/articles/2024-11-06/how-5-key-demographic-groups-helped-trump-win-the-2024-election.

16. Johnson and David.

17. Amnesty International, "National Security and Human Rights," accessed July 29, 2024, https://www.amnestyusa.org/issues/national-security.

18. "A Letter from 18 Writers," *Nation*, August 18, 2006, https://www.thenation.com/article/archive/letter-18-writers/tnamp.

19. "Author Toni Morrison Endorses Barack Obama," NBC News, January 28, 2008, https://www.nbcnews.com/id/wbna22879780.

ESSAY 24: VERY REAL OPEN LETTER TO MR. BARACK OBAMA
CONCERNING HIS SPEECH ACCUSING BLACK MEN OF SEXISM BECAUSE
SOME HADN'T PLANNED TO VOTE FOR VICE PRESIDENT KAMALA HARRIS
IN THE 2024 ELECTION

1. Erica L. Green and Katie Rogers, "A Stern Obama Tells Black Men to Drop 'Excuses' and Vote for Kamala Harris," *New York Times*, October 10, 2024, https://www.nytimes.com/2024/10/10/us/politics/obama-harris-pittsburgh-democrats.html/.

2. Barack Obama, *The Audacity of Hope* (Crown Publishers, 2006), 253.

3. For Barack Obama's praising of David Patrick Moynihan, see Barack Obama, The Audacity of Hope (Crown Publishers, 2006), 254. For further discussion of Obama's views on African American single parent homes, see "Text of Obama's Father's Day Speech," *Politico*, June 15, 2008, https://www.politico.com/story/2008/06/text-of-obamas-fatherhood-speech-011094.

ESSAY 25: THE LITTLE BOY WHO WILL BE MY FATHER

1. Originally published in Honorée Fanonne Jeffers, *Red Clay Suite* (Southern Illinois University Press, 2007), 51–52.

2. <COMP: Delete note number.>

ESSAY 26: MY LIFE WITH ROOTS

1. Jacobs, *Incidents in the Life*, 45–46.

2. Lobban, "Slavery, Insurance and the Law."

ESSAY 27: BLUES FOR BOYS, BLUES FOR MEN

1. Federal Bureau of Investigation, "Lance Jeffers," Internet Archive, https://archive.org/details/fbeyesjefferslance8136.

ESSAY 28: LEXICON

1. Originally published in Honorée Fanonne Jeffers, *Red Clay Suite* (Southern Illinois University Press, 2007), 46–47.

ESSAY 29: BLUES FOR PARADISE

1. "Carlton Papers—Book of Negroes, 1783," Library and Archives, Canada, https://www.bac-lac.gc.ca/eng/discover/military-heritage/loyalists/book-of-negroes/Pages/introduction.aspx.

2. Alpern, *Amazons of Sparta*.

3. For a discussion of the Dahomeyean poems of Lucille Clifton, see Jeffers, "Go Back and Fetch It."

4. Maxwell, *F.B. Eyes*, 59–126.

5. Maxwell.

6. Johnson, *DeWolf and the Slave Trade*, 23–31.

7. Manisha Kabi, "Onesimus: The Enslaved Man That Helped Save Bostonians During a Smallpox Epidemic," University of Toronto Emerging & Pandemic Infections Consortium, February 2, 2024, https://epic.utoronto.ca/onesimus-the-enslaved-man-that-helped-save-bostonians-during-a-smallpox-epidemic.

8. Johnson, *DeWolf and the Slave Trade*, 23–31.

9. Macgregor, "Some Notes on Nsibidi."

10. Phillis Wheatley [Peters], "To the Right Honorable William, Earl of Dartmouth," in *Poems on Various Subjects, Religious and Moral* (A. Bell, 1773), 74.

11. "Senegal President Tells P.E.N. Culture of U.S. Lacks Feeling." *New York Times*, May 31, 1971, https://www.nytimes.com/1975/05/31/archives/senegal-president-tells-pen-culture-of-us-lacks-feeling.html.

12. Name changed for privacy.

13. Name changed for privacy.

14. For a complete discussion of the *signares*, the willing African/Afro-European mistresses of slave-trading Europeans, as well as the mixed-race social hierarchy of Gorée and Saint-Louis under French colonizers, see Jones, *Metis of Senegal*.

ESSAY 31: A BRIEF NOTE CONCERNING ANOTHER LATE BROTHER-FRIEND WHO LED ME TO THIS DISCUSSION OF THE BLACK WOMAN AS SOUL SISTER SHAPESHIFTER IN THESE UNITED STATES

1. Woodard, "Shapeshifter Figure."

2. For a discussion of the Middle Passage as a transformative, queering event, see Tinsley, "Black Atlantic, Queer Atlantic."

3. Gilroy, "Living Memory," 178.

4. Jeffers, "Du Bois's Dark Modernism."

ESSAY 34: BLUES FOR THE SANCTUARY

1. Gaines, "The Sky Is Gray," 97.

2. Cannon, *Katie's Canon*, 19–34.

3. Cannon, 75–84.

4. Cannon, 75–84.

5. Lee, *Religious Experience and Journal*, 4.

6. Lee, 12.

7. Lee, 12.

8. Jericho Brown, email message to author, January 27, 2024.

9. Michelle Martin, "Slave Bible from the 1800s Omitted Key Passages

That Could Incite Rebellion," NPR, December 9, 2018, https://www. npr.org/2018/12/09/674995075/slave-bible-from-the-1800s-omitted-key-passages-that-could-incite-rebellion.

ESSAY 35: TONI MORRISON DID THAT

1. Toni Morrison, interview by Charlie Rose, *The Charlie Rose Show*, aired January 19, 1998, https://charlierose.com/videos/17664.
2. Morrison.
3. Morrison.
4. Morrison, "Recitatif."
5. Morrison, *Playing in the Dark*, 16.
6. Abel, "Black Writing, White Reading"; Rayson, " Morrison's 'Recitatif.' "
7. hooks, *Black Looks*, 14.
8. Morrison, *Playing in the Dark*, 22; and Baldwin, *Fire Next Time*, 5.
9. Kant, *Essays and Treatises*, 73.
10. Lewis, "Kant 200 Years On."

ESSAY 36: IN SEARCH OF OUR MOTHERS' TAR BABY

1. The Uncle Remus Museum, https://www.uncleremusmuseum.org.
2. Walker, "Uncle Remus."
3. Harris, *Uncle Remus*, 12.
4. Jeffers, *Red Clay Suite*, 32.
5. Gaudet, "Bouki, the Hyena."
6. Anderson, "Re-Animalating Native Realities," 269.
7. Swanton, "Orphan."
8. For a discussion on cultural borrowing between southeastern Indigenous and African American folklore(s), see Baringer, "Brer Rabbit."
9. Wagner, *Tar Baby*, x.
10. For a discussion of the failed efforts of the Daughters of the Confederacy to erect a monument to the southern African American Mammy in 1923, see Katrina Dyonne Thompson, "'Taking Care of White Babies, That's What I Do': The Help and Americans' Obsession with the Mammy," in Claire Oberon Garcia, Vershawn Ashanti Young, and Charise Pimentel, From Uncle Tom's Cabin to The Help: *Critical Perspectives on White-Authored Narratives of Black Life* (Palgrave McMillan, 2014), 52–64.
11. Harris, *Told by Uncle*, 5.
12. Harris, 5.

ESSAY 38: ON BEING FANNIE LOU HAMER TIRED

1. Leslie Podell, "Compare the Two Speeches," Sojourner Truth Project, /

https://www.thesojournertruthproject.com/compare-the-speeches/
2. Painter, "Sojourner Truth in Life and Memory."
3. Hamer, "Sick and Tired," 63.
4. Blain, *Until I Am Free*," x.
5. Blain, 77.
6. Jeffers, review of *Sacriligion*, 163.
7. Jerry Mitchell, "On This Day in 1963," June 9, 2024, https://mississippitoday.org/2024/06/09/on-this-day-in-1963-fannie-lou-hamer-was-jailed-and-beaten-for-defying-segregation-on-bus.
8. Hamer, "Sick and Tired," 63.
9. Blain, *Until I Am Free*," x.

ESSAY 39: DRIVING INTERSTATE WEST THROUGH GEORGIA

1. Originally published in Honorée Fanonne Jeffers, *Red Clay Suite* (Southern Illinois University Press, 2007), 24.

PART VII: IN SEARCH OF OUR MOTHERS' FORGIVENESS

1. These journal entries are irregular. Many days from July through October 2023 weren't recorded in my journal. For example, entries for October 10–15, 2023, are missing.
2. <Comp: Delete this note.>

ESSAY 40: AUGUST 2023

1. Morrison, *Beloved*, 321.
2. Morrison, 137.

ESSAY 41: SEPTEMBER 2023

1. "Dear Phillis: Radio 3 Sunday Feature," produced by Tej Adeleye, British Broadcasting Corporation, September 3, 2023, https://www.bbc.co.uk/sounds/play/m001078w.

ESSAY 42: OCTOBER 2023

1. Name changed for privacy.

Bibliography

Abel, Elizabeth. "Black Writing, White Reading: Race and the Politics of Feminist Interpretation." *Critical Inquiry* 19, no. 3 (1993): 470–98. http://www.jstor.org/stable/1343961.

Alpern, Stanley. *Amazons of Sparta: The Women Warriors of Dahomey*. New York University Press, 2011. Kindle.

Anderson, Joshua T. "Re-Animalating Native Realities: The Funny Animals and Indigenous First Beings of Native Realities Press." *Inks: The Journal of the Comics Studies Society* 3, no. 3 (2019): 249–72. https://dx.doi.org/10.1353/ink.2019.0032.

Angelou, Maya. *The Complete Collected Poems of Maya Angelou*. Random House, 1994.

Bailey, Moya. *Misogynoir Transformed: Black Women's Digital Resistance*. New York University Press, 2021.

Baldwin, James. *Evidence of Things Not Seen*. Henry Holt, 1985.

———. "My Dungeon Shook." In *The Fire Next Time*, 1–10. Vintage, 1993. Kindle.

Ballvé, Javier Á Cancio-Donlebún. "The King of Spain's Slaves in St. Augustine, Florida (1580–1618)." *Estudios del Observatorio / Observatorio Studies* 74 (2021): 1–81. https://cervantesobservatorio.fas.harvard.edu/en/reports/king-spains-slaves-st-augustine-florida-1580-1618.

Banks, Taunya Lovell. "Dangerous Woman: Elizabeth Key's Freedom Suit—Subjecthood and Racialized Identity in Seventeenth-Century Colonial Virginia." *Akron Law Review* 41 (2008): 799–837.

———. "Elizabeth Key, Seventeenth-Century Virginia." In *As If She Were Free: A Collective Biography of Women and Emancipation in the Americas*, edited by Erica L. Ball, Tatiana Seijas, and Terri L. Snyder. Cambridge University Press, 2020. Kindle.

Bardaglio, Peter W. "Rape and the Law in the Old South: 'Calculated to Excite Indignation in Every Heart.'" *Journal of Southern History* 60, no. 4 (November 1994): 749–72.

Baringer, Sandra K. "Brer Rabbit and His Cherokee Cousin: Moving Beyond the Appropriation Paradigm." In *When Brer Rabbit Meets Coyote: African-Native Literature*, edited by Jonathan Brennan, 114–38. University of Illinois Press, 2003.

Bell, Karen Cook. *Running from Bondage: Enslaved Women and Their Remarkable Fight for Freedom in Revolutionary America*. Cambridge University Press, 2021. Kindle.

Bernier, François. "Nouvelle division de la terre, par les différents Especes ou Race d'hommes qui l'habitent, envoyée par un fameux voyageur, à M. l'Abbé de la w** à peu prés en ces termes." *Journal des sçavans*, April 24, 1684, 135. Translated by Honorée Fanonne Jeffers. /https://archive.org/details/JournalDesScavans1684/page/n136/mode/1up/

Billings, Warren M., ed. *The Old Dominion in the Seventeenth Century: A Documentary History of Virginian, 1606–1689*. University of North Carolina, 1975.

Blain, Keisha. *"Until I Am Free": Fannie Lou Hamer's Enduring Message to America*. Beacon Press, 2021.

Brown, Kathleen M. *Good Wives, Nasty Wenches, and Anxious Patriarchs: Gender, Race, and Power in Colonia Virginia*. University of North Carolina Press, 1996.

Cannon, Katie. *Katie's Canon: Womanism and the Soul of the Black Community*. Fortress Press, 2021.

Césaire, Aimé. *Discours sur le colonialisme*. Présence Africaine, 1955.

Clifton, Lucille. *The Collected Poems of Lucille Clifton, 1965–2010*. Edited by Kevin Young and Michael Glaser. BOA Editions, 2012.

Cohen, Cathy J. "Punks, Bulldaggers, and Welfare Queens: The Radical Potential of Queer Politics." *GLQ: Gay and Lesbian Quarterly* 3, no. 4 (1997): 437–65.

Crawford, Margo Natalie. "When Hortense Spillers and Toni Morrison Meet in the Clearing: The Hieroglyphics of Marking and Unmarking." *boundary 2* 51, no. 1 (February 2024): 77–93. https://doi-org.ezproxy.lib.ou.edu/10.1215/01903659-10887541.

Crenshaw, Kimberlé. "The Curious Resurrection of First Wave Feminism in the U.S. Elections: An Intersectional Critique of the Rhetoric of Solidarity and Betrayal." In *Sexuality, Gender, and Power: Intersectional and Transnational Perspectives*, edited by Anna G. Jónasdóttir, Valerie Bryson, and Kathleen B. Jones. Routledge, 2011. https://bookshelf.vitalsource.com/reader/books/9781136852800/pageid/241.

———. "Demarginalizing the Intersection of Race and Sex: A Black Feminist Critique of Antidiscrimination Doctrine, Feminist Theory and Antiracist Politics." *University of Chicago Legal Forum*, no. 1 (1989): 139–67. http://chicagounbound.uchicago.edu/uclf/vol1989/iss1/8.

Custolow, Dr. Linwood "Little Bear" and Angela L. "Silver Star" Daniel. *The True Story of Pocahontas: The Other Side of History*. Fulcrum, 2007. Kindle.

Czachor, Emily. "Lauren Boebert's Tweet History Scrutinized amid Questions on Her Capitol Insurrection Role." *Newsweek*, January 16, 2021. https://www.newsweek.com/lauren-boeberts-tweet-history-scrutinized-amid-questions-her-capitol-insurrection-role-1562255.

Davis, Thadious M. *Understanding Alice Walker*. University of South Carolina Press, 2021.

Du Bois, W. E. B. *Black Reconstruction: An Essay Toward a History of the Part Which Black Folk Played in the Attempt to Reconstruct Democracy in America, 1860–1880*. Harcourt, Brace, 1935.

———. *Darkwater: Voices from Within the Veil*. Harcourt Brace, 2020. Reprint, with introduction by Honorée Fanonne Jeffers and preface by Marable Manning, Verso Books, 2022.

Dunbar, Paul Lawrence. "Little Brown Baby." In *The Book of American Negro Poetry, edited by*

Johnson, James Weldon. Harcourt, Brace, 1922. https://archive.org/details/bookofamericanne00johnrich.

Epstein, Rebecca, Jamilia Blake, and Thalia González. "Girlhood Interrupted: The Erasure of Black Girls' Childhood," June 27, 2017. SSRN. http://dx.doi.org/10.2139/ssrn.3000695.

Farmer, Ashley. "Archiving While Black." *Chronicle of Higher Education*, July 22, 2018. https://www.chronicle.com/article/archiving-while-black.

Feinstein, Rachel A. *When Rape Was Legal: The Untold History of Sexual Violence During Slavery*. Routledge, 2019.

Franklin, John Hope. " 'Legal' Disfranchisement of the Negro." *Journal of Negro Education* 26, no. 3 (1957): 241–48. https://doi.org/10.2307/2293406.

Gaines, Ernest. "The Sky Is Gray." In *Bloodline: Five Stories*, 83–120. Vintage, 1997.

Gates, Henry Louis, Jr. *The Signifying Monkey: A Theory of African American Criticism*. Oxford University Press, 1998.

Gaudet, Marcia. "Bouki, the Hyena, in Louisiana and African Tales." *Journal of American Folklore* 105, no. 415 (Winter 1992): 66–72. https://www.jstor.org/stable/542000.

Geary, Daniel. *Beyond Civil Rights: The Moynihan Report and Its Legacy*. University of Pennsylvania Press, 2015. Kindle.

Gershenhorn, Jerry. "*Hocutt v. Wilson* and Race Relations in Durham, North

Carolina, during the 1930s." *North Carolina Historical Review* 78, no. 3 (2001): 275–308. http://www.jstor.org/stable/23522330.

Gilroy, Paul. "Living Memory: A Meeting with Toni Morrison." In *Small Acts: Thoughts on the Politics of Black Cultures*, 175–82. Serpent's Tail, 1993.

Godwyn, Morgan. *The Negro's and Indians Advocate, suing for their Admission into the Church: or, a Persuasive to the Instructing and Baptizing of the Negro's and Indians in our Plantations [. . .].* 1680. https://archive.org/details/bim_early-english-books-1641-1700_the-negros-indians-ad_godwin-morgan_1680.

Goetz, Rebecca Anne. *The Baptism of Early America: How Christianity Created Race.* Johns Hopkins University Press, 2012. Kindle.

Goldenberg, David M. *The Curse of Ham: Race and Slavery in Early Judaism, Christianity, and Islam.* Princeton University Press, 2003. https://doi-org.ezproxy.lib.ou.edu/10.1515/9781400828548.

Gomez, Michael A. *African Dominion: A New History of Empire in Early and Medieval West Africa.* Princeton University Press, 2018.

Gordon-Reed, Annette. *The Hemingses of Monticello.* W. W. Norton, 2004. Kindle.

———. *Thomas Jefferson and Sally Hemings: An American Controversy.* University of Virginia Press, 1997.

Grantham, Dewey W. "Georgia Politics and the Disfranchisement of the Negro." *Georgia Historical Quarterly* 32, no. 1 (1948): 1–21. http://www.jstor.org/stable/40577090.

Griffin, Farah Jasmine. " 'Ironies of the Saint': Malcolm X, Black Women, and the Price of Protection." In *Sisters in the Struggle: African American Women in the Civil Rights-Black Power Movement*, edited by Bettye Collier-Thomas and V. P. Franklin, 214–29. New York University Press, 2001. https://doi-org.ezproxy.lib.ou.edu/10.18574/nyu/9780814790380.003.0016.

Hamer, Fannie Lou. "I'm Sick and Tired of Being Sick and Tired," speech delivered with Malcolm X at the Williams Institutional CME Church, Harlem, New York, December 20, 1964. In *The Speeches of Fannie Lou Hamer: To Tell It Like It Is*, edited by Maegan Park Brooks and Davis W. Houck. University Press of Mississippi, 2011. Kindle.

Hamlin, Kimberly. "What Raising the Age of Sexual Consent Taught Women About the Vote." *Smithsonian Magazine*, August 26, 2020. https://www.smithsonianmag.com/history/what-raising-age-sexual-consent-taught-women-about-vote-180975658.

Hammond, John. *Leah and Rachel, or, the two fruitfull sisters Virginia and Maryland: their present condition, impartially stated and related [. . .].* In *Original Narratives of Early American History: Narratives of Early Maryland, 1633–1684*, edited by Clayton Colman Hall. Charles Scribner's Sons, 1910.

Harris, Joel Chandler. *Uncle Remus: His Songs and His Sayings: The Folk-Lore of the Old Plantation.* D. Appleton, 1881. https://archive.org/details/uncleremushisson01harr.

———. *Told by Uncle Remus: New Stories of the Old Plantation.* McKinlay, Stone & Mackenzie, 1905. https://archive.org/details/toldbyuncleremus0harri/page/n5/mode/2up

Hartman, Saidiya. *Lose Your Mother: A Journey Along the Atlantic Slave Route.* Farrar, Straus and Giroux, 2007.

———. "Venus in Two Acts." *Small Axe* 12, no. 2 (2008): 1–14. https://doi.org/10.1215/-12-2-1.

Hening, William Waller. *The Statutes at Large; Being a Collection of All the Laws of Virginia, from the First Session of the Legislature, in the Year 1619 [. . .].* 2 vols. R. & W. & G. Bartow, 1823 https://archive.org/details/statutesatlargeb02virg.

Herskovitz, Melville. *The Myth of the Negro Past.* Harper & Brothers, 1941. Reprint, with introduction by Sidney W. Mintz, Beacon Press, 1990. Citations refer to the Beacon Press edition.

Higginbotham, Evelyn Brooks. *Righteous Discontent: The Women's Movement in the Black Baptist Church, 1880–1920.* Harvard University Press, 1993.

hooks, bell. *Black Looks: Race and Representation.* Routledge, 2015. Kindle.

———. *Feminism Is for Everybody: Passionate Politics.* Routledge, 2015. Kindle.

———. *We Real Cool: Black Men and Masculinity.* Routledge, 2004. Kindle.

Hotten, John Camden, ed. *The Original Lists of Persons of Quality; Emigrants; Religious Exiles; Political Rebels; Serving Men Sold for a Term of Years; Apprentices; Children Stolen; Maidens Pressed; and Others Who Went from Great Britain to the American Plantations, 1600–1700 [. . .].* John Camden, 1874. https://archive.org/details/originallistsofp00hottuoft.

Human Rights Watch. "We Need to Take Away Children." Last modified December 16, 2024. https://www.hrw.org/report/2024/12/16/we-need-take-away-children/zero-accountability-six-years-after-zero-tolerance

Jacobs, Harriet. *Incidents in the Life of a Slave Girl. Written by Herself.* Published by the author, 1861. https://docsouth.unc.edu/fpn/jacobs/jacobs.html.

Jeffers, Honorée Fanonne. *The Age of Phillis.* Wesleyan University Press, 2020.

———. "Du Bois's Dark Modernism." Introduction to the 2022 Verso edition of Du Bois, *Darkwater*, ix–xvi.

———. "Go Back and Fetch It." Poetry Foundation, November 30, 2020. https://www.poetryfoundation.org/articles/154884/go-back-and-fetch-it.

———. *The Love Songs of W. E. B. Du Bois: A Novel.* HarperCollins, 2021.

————. *Red Clay Suite*. Southern Illinois University Press, 2007.

————. Review of *Sacriligion* by L. Lamar Wilson; *The Big Smoke*, by Adrian Matejka; and *Catastrophic Bliss*, by Myronn Hardy. *Prairie Schooner* 88, no. 3 (Fall 2014): 163.

————. "Toni Morrison's Only Short Story Addresses Race by Avoiding Race." *New York Times*, January 28, 2022. https://www.nytimes.com/2022/01/28/books/review/toni-morrison-recitatif.html.

Jeffers, Lance. *When I Know the Power of My Black Hand*. Broadside Press, 1974.

Jeffers, Trellie. "The Black Black Woman and the Black Middle Class." *Black Scholar* 4, no. 6-7 (1973): 37–41. doi:10.1080/00064246.1973.11760857.

————. " 'From the Old Slave Shack': Memoirs of A Teacher." *PoemMemoirStory* 8 (2008): 119–28. https://digitalcommons.library.uab.edu/pms/vol08/iss2008/53.

Jefferson, Thomas. *Notes on the State of Virginia*. 1781.

Johnson, Cynthia Mestad. *James DeWolf and the Rhode Island Slave Trade*. History Press, 2014.

Jones, Hilary. *The Metis of Senegal: Urban Life and Politics in French West Africa*. Indiana University Press, 2013.

Jones, Martha S. *Vanguard: How Black Women Broke Barriers, Won the Vote and Insisted on Equality for All*. Hachette, 2020.

Kant, Immanuel. *Essays and Treatises on Moral, Political, and Various Philosophical Subjects*. Vol. 2. Printed for the translator, 1799. https://archive.org/details/essaysandtreati00kantgoog/page/n97/.

King, Wilma. *Stolen Childhood: Slave Youth in Nineteenth-Century America*. 2nd ed. Indiana University Press, 2011. Kindle.

Kingsbury, Susan Myra, and Carola Woerishoffer, eds. *The Records of the Virginia Company of London*. Vol. 3, *Documents 1*. US Government Printing Office, 1933. https://archive.org/details/recordsofvirgini03virg.

Knight, Lucien Lamar. *A Standard History of Georgia and Georgians*. Vol. 5. Lewis, 1917.

Landers, Jane. "Slavery in the Lower South." *OAH Magazine of History* 17, no. 3 (2003): 23–27. https://www.deepdyve.com/lp/oxford-university-press/slavery-in-the-lower-south-azj0VGYfdD.

Laslett, Peter. "Age at Menarche in Europe since the Eighteenth Century." *Journal of Interdisciplinary History* 2, no. 2 (1971): 221–36. https://doi.org/10.2307/202843.

Lee, Jarena. *Religious Experience and Journal of Mrs. Jarena Lee, Giving an Account of Her Call to Preach the Gospel*. Published by the author, 1849. https://www.gutenberg.org/cache/epub/66953/pg66953-images.html.

Lewis, Rick. "Kant 200 Years On." *Philosophy Now: A Magazine of Ideas.* https://philosophynow.org/issues/49/Kant_200_Years_On#.

Ligon, Richard. *A True and Exact History of the Island of Barbados: Illustrated with a Mapp of the Island, as also the Principall Trees and Plants There [. . .].* Humphrey Moseley, 1657. https://archive.org/details/trueexacthistory00ligo.

Lobban, Michael. "Slavery, Insurance and the Law." *Journal of Legal History* 28, no. 3 (December 2007): 319–28.

London, Kathleen. "The History of Birth Control." In *The Changing American Family: Historical and Comparative Perspectives.* Curriculum Units by Fellows of the Yale-New Haven Teachers Institute, vol. 6. Yale-New Haven Teachers Institute, 1982. https://teachersinstitute.yale.edu/curriculum/units/files/82.06.03.pdf.

Long, Michael G. *Martin Luther King Jr., Homosexuality, and the Early Gay Rights Movement: Keeping the Dream Straight?* Palgrave McMillan, 2012. Kindle.

Macgregor, J. K. "Some Notes on Nsibidi." *Journal of the Royal Anthropological Institute of Great Britain and Ireland* 39 (1909): 209–19. https://doi.org/10.2307/2843292.

Marshall, Susan E. *Splintered Sisterhood: Gender and Class in the Campaign Against Woman Suffrage.* University of Wisconsin Press, 1997.

Martin, Lawrence. "The Genesis of Godey's Lady's Book." *New England Quarterly* 1, no. 1 (1928): 41–70. https://doi.org/10.2307/359723.

Martin, Michelle. "Slave Bible from the 1800s Omitted Key Passages That Could Incite Rebellion." December 9, 2018. https://www.npr.org/2018/12/09/674995075/slave-bible-from-the-1800s-omitted-key-passages-that-could-incite-rebellion.

Maxwell, William J. *F.B. Eyes: How J. Edgar Hoover's Ghostreaders Framed African American Literature.* Princeton University Press, 2015. http://www.jstor.org/stable/j.ctt9qh0jx.6.

McDonald, Laughlin. *A Voting Rights Odyssey: Black Enfranchisement in Georgia.* Cambridge University Press, 2003.

Mitchell, Jerry. "On This Day in 1963." June 9, 2024. https://mississippitoday.org/2024/06/09/on-this-day-in-1963-fannie-lou-hamer-was-jailed-and-beaten-for-defying-segregation-on-bus.

Morgan, Jennifer L. *Laboring Women: Reproduction and Gender in New World Slavery.* University of Pennsylvania Press, 2004. Kindle.

———. "Partus Sequitur Ventrem: Law Race and Reproduction in Colonial Slavery," *Small Axe* 22, no 1 (March 2018): 1–17. https://muse.jhu.edu/pub/4/article/689365.

Morrison, Toni. *Beloved.* Vintage, 2004. Kindle.

———. *Playing in the Dark: Whiteness and the Literary Imagination.* Vintage, 1993. Kindle.

———. "Recitatif." In *Confirmation: An Anthology of African American Women,* edited by Amiri Baraka and Amina Baraka, 243–61. Quill, 1983.

———. "Rememory." In Morrison, *Source of Self-Regard,* 323–24.

———. *The Source of Self-Regard: Selected Essays, Speeches, and Meditations.* Alfred A. Knopf, 2019. Kindle.

Newton, John, and William Cowper. *Olney Hymns in Three Books.* W. Oliver, 1779. https://www.loc.gov/item/2006700069.

Obama, Barack. *The Audacity of Hope.* Crown Publishers, 2006.

Painter, Nell Irvin. "Sojourner Truth in Life and Memory: Writing the Biography of an American Exotic." *Gender and History* 2, no. 1 (Spring 1990): 3–16. http://www.nellpainter.com/assets/pdfs/articles/A29_SojTruthExotic.pdf.

Pennington, James W. C. *The Fugitive Blacksmith; or, Events in the History of James W. C. Pennington, Pastor of a Presbyterian Church, New York, Formerly a Slave in the State of Maryland, United States.* 2nd ed. Charles Gilpin, 1849. https://docsouth.unc.edu/neh/penning49/penning49.html.

Perkins-Valdez, Dolen. *Wench.* Amistad, 2010.

Peterson, Beverly. "Mrs. Hale on Mrs. Stowe and Slavery." *American Periodicals* 8 (1998): 30–44. http://www.jstor.org/stable/20771111.

Rayson, Ann. "Toni Morrison's 'Recitatif' and Being White, Teaching Black." In *Changing Representations of Minorities East and West: Selected Essays,* vol. 11, edited by Larry E. Smith and John Reader, 41–46. University of Hawaii Press, 1996.

Richardson, Cathy J. "Punks, Bulldaggers, and Welfare Queens: The Radical Potential of Queer Politics." *GLQ: Gay and Lesbian Quarterly* 3, no. 4 (1997): 452.

Richardson, Riché. *Black Masculinity and the U.S. South: From Uncle Tom to Gangsta.* University of Georgia Press, 2007.

Schroeder, Patricia R. *Robert Johnson: Mythmaking and Contemporary American Culture.* University of Illinois Press, 2004.

Sheeler, J. Reuben. "Servitude and Slavery of Virginia in Seventeenth Century." *Negro History Bulletin* 10, no. 7 (April 1947): 161–64. http://www.jstor.org/stable/44174714.

Strackey, William. *The Historie of Travaile into Virginia Britannia: Expressing the Cosmographie and Comodities of the Country, Togither with the Manners and Customes of the People.* Edited by Richard Henry Major. Hakluyt Society, 1849. https://archive.org/details/dli.ministry.02639/page/20.

Spillers, Hortense J. "Mama's Baby, Papa's Maybe: An American Grammar Book."

Diacritics 17, no. 2 (Summer 1987): 64–81. https://chromaticcabinet.swarthmore.edu/wp-content/uploads/2017/02/Spillers.pdf.

Stauffer, Tema. *Southern Fiction: Photographs by Tema Stauffer.*" Daylight Community Arts Foundation, 2022.

Swanton, John R. "The Orphan and the Origin of Corn." In *Myths and Tales of the Southeastern Indians*, 15–17. University of Oklahoma Press, 1995.

Tallman, Jamie Q. *The Notorious Dr. Flippin: Abortion and Consequence in the Early Twentieth Century*. Texas Tech University Press, 2011.

Thompson, Katrina Dyonne. "Taking Care of White Babies, That's What I Do": *The Help* and Americans' Obsession with the Mammy." In *From* Uncle Tom's Cabin *to* The Help: *Critical Perspectives on White-Authored Narratives of Black Life.* Edited by Claire Oberon Garcia, Vershawn Ashanti Young, and Charise Pimentel. Palgrave McMillan, 2014.

Thorndale, William. "The Virginia Census of 1619." *Magazine of Virginia Genealogy* 33, no. 3 (Summer 1995): 155–70. https://www.vgs.org/vgs_mag_33-3_1995.

Tinsley, Omise'eke Natasha. "Black Atlantic, Queer Atlantic: Queer Imaginings of the Middle Passage." *GLQ: A Journal of Lesbian and Gay Studies* 14, nos. 2–3 (2008): 191–216. http://muse.jhu.edu/journals/glq/summary/v014/14.2-3.tinsley.html.

Turner, Jennifer, Mariana Olaizola Rosenblat, Nino Guruli, et al. *Captive Labor: Exploitation of Incarcerated Workers.* ACLU and GHRC Research Report. University of Chicago Law School/Global Human Rights Clinic, 2022. Accessed October 7, 2024. https://chicagounbound.uchicago.edu/cgi/viewcontent.cgi?article=1003&context=ghrc.

Turner, Steve. *Amazing Grace: The Story of America's Most Beloved Song.* HarperCollins, 2008. Kindle.

Wagner, Brian. *The Tar Baby: A Global History*. Princeton, NJ: Princeton University Press, 2017.

Walker, Alice. *The Color Purple.* Penguin Books, 2022. Kindle.

———. *In Search of Our Mothers' Gardens*. HarperCollins, 1983.

———. "Uncle Remus, No Friend of Mine." *Georgia Review* 66, no. 3 (2012): 635–37. http://www.jstor.org/stable/23268234.

Weaver, Afaa M., ed. *These Hands I Know*. Sarabande Books, 2002.

Welch, Ashton Welsey. "Law and the Making of Slavery in Colonia Virginia." *Ethnic Studies Review* 27, no. 1 (2004): 1–22.

Welter, Barbara. "The Cult of True Womanhood, 1820–1860." *American Quarterly* 18, no. 2 (1966): 151–74.

Wexler, Laura. *Fire in a Canebrake: The Last Mass Lynching in America*. Scribner, 2003.

Wheatley [Peters], Phillis. *Poems on Various Subjects, Religious and Moral*. A. Bell, 1773.

Wiencek, Henry. *Master of the Mountain: Thomas Jefferson and His Slaves*. Farrar, Straus and Giroux, 2012. Kindle.

Wilson, Theodore Brantner. *The Black Codes of the South*. University of Alabama Press, 1965.

Woodard, Vincent Maurice. "The Shapeshifter Figure: A New Cartography of Sex and Gender Formation Within Radical Black Antebellum Culture." PhD diss., University of Texas at Austin, 2002. http://hdl.handle.net/2152/11909.

ONLINE ARCHIVES CONSULTED

American Dictionary of the English Language: Webster's Dictionary 1828, https://webstersdictionary1828.com/

Ancestry, www.ancestry.com

Civil Rights Movement Archive, https://www.crmvet.org/

Digital North Carolina Newspapers, https://www.digitalnc.org/newspapers/

Documenting the American South, https://docsouth.unc.edu/

Encyclopedia Virginia, https://encyclopediavirginia.org/

Eighteenth Century Collections Online, https://www.gale.com/primary-sources/eighteenth-century-collections-online

Find a Grave, https://www.findagrave.com/

George Washington's Mount Vernon, www.mountvernon.org/

HathiTrust, www.hathitrust.org

Historical Newspapers, https://go.newspapers.com/

Internet Archive, https://archive.org/

Library of Congress, www.loc.gov

Project Gutenburg, www.gutenberg.org

Thomas Jefferson Monticello, www.monticello.org

Virginia Genealogical Society, www.vgs.org

Virtual Jamestown, https://www.virtualjamestown.org/

About the Author

To Come